Warwick William Wroth, A

The London Pleasure Gardens of the Eighteenth Century

Warwick William Wroth, Arthur Edgar Wroth

The London Pleasure Gardens of the Eighteenth Century

ISBN/EAN: 9783741134425

Manufactured in Europe, USA, Canada, Australia, Japa

Cover: Foto ©Thomas Meinert / pixelio.de

Manufactured and distributed by brebook publishing software
(www.brebook.com)

Warwick William Wroth, Arthur Edgar Wroth

The London Pleasure Gardens of the Eighteenth Century

THE LONDON
PLEASURE GARDENS

OF

THE EIGHTEENTH CENTURY

BY

WARWICK WROTH, F.S.A.

OF THE BRITISH MUSEUM

ASSISTED BY

ARTHUR EDGAR WROTH

WITH SIXTY-TWO ILLUSTRATIONS

London

MACMILLAN AND CO., Ltd.

NEW YORK: THE MACMILLAN CO.

1896

"A great deal of company, and the weather and garden pleasant and it is very cheap and pleasant going thither. . . . But to hear the nightingale and the birds, and here fiddles and there a harp, and here a Jew's trump, and here laughing and there fine people walking is mighty divertising."—SAMUEL PEPYS.

PREFACE

In the following pages an attempt has been made to write, for the first time, a history of the London pleasure gardens of the last century. Scattered notices of these gardens are to be found in many histories of the London parishes and in other less accessible sources, and merely to collect this information in a single volume would not, perhaps, have been a useless task. It is one, however, that could not have been undertaken with much satisfaction unless there was a prospect of making some substantial additions—especially in the case of the less known gardens—to the accounts already existing. A good deal of such new material it has here been possible to furnish from a collection of newspapers, prints, songs, &c., that I have been forming for several years to illustrate the history of the London Gardens.[1]

The information available in the writings of such laborious topographers as Wilkinson, Pinks, and Nelson is, of course, indispensable, and has not been here

[1] Some of the rarer items of the collection which it seemed desirable to cite as authorities are marked W. or W. Coll.

neglected ; yet even in the treatment of old material there seemed room for improvement, at least in the matter of lucidity of arrangement and chronological definiteness. For, if the older histories of the London parishes have a fault, it is, perhaps, that, owing to their authors' anxiety to omit nothing, they often read more like *materials* for history than history itself. Thus, we find advertisements and newspaper paragraphs set forth at inordinate length and introduced without being properly assimilated with the context, and the reader is often left to find his own way through a mass of confusing and trivial detail.

The principal sources of information consulted are named in the notes and in a section at the end of each notice, and, wherever practicable, a list has been added of the most interesting views of the various gardens. The Introduction contains a brief sketch of some of the main characteristics of the pleasure resorts described in the volume, and it is only necessary here to add that even our long list of sixty-four gardens does not by any means exhaust the outdoor resources of the eighteenth-century Londoner, who had also his Fairs, and his Parks, and his arenas for rough sport, like Hockley-in-the-Hole. But these subjects have already found their chroniclers.

In preparing this work for press I have had the assistance of my brother, Mr. Arthur E. Wroth, who has, moreover, made a substantial contribution to the volume by furnishing the accounts of Sadler's Wells, White Conduit House, Bagnigge Wells, and Hampstead

Wells, and by compiling ten shorter notices. For the remaining fifty notices, for the Introduction, and the revision of the whole I am myself responsible.

Although the book has not been hastily prepared, and has been written for pleasure, I cannot hope that it is free from errors. I trust, however, that the shortcomings of a work which often breaks new ground and which deals with many miscellaneous topics will not be harshly judged.

WARWICK WROTH.

London,
  September, 1896.

CONTENTS

I. CLERKENWELL AND CENTRAL GROUP

LIST OF ILLUSTRATIONS

ILLUSTRATIONS IN THE TEXT

LONDON   PLEASURE   GARDENS

INTRODUCTION

An entry in the diary of Samuel Pepys records how
on the 7th of June, 1665, " the hottest day (he says)
that ever I felt in my life," he took water to the Spring
Garden at Fox-hall and there stayed, pleasantly walking,
and spending but sixpence, till nine at night.   The
garden that he visited was that which formed the
nucleus of those Vauxhall Gardens which, seventy or
eighty years later, became the most favoured summer
resort of pleasure-seeking Londoners.   Vauxhall with
its great concourse of high and low, its elaborate concerts, its lamps and brightly painted supper-boxes, is far
removed from the simple garden in which Mr. Pepys
delighted to ramble, but not only Vauxhall, but several
other pleasure gardens of the eighteenth century may
be traced to comparatively humble beginnings in the
period between the Restoration and the reign of Anne.[1]

In the early days of these gardens no charge was
made for admission, but a visitor would naturally spend

[1] Several London pleasure gardens were in existence *before* the
Restoration, the Mulberry Garden on the site of Buckingham
Palace and the Spring Gardens at Charing Cross being well-known
instances.   But in the present volume only such seventeenth-
century gardens as survived till the succeeding century are noticed.

B

a trifle in cheese-cakes and syllabubs for the ladies, and would order for himself some bottle-ale and such substantial viands as were afforded by the tavern or the master's dwelling-house attached to the garden. The musical entertainments that afterwards became a feature of the principal gardens were originally of little account. The Wells of Lambeth (1697) and Hampstead (1701) provided a concert of some pretensions, but Mr. Pepys at the Spring Garden was content with the harmony of a harp, a fiddle, and a Jew's trump.

In some places, however, a Long (or Great) Room was at an early period built for the dancing that generally took place there in the morning or the afternoon ; and booths and raffling-shops were set up for the benefit of card-players and gamblers. The quiet charm of a garden was, moreover, sometimes rudely broken by the incursion of gallants like " young Newport " and Harry Killigrew—" very rogues (says Pepys) as any in the town." At last, about 1730–40, the managers of the principal public gardens found it desirable to make a regular charge for admission : they requested gentlemen " not to smoak on the walks," sternly prohibited the entrance of servants in livery, and, generally, did their best to exclude improper characters.

The author of the *Sunday Ramble*, a little guidebook of the last century often quoted in this work, visited, or says that he visited, on a single Sunday all the best known gardens near town But it would have required an abnormally long life and a survey far less hurried to make acquaintance with all the open-air resorts that flourished during the whole, or part, of the eighteenth century. Such a long-lived Rambler who wished to know his gardens at first hand would probably have visited them (as in this volume we invite the reader to do) in five or six large groups, paying little heed to what might seem the pedantry of Parishes and Hundreds.

Beginning in what are now the densely populated districts of Clerkenwell and central London, he would find himself in the open fields and in a region abounding in mineral springs. Islington Spa (1684–1840) and its opposite neighbour Sadler's Wells (from 1683) had chalybeate springs that claimed to rival the water ("so mightily cry'd up") of Tunbridge Wells in Kent, and if the water itself was unpalatable, the adjoining pleasure gardens and Long Rooms, with their gay company, tended to make the drinking of medicinal water both pleasant and seductive. At no great distance from Sadler's Wells were the Wells of Bagnigge (from 1759), the London Spa (from 1685), St. Chad's Well, and Pancras Wells (from *circ.* 1697); and a walk to Old Street would be rewarded by a plunge in the clear waters of the Peerless Pool, or by a basket of carp and tench caught in the fish pond close by.

Behind the Foundling Hospital there might be found a bowling green; at the Mulberry Garden (Clerkenwell) a skittle-ground and an evening concert; in Rosoman Street, a wonderful grotto and an enchanted fountain[1] and (at the New Wells, *circ.* 1737–1750), a complete "variety" entertainment.

Sunday afternoon, if you did not mind the society of prentices and milliners, might be spent in Spa Fields at the Pantheon tea-house and garden (1770–1776), or at the Adam and Eve Gardens at Tottenham Court.

Farther west lay the Marylebone Bowling Green and Garden, developed in 1738 into the well-known Marylebone Gardens, and in this neighbourhood were several humbler places of entertainment, the Jew's Harp House, The Queen's Head and Artichoke, and The Yorkshire Stingo.

Islington and North London were full of rural resorts, the Sunday haunts of the London "cit" and his family. In Penton Street was the renowned White

---

[1] The English Grotto.

Conduit House, and near it Dobney's Bowling Green, both visited in early days for their delightful prospects of the distant country. The Three Hats in Islington attracted visitors who wished to see the surprising horsemanship of Sampson and of Johnson "the Irish Tartar." Canonbury, Highbury, Kentish Town, and Hornsey were pleasant places farther afield.

Still farther north were Belsize House, with its fashionable gambling and racing ; the popular Wells of Hampstead, and the Kilburn Wells. The Spaniards, and New Georgia with its maze and mechanical oddities, were Sunday attractions in Hampstead for the good wives and daughters of tradesmen like Zachary Treacle.[1]

Chelsea could boast of at least two gardens in addition to the famous gardens and Rotunda of Ranelagh. In Pimlico was Jenny's Whim. At Brompton, the Florida (or Cromwell's) Gardens, a pleasant place, half garden, half nursery, where you could gather cherries and straw-berries "fresh every hour in the day."

London south of the Thames was not less well pro-vided for. Nearly opposite Somerset House were Cuper's Gardens (*circ.* 1691–1759). Lambeth had its wells and its Spring Garden (Vauxhall Gardens). In St. George's Fields and Southwark were the mineral springs of the notorious Dog and Duck ; the Restora-tion Spring Gardens, and Finch's Grotto Gardens. Farther east were the Bermondsey Spa, and the St. Helena Gardens at Rotherhithe.

Such was the geographical distribution of the London pleasure gardens. "A mighty maze—but not without a plan." Or, at least a clue to their intricacies may be found by arranging them in three groups, each with its distinctive characteristics.

In our first division we may place pleasure resorts of the Vauxhall type, beginning with the four great

[1] Cp. *The Idler*, No. 15, July 1758.

London Gardens—Cuper's Gardens, the Marylebone Gardens, Ranelagh, and Vauxhall itself. These were all well-established in popular favour before the middle of the last century, and all depended for their reputation upon their evening concerts, their fireworks,[1] and their facilities for eating and drinking. Ranelagh relied less on the attractions of its gardens than did the other resorts just mentioned. Here the great Rotunda over-shadowed the garden, and the chief amusement was the promenade in an "eternal circle" inside the building. Except on gala nights of masquerades and fireworks, only tea, coffee and bread and butter were procurable at Ranelagh ; and a Frenchman about 1749 hints at more than a suspicion of dulness in the place when he comments "on s'ennuie avec de la mauvaise musique, du thé, et du beurre."

Imitations of the principal gardens were attempted in various parts of London. Thus the Mulberry Garden (*circ.* 1742), the Sir John Oldcastle and the Lord Cobham's Head in Clerkenwell had their fireworks, and their concerts by local celebrities, described in the ad-vertisements as a " Band of the best Masters." Finch's Grotto Garden in Southwark (1760—*circ.* 1773), though not a fashionable resort, was illuminated on certain evenings of the week, and provided very creditable concerts, in which performers of some repute occasionally took part. Bermondsey Spa, from about 1784, had, like Vauxhall, its Grand Walk and coloured lamps, and kept its own poet and musical composer (Jonas Blewitt, the organist).[2] Two places called the Temple of Apollo (or Apollo Gardens) and the Temple of Flora, in the Westminster Bridge Road, also endea-voured to acquire something of a Vauxhall tone, at

---

[1] At Vauxhall fireworks were not introduced till 1798, but illuminations were always a feature of the gardens.

[2] Bermondsey Spa and Finch's Grotto, above mentioned, might be classed among the spas and springs, but their amusements resembled those of Vauxhall.

least to the extent of having painted boxes, illuminations and music, and a variety of (imitation) singing-
birds. These Temples were set up late in the eighteenth
century, and came to a bad end.

To a second division belong the gardens connected
with mineral springs. Several of these, as we have
already seen, date from the end of the seventeenth century—Islington Spa, Sadler's Wells, and the Wells of
Pancras, Hampstead, and Lambeth. The Dog and Duck,
Bagnigge Wells, and other springs did not become well
known till the eighteenth century. Such places were
usually day resorts, opening early in the morning and
providing something in the way of breakfasting, dancing, and music. The waters were advertised, and by
many accepted, as Universal Medicines. A rising of
the vapours, a scorbutic humour, an inveterate cancer
could all be cured (as "eminent physicians" constantly
testified) by drinking these unpleasant, but probably
harmless, beverages—if possible, on the spot, or at
any rate in bottles sent out by the dozen and stamped
with the proprietor's seal. Islington Spa became the
vogue in 1733 when the Princess Amelia regularly
attended it. The Dog and Duck waters were recommended to Mrs. Thrale by Dr. Johnson, and many
cures vouched for by a physician attested the efficacy
of the purging and chalybeate Wells of Bagnigge.

But the adventitious attractions of these places had
a tendency to obscure their importance as spas. Bagnigge Wells and, to some extent, Islington Spa became
after a time little more than tea-gardens. Sadler's lost
sight of its Wells early in the eighteenth century, and
relied for profit on the development of the rope-dancing
and pantomime in its theatre. The Dog and Duck
(St. George's Spa) became at last a tea-garden and a
dancing-saloon which had to be suppressed as the haunt
of "the riff-raff and scum of the town." Finch's Grotto
and Bermondsey Spa, on the other hand, when their

springs had ceased to attract, developed (as we have shown) into minor Vauxhalls.

The third division of the London gardens consists of those that were mainly tea-gardens. Many of these though small and unpretending possessed a distinctly rural charm. Such were Highbury Barn, and the Canonbury House tea-gardens, Hornsey with its romantic wood, and Copenhagen House standing alone in the hayfields. Bagnigge Wells and White Conduit House, the classic tea-gardens of London, were prettily laid out and pleasantly situated, but in their later days became decidedly cockneyfied. The great day at these gardens was Sunday, especially between five and nine o'clock. The amusements were of a simple kind—a game of bowls or skittles, a ramble in the maze, and a more or less hilarious tea-drinking in the bowers and alcoves which every garden provided. In the Long Rooms of Bagnigge Wells, White Conduit House, and the Pantheon the strains of an organ, if the magistrates allowed the performance, might also be enjoyed.

The season at most of the London gardens began in April or May, and lasted till August or September. The principal gardens were open during the week (not, regularly, on Sundays) on three or more days, and those of the Vauxhall type were usually evening resorts. Much depended, it need hardly be said, upon the state of the weather, and sometimes the opening for the season had to be postponed. When the rain came, the fireworks were hopelessly soaked and people took refuge as they could under an awning or a colonnade or in a Great Room. A writer in *The Connoisseur* of 1755 (May 15th) only too justly remarks that our Northern climate will hardly allow us to indulge in the pleasures of a garden so feelingly described by the poets : " We dare not lay ourselves on the damp ground in shady groves or by the purling stream," unless at least " we fortify our insides against the cold

by good substantial eating and drinking. For this
reason the extreme costliness of the provisions at our
public gardens has been grievously complained of by
those gentry to whom a supper at these places is as
necessary a part of the entertainment as the singing or
the fireworks." More than seventy years later Tom
Moore (*Diary*, August 21st, 1829) describes the misery
of a wet and chilly August night at Vauxhall—the
gardens illuminated but empty, and the proprietor comparing the scene to the deserts of Arabia. On this
occasion, Moore and his friends supped between twelve
and one, and had some burnt port to warm themselves.

The charge for admission at Vauxhall, Marylebone
Gardens, and Cuper's was generally not less than a
shilling. Ranelagh charged half-a-crown, but this
payment always included " the elegant regale " of tea,
coffee, and bread and butter. The proprietors of the
various Wells made a regular charge of threepence
or more for drinking the water at the springs and
pump rooms. At some of the smaller gardens a charge of
sixpence or a shilling might be made for admission, but
the visitor on entering was presented with a metal check
which enabled him to recover the whole or part of his
outlay in the form of refreshments.

Vauxhall, Marylebone, Cuper's, and Ranelagh often
numbered among their frequenters people of rank and
fashion, who subscribed for season-tickets, but (with the
possible exception of Ranelagh) were by no means exclusive or select. The Tea-gardens, and, as a rule, the
Wells, had an aristocracy of aldermen and merchants,
young ensigns and templars, and were the chosen
resorts of the prentice, the sempstress, and the small
shopkeeper.

The proprietors of gardens open in the evening found
it necessary to provide (or to announce that they provided) for the safe convoy of their visitors after nightfall. Sadler's Wells advertised " it will be moonlight,"

and provided horse patrols to the West End and the City. The proprietor of Belsize House, Hampstead, professed to maintain a body of thirty stout fellows " to patrol timid females or other." Vauxhall—in its early days usually approached by water—seems to have been regarded as safe, but Ranelagh and the Marylebone Gardens maintained regular escorts.

In the principal gardens, watchmen and " vigilant officers " were always supposed to be in attendance to keep order and to exclude undesirable visitors. Unsparing denunciation of the morals of the chief gardens, such as is found in the lofty pages of Noorthouck, must, I am inclined to think, be regarded as rhetorical, and to a great extent unwarranted. On the other hand, one can hardly accept without a smile the statement of a Vauxhall guide-book of 1753, that " even Bishops have been seen in this Recess without injuring their character," for it cannot be denied that the vigilant officers had enough to do. There were sometimes scenes and affrays in the gardens, and Vauxhall and Cuper's were favourite hunting-grounds of the London pickpocket. At the opening Ridotto at Vauxhall (1732) a man stole fifty guineas from a masquerader, but here the watchman was equal to the occasion, and " the rogue was taken in the fact." At Cuper's on a firework night a pickpocket or two might be caught, but it was ten to one that they would be rescued on their way to justice by their confederates in St. George's Fields.

The dubious character of some of the female frequenters of the best known gardens has been necessarily indicated in our detailed accounts of these gardens, though always, it is hoped, in a way not likely to cause offence. The best surety for good conduct at a public garden was, after all, the character of the great mass of its frequenters, and it is obvious that they were decent people enough, however wanting in graces of good-breeding and refinement. Moreover, from the end of

the year 1752, when the Act was passed requiring
London gardens and other places where music and
dancing took place to be under a license, it was generally
the interest of the proprietor to preserve good order for
fear of sharing the fate of Cuper's, which was unable
to obtain a renewal of its license after 1752, and had to
be carried on as a mere tea-garden.   The only places,
perhaps, at which disreputable visitors were distinctly
welcome were those garish evening haunts in St. George's
Fields, the Dog and Duck, the Temples of Flora and
Apollo and the Flora Tea-Gardens.   All these were
suppressed or lost their license before the end of the
eighteenth century.

Of the more important gardens, Marylebone and
Cuper's ceased to exist before the close of the last
century.   Ranelagh survived till 1803 and Vauxhall
till 1859.   Finch's Grotto practically came to an end
about 1773 and Bermondsey Spa about 1804.   Many
of the eighteenth-century tea-gardens lasted almost to
our own time, but the original character of such places
as Bagnigge Wells (closed 1841), White Conduit House
(closed 1849), and Highbury Barn (closed 1871) was
greatly altered.

During the first thirty or forty years of the nineteenth
century numerous gardens, large and small, were flour-
ishing in or near London.   Some of these, like Bagnigge Wells, had been well-known gardens in the
eighteenth century, while the origin of others, such
as Chalk Farm, Camberwell Grove House, the Rose-
mary Branch Gardens at Islington, or rather Hoxton,
the Mermaid Gardens, Hackney, and the Montpelier
Gardens, Walworth, may be probably, or certainly,
traced to the last century.   These last-mentioned places,
however, had little or no importance as public gardens
till the nineteenth century, and have not been described
in the present work.

Many new gardens came into existence, and of these

the best known are the Surrey Zoological Gardens
(1831–1856); Rosherville (established 1837); Cremorne (*circ.* 1843–1877); and the Eagle Tavern and
Gardens (*circ.* 1825–1882), occupying the quiet domain
of the old Shepherd and Shepherdess.

The sale of Vauxhall Gardens in August 1859, or
perhaps the closing of Highbury Barn in 1871, may be
held to mark the final disappearance of the London
Pleasure Gardens of the eighteenth century. " St.
George's Fields are fields no more ! " and hardly a
tree or shrub recalls these vanished pleasances of our
forefathers. The site of Ranelagh is still, indeed, a
garden, and Hampstead has its spring and Well Walk.
But the Sadler's Wells of 1765 exists only in its theatre,
and its gardens are gone, its spring forgotten, and its
New River covered in. The public-house, which in
London dies hard, has occupied the site, and preserved
the name of several eighteenth-century gardens, including
the London Spa, Bagnigge Wells, White Conduit
House and the Adam and Eve, Tottenham Court, but
the gardens themselves have been completely swept
away.

Vauxhall, Belsize House, and the Spa Fields Pantheon,
none of them in their day examples of austere morality,
are now represented by three churches. From the
Marylebone Gardens, the Marylebone Music Hall
may be said to have been evolved. Pancras Wells
are lost in the extended terminus of the Midland
Railway, and the Waterloo Road runs over the
centre of Cuper's Gardens. Finch's Grotto, after
having been a burial ground and a workhouse, is now
the headquarters of our London Fire Brigade. Copenhagen House with its fields is the great Metropolitan
Cattle Market. The Three Hats is a bank ; Dobney's
Bowling Green, a small court ; the Temple of Apollo,
an engineer's factory, and the sign of the Dog and Duck
is built into the walls of Bedlam.

I

CLERKENWELL AND CENTRAL GROUP

ISLINGTON SPA, OR NEW TUNBRIDGE WELLS

A poetical advertisement of the year 1684 [1] refers
to " the sweet gardens and arbours of pleasure " at this
once famous resort, situated opposite the New River
Head, Clerkenwell. The chalybeate spring in its
grounds was discovered at or shortly before that date,
and the proprietor in 1685 is described in the *London
Gazette* [2] as " Mr. John Langley, of London, merchant,
who bought the rhinoceros and Islington Wells."

The original name of the Spa was Islington Wells,
but it soon acquired (at least as early as 1690) the
additional title of New Tunbridge, or New Tunbridge
Wells, by which it was generally known until about
1754, when the name of Islington Spa came into use,
though the old title, New Tunbridge, was never quite
abandoned. [3]

[1] *Islington Wells, a song of all the virtues of those old waters newly
found out.* London, 1684 (Brit. Mus.). cp. *A morning ramble ; or
Islington Wells burlesqt.* London, 1684 (Cunningham, *London*,
1850, s.v. "Islington ").

[2] *London Gazette*, 24 September, 1685.

[3] Nearly all modern writers—Mr. Pinks is an exception—have in
some way or other confused Sadler's Wells with New Tunbridge
Wells (Islington Spa). The mistake may have first arisen from the
circumstance that Sadler, in his printed prospectus concerning the
discovery of the wells on his premises, describes them as "Sadler's
New Tunbridge Wells near Islington." The sub-title of New
Tunbridge Wells never, however, took root at Sadler's, though it

Although the place could not at any period boast of
the musical and "variety" entertainments of its neighbour Sadler's Wells, it soon acquired greater celebrity
as a Spa, and from about 1690 to 1700 was much
frequented.   The gardens at this period [1] were shaded
with limes and provided with arbours ; and, in addition
to its coffee-house, the Spa possessed a dancing-room
and a raffling shop.[2]   The charge for drinking the
water was threepence, and the garden was open on
two or three days in the week from April or May
till August.

As early as seven o'clock in the morning a few vale-
tudinarians might be found at the Well, but most of
the visitors did not arrive till two or three hours later.
Between ten and eleven the garden was filled with a gay
and, in outward seeming, fashionable throng. The company, however, was extraordinarily mixed.   Virtue and
Vice ; Fashion and the negation of Fashion had all their
representatives.   Sir Courtly Nice drove up to the gate
in his gilt coach, and old Sir Fumble brought his lady
and daughter.   Modish sparks and fashionable ladies,
good wives and their children, mingled with low women
and sempstresses in tawdry finery ; with lawyers' clerks,
and pert shopmen ; with sharpers, bullies, and decoys.
A doctor attended at the Well to give advice to the
drinkers, not a few of whom came for the serious
purpose of benefiting their health.

But the chief attraction was the Walks ; the promenade where the beau strutted with his long sword
beribboned with scarlet, and ladies fragrant with Powder

was soon permanently adopted (as is stated in our text) by the rival
Islington Wells, *i.e.* Islington Spa.

[1] The following details are mainly derived from *Islington Wells,
or the Threepenny Academy*, 1691, and from Edward Ward's *Walk to
Islington*, 1699, fol.   (Ward's *Works*, ii. 63, ff. ed. 1709).

[2] Ward describes the gambling places as an outhouse with sheds
and a hovel adjoining.

Richard Temple Viscount Cobham &c.

of Orange and Jessamine discussed one another and the
fashions :—

> Lord ! madam, did you e'er behold
> (Says one) a dress so very old ?
> Sure that commode was made, i' faith,
> In days of Queen Elizabeth ;
> Or else it was esteemed the fashion
> At Charles the Second's coronation :
> The lady, by her mantua's forebody,
> Sure takes a pride to dress like nobody.[1]

Others of more plebeian estate preferred the seclu-
sion of an arbour shaded with climbing shrubs and
sycamore, where sweethearts could chat, or, if so
minded, enjoy a late breakfast of plum-cake and ale.
Older people retired to the coffee-house to smoke and
talk politics over their coffee, but the man about town
and his female friends were to be found deep at play
in the raffling shop, or speculating in the Royal Oak
Lottery.[2] Again and again it was the *Board* that won,
while the projector and the man with cogged dice in his
pocket looked cynically on. At about eleven a.m. the
dancing began. Music for dancing all day long was
advertised in 1700 for every Monday and Thursday of
the summer season. But the music of that period seems
to have been only the harmony of three or four by no
means accomplished fiddlers, and it is doubtful if the
dancing ever continued beyond the morning and afternoon.

In the early years of the eighteenth century the Spa
seems to have gone out of fashion,[3] and in 1714 *The
Field Spy* speaks of it as a deserted place :—

> The ancient drooping trees unprun'd appear'd ;
> No ladies to be seen ; no fiddles heard.

---

[1] *Islington Wells, or the Threepenny Academy.*

[2] Cp. E. Ward, " The Infallible Predictor " (*Works*, ii. p. 355,
ed. 1709).

[3] An advertisement of 23 May, 1712 (Percival's Sadler's Wells

The patronage of royal personages at last revived its fortunes. In the months of May and June 1733, the Princess Amelia, daughter of George II., and her sister Caroline came regularly to drink the waters. On some occasions the princesses were saluted by a discharge of twenty-one guns, and the gardens were thronged. On one morning the proprietor took £30, and sixteen hundred people are said to have been present. New Tunbridge Wells once more, for a few years, became the vogue. Pinchbeck, the toyman, prepared a view of the gardens which he sold as a mount for his fans. A song of the time, *The Charms of Dishabille*, which George Bickham illustrated with another view of the gardens, gives a picture of the scene (1733–1738) :

> Behold the Walks, a chequer'd shade,
> In the gay pride of green array'd ;
> How bright the sun ! the air how still !
> In wild confusion there we view
> Red ribbons grouped with aprons blue ;
> Scrapes, curtsies, nods, winks, smiles and frowns,
> Lords, milkmaids, duchesses and clowns,
> In their all-various dishabille.

The same mixed company thus frequented the Spa as of old, and when my Lord Cobham honoured the garden with a visit, there were light-fingered knaves at hand to relieve him of his gold repeater. The physician who at this time attended at the Well was " Dr." Misaubin, famous for his pills, and for his design to ruin the University of Cambridge (which had refused him a doctor's degree) by sending his son to the University of Oxford. Among the habitués of the garden was an eccentric person named Martin, known as the Tunbridge Knight. He wore a yellow cockade and carried a hawk on his fist,

Coll.) announces the performances from six to ten in the morning and from four till eight in the evening of two wonderful posture-makers, a man and a child of nine, to take place in the dancing-room of New Tunbridge Wells.

The Charms of Dishabille, or New Tunbridge Wells at Islington.

Whence comes it that ỷ shining Great, To Titles born & anful State, Thus condescend thus

check their Wills, And send away to Tunbridge Wells, To mix with vulgar Beaus & Belles. Ye

Sages your fam'd Glasses raise Survey this Meteors dazzling Blaze, And say, portends it Good or Ill?

Soon as Aurora gilds the Skies.
With brighter Charms ỷ ladies rise,
To dart forth Beams that save or kill.
No Homage at the Toilette paid,
(Their lovely Features unsurvey'd)
Sweet Negligence her Influence lend,
And all ỷ artless Graces blends,
That form ỷ tempting Dishabille.

Behold ỷ Walks, a cheequer'd Shade.
In ỷ gay Pride of Green array'd;
How bright ỷ Sun ỷ fler how still!
In wild Confusion there we view,
Red Ribbons groop'd with Aprons blew:
Scrapes Curtzies Nods, Winks Smiles & Frowns,
Lords, Milkmaids, Dutchesses and Clowns,
In their all various Dishabille.

Thus, in the famous Age of Gold,
(Not quite romantic tho' so old)
Mankind were merely Jack & Gill.
On flow'ry Banks, by murm'ring Streams,
They tattl'd, walk'd, had pleasing Dreams,
But dress'd indeed, like awkward Folks;
Not Steeple Hats, Surtouts, short Cloaks;
Fig-leaves the only Dishabilles

For the Flute.

G.Bickham jun. sculp.

The Words by M. Lockman Written in 1733.

To ỷ Tune of ỷ Black Joke.

ISLINGTON SPA IN 1733. BY GEORGE BICKHAM.

which he named Royal Jack, out of respect to the Royal Family.

Fashion probably soon again deserted the Spa; but from about 1750 to 1770 it was a good deal frequented by water-drinkers and visitors who lodged for a time at the Wells. One young lady of good family, who was on a visit to London in June 1753, wrote home to her friends [1] that New Tunbridge Wells was " a very pretty Romantick place," and the water " very much like Bath water, but makes one vastly cold and Hungary." A ticket costing eighteenpence gave admission to the public breakfasting [2] and to the dancing from eleven to three. It was endeavoured to preserve the most perfect decorum, and no person of exceptionable character was to be admitted to the ball-room.[3] This invitation to the dance reads oddly at a time when the Spa was being industriously recommended to the gouty, the nervous, the weak-kneed, and the stiff-jointed.[4]

In 1770 the Spa was taken by Mr. John Holland, and from that year, or somewhat earlier, the place was popular as an afternoon tea-garden. The " Sunday Rambler " describes it as genteel, but judging from George Colman's farce, *The Spleen; or Islington Spa*

[1] Extract from family correspondence communicated by C. L. S. to *Notes and Queries*, 8th ser. vi. 1894, p. 69.

[2] In 1760 the breakfasting was ninepence, the afternoon tea sixpence, and the coffee eightpence. No stronger beverages were sold.

[3] A serious attempt seems to have been made to keep this rule. The *London Daily Advertiser* for 25 June, 1752, records that a beautiful though notorious woman, who had appeared at the dancing at New Tunbridge on June 24, was, on being recognised by the company, turned out by a constable.

[4] Dr. Russel, who analysed the water about 1733, says that it had a taste of iron and (unless mixed with common water) was apt to make the drinker giddy or sleepy. This was the experience of Lady Mary Wortley Montagu, who, however, expatiates on the benefit she had derived from the Spa.

(first acted in 1776), its gentility was that of publicans and tradesmen. " The Spa (says Mrs. Rubrick) grows as genteel as Tunbridge, Brighthelmstone, Southampton or Margate. Live in the most social way upon earth : all the company acquainted with each other. Walks, balls, raffles and subscriptions. Mrs. Jenkins of the Three Blue Balls, Mrs. Rummer and family from the King's Arms ; and several other people of condition, to be there this season ! And then Eliza's wedding, you know, was owing to the Spa. Oh, the watering-places are the only places to get young women lovers and husbands ! "

In 1777, Holland became bankrupt, and next year a Mr. John Howard opened the gardens in the morning and afternoon, charging the water-drinkers sixpence or threepence, or a guinea subscription. He enriched the place with a bowling-green [1] and with a series of " astronomical lectures in Lent, accompanied by an orrery." A band played in the morning, and the afternoon tea-drinking sometimes (1784) took place to the accompaniment of French horns.[2] Sir John Hawkins, the author of *The History of Music*, frequented the Spa for his health in 1789. On returning home after drinking the water one day in May (Wednesday 20th, 1789) he complained of a pain in his head and died the next morning of a fever in the brain. " Whether (as a journalist of the time observes) it was owing to the mineral spring being taken when the blood was in an improper state to receive its salubrious effect, or whether it was the sudden visitation of Providence, the sight of the human mind is incompetent to discover."

The Spa continued to be resorted to till the beginning of the present century when the water and

---

[1] This was between the main part of the Spa gardens and St. John's Street Road ; cp. Wallis's *Plan*, 1808.

[2] A band had played in the morning under Holland's management (advertisement in the *Public Advertiser*, 5 May, 1775).

tea-drinking began to lose their attractions. The author of *Londinium redivivum*, writing about 1803,[1] speaks, however, of the gardens with enthusiasm as " really very beautiful, particularly at the entrance. Pedestals and vases are grouped with taste under some extremely picturesque trees, whose foliage (is) seen to much advantage from the neighbouring fields." At last, about 1810, the proprietor, Howard, pulled down the greater part of the old coffee-house,[2] and the gardens were curtailed by the formation of Charlotte Street (now Thomas Street). At the same time the old entrance to the gardens, facing the New River Head, was removed for the building of Eliza Place.[3] A new entrance was then made in Lloyd's Row, and the proprietor lived in a house adjoining. A later proprietor, named Hardy, opened the gardens in 1826 as a Spa only. The old Well was enclosed, as formerly, by grotto work and the garden walks were still pleasant. Finally in 1840, the two rows of houses called Spa Cottages were built upon the site of the gardens.

A surgeon named Molloy, who resided about 1840–1842 in the proprietor's house in Lloyd's Row, preserved the Well, and by printed circulars invited invalids to drink the water for an annual subscription of one guinea, or for sixpence each visit. In Molloy's time the Well was contained in an outbuilding attached to the east side of his house. The water was not advertised after his tenancy, though it continued to flow as late as 1860. In the autumn of 1894, the writers of this volume visited the house and found the outbuilding occupied as a dwelling-room of a very humble descrip-

---

[1] Malcolm, *Lond. rediv.* iii. 230, 231.

[2] The orchestra connected with it was pulled down in 1827 ; Cromwell's *Clerkenwell*, p. 357.

[3] No. 6, Eliza Place, stood on the site of the old entrance (Pinks).

tion. Standing in this place it was impossible to realise that we were within a few feet of the famous Well. A door, which we had imagined on entering to be the door of a cupboard, proved to be the entrance to a small cellar two or three steps below the level of the room. Here, indeed, we found the remains of the grotto that had once adorned the Well, but the healing spring no longer flowed.[1]

Eliza Place was swept away for the formation of Rosebery Avenue, and the two northernmost plots of the three little public gardens, opened by the London County Council on 31 July, 1895,[2] as Spa Green, are now on part of the site of the old Spa. The Spa Cottages still remain, as well as the proprietor's house in Lloyd's Row, and beneath the coping-stone of the last-named the passer-by may read the inscription cut in bold letters : ISLINGTON SPA OR NEW TUNBRIDGE WELLS.

[Besides the authorities cited in the text and notes and in the account in Pinks's *Clerkenwell*, p. 398, ff., the following may be mentioned :—*Experimental observations on the water of the mineral spring near Islington commonly called New Tunbridge Wells*. London, 1751, 8vo ; another ed., 1773, 8vo (the Brit. Mus. copy of the latter contains some newspaper cuttings) ; Dodsley's *London*, 1761, s.v. "Islington " ; Kearsley's *Strangers' Guide*, s.v. "Islington " ; Lewis's *Islington ; Gent. Mag.* 1813, pt. 2, p. 554, ff. ; advertisements, &c., in Percival's Sadler's Wells Collection and in W. Coll.; Wheatley's *London*, ii. 268, and iii. p. 199.]

VIEWS.

1. View of the gardens, coffee-house, &c., engraved frontispiece

---

[1] Mr. Philip Norman, writing in *Notes and Queries*, 8th ser. vi. 1894, p. 457, says :—"I have seen (in the cellar of No. 6, Spa Cottages, behind the house at the corner of Lloyd's Row) grotto work with stone pilasters and on each side steps descending. Here, I believe, was the chalybeate spring. For many years it has ceased to flow."

[2] *Daily Telegraph*, 1 August, 1895.

to Lockman's poem, *The Humours of New Tunbridge Wells at Islington*, London, 1734, 8vo (cp. Pinks, 401, note, and 402).

2. View of the gardens, well, coffee-house, &c., engraved by G. Bickham, jun., as the headpiece of " The Charms of Dishabille or New Tunbridge Wells " (Bickham's *Musical Entertainer*, 1733, &c., vol. i. No. 42).

3. Engravings of the proprietor's house in Lloyd's Row ; Cromwell's *Clerkenwell*, 352 ; Pinks, 405. The house is still as there represented.

THE PANTHEON, SPA FIELDS

THE Spa Fields Pantheon stood on the south side of the present Exmouth Street, and occupied the site of the Ducking Pond House,[1] a wayside inn, with a pond in the rear used for the sport of duck-hunting.

The Ducking Pond premises having been acquired by Rosoman of Sadler's Wells, were by him sub-let to William Craven, a publican, who, at a cost of £6,000, laid out a garden and erected on the site of the old inn a great tea-house called the Pantheon, or sometimes the Little Pantheon, when it was necessary to distinguish it from " the stately Pantheon " in Oxford Street, built in 1770–1771, and first opened in January 1772.[2]

The Spa Fields Pantheon was opened to the public early in 1770, and consisted of a large Rotunda, with two galleries running round the whole of the interior, and a large stove in the centre.

The place was principally resorted to by apprentices and small tradesmen, and on the afternoon and evening of Sunday, the day when it was chiefly frequented, hundreds of gaily-dressed people were to be found in

[1] A newspaper paragraph of April 1752, mentions the little summer house at the Ducking Pond House in Spa Fields, as being lately stripped of its chairs and tables by some pitiful rogues.

[2] In *The Macaroni and Theatrical Magazine* for January 1773 (p. 162) is the notice : --

" Pantheons : The *Nobility's*, Oxford Road ; the *Mobility's*, Spawfields."

the Rotunda, listening to the organ,[1] and regaling themselves with tea, coffee and negus, or with supplies of punch and red port. A nearer examination of this crowded assembly showed that it consisted of journeymen tailors, hairdressers, milliners and servant maids, whose behaviour, though boisterous, may have been sufficiently harmless.

The proprietor endeavoured to secure the strict maintenance of order by selling nothing after ten o'clock in the evening. But his efforts, it would seem, were not entirely successful. "Speculator," a correspondent of the *St. James's Chronicle*, who visited the place in May 1772, "after coming from church," looked down from his vantage-ground in one of the galleries upon what he describes as a dissipated scene. To his observation the ladies constituted by far the greater part of the assembly, and he was shocked more than once by the request, "Pray, Sir, will you treat me with a dish of tea?"

A tavern with tea-rooms for more select parties stood on the east of the Rotunda. Behind the buildings was a pretty garden, with walks, shrubs and fruit trees. There was a pond or canal stocked with fish, and near it neat boxes and alcoves for the tea-drinkers. Seats were dispersed about the garden, the attractions of which were completed by a summer-house up a handsome flight of stone steps, and a statue of Hercules, with his club, on a high pedestal. The extent of the garden was about four acres.

A writer in the *Town and Country Magazine* for April 1770 (p. 195), speaks contemptuously of the canal "as about the size of a butcher's tray, where

---

[1] The organ appears, about 1772, to have been silenced on Sundays, at least for a time. A correspondent in *The Gazetteer and New Daily Advertiser* for 20 June, 1772, refers to the Middlesex Justices who will not suffer the organs to be played at the Little Pantheon, White Conduit House, Bagnigge Wells, &c.

citizens of *quality* and their spouses come on Sunday to view the amorous flutterings of a duck and drake." This, however, is the opinion of a fashionable gentleman who goes alternately to Almack's and Cornelys's, while Ranelagh (he says) "affords me great relief."

The career of the Pantheon was brief ; for in March 1774 the building and its grounds were announced for sale on account of Craven's bankruptcy. According to the statement of the auctioneer the place was then in full trade, and the returns almost incredible, upwards of one thousand persons having sometimes been accommodated in the Rotunda. It is uncertain if another proprietor tried his hand, if so he was probably unsuccessful, for the Pantheon was certainly closed as a place of amusement in 1776.

In July 1777 the Rotunda, after having been used for a time as a depot for the sale of carriages, was opened for services of the Church of England under the name of Northampton Chapel. One of the preachers, moralising on the profane antecedents of the place, adopted the text, "And he called the name of that place Bethel, but the name of that city was called Luz at the first."

The building was afterwards purchased by the Countess of Huntingdon, and opened in March 1779 under the name of Spa Fields Chapel as a place of worship in her connexion. Various alterations were at that time, and subsequently, made in the building, and a statue of Fame, sounding a trumpet, which had stood outside the Pantheon on the lantern surmounting the cupola was removed. The tavern belonging to the Pantheon, on the east side of the Rotunda, was occupied by Lady Huntingdon as her residence. It was a large house partly covered by branches of jessamine.

The gardens, in the rear of the Rotunda, were converted in 1777 into the Spa Fields burial-ground, which became notorious in 1843 for its over-crowded and pestilential condition, and for some repulsive disclosures as to the systematic exhumation of bodies in order to make room for fresh interments.

Spa Fields Chapel was pulled down in the beginning of 1887, and the present church of the Holy Redeemer was erected on its site, and consecrated for services of the Church of England on 13 October, 1888. Such have been the strange vicissitudes of the Pantheon tea-house and its gardens.

[Pinks's *Clerkenwell;* Walford, *O. and N. London; The Sunday Ramble;* Tomlins's *Perambulation of Islington,* p. 158 ; *Notes and Queries,* 1st ser. ii. p. 404 ; *Spa Fields Chapel and its Associations,* London, 1884.]

VIEWS.

1. View of Northampton or Spa Fields Chapel, with the Countess of Huntingdon's house adjoining. Hamilton, del., Thornton sculp., 1783. Crace, *Cat.* p. 589, No. 43.

2. Exterior of Chapel and Lady Huntingdon's house, engraving in Britton's *Picture of London,* 1829, p. 120.

3. Later views of the Chapel (interior and exterior) engraved in Pinks's *Clerkenwell,* pp. 146, 147.

THE LONDON SPA

THE London Spa public-house, standing at the corner of Rosoman Street and Exmouth Street, marks the site of a seventeenth-century inn called The Fountain.

A spring of chalybeate water was discovered on the premises of this inn about 1685, and was a special inducement held out to the public by the proprietor, John Halhed, vintner, to visit his house. In August 1685, Halhed, in advertising the virtues of the water, stated that no less an authority than Robert Boyle, the chemist, had adjudged and openly declared it to be the strongest and very best of these late found out medicinal waters. The honest vintner, in giving other local wells their due, maintained that his was equivalent, if not better, in virtue, goodness, and operation, to that of Tunbridge (so mightily cry'd up) or any other water yet known. On 14 July, 1685, the house was solemnly nominated and called the London Spaw, by Robert Boyle, in the presence of " an eminent, knowing, and more than ordinary ingenious apothecary . . . besides the said John Halhed and other sufficient men." The name of the Fountain seems thenceforth to have been superseded by that of the London Spa. In inviting persons of quality to make a trial of the spring, Halhed expressed the wish that the greatness of his accommodation were suitable to the goodness of his waters, although he was not without convenient apartments and walks for both sexes. The poor were to be supplied with the water gratis.

For a few years subsequent to 1714 the place appears to have fallen into neglect ; but it afterwards was once more frequented, and in 1720 the author of *May Day* [1] writes :—

> Now nine-pin alleys, and now skettles grace,
> The late forlorn, sad, desolated place ;
> Arbours of jasmine fragrant shades compose
> And numerous blended companies enclose.

On May-day the milk-maids and their swains danced in the gardens to the music of the fiddler. Holiday folk flocked to test the virtues of the spring, and from this time onwards, the London Spa enjoyed some degree of popularity. In the summer of 1733, *Poor Robin's Almanack* records how—

> Sweethearts with their sweethearts go
> To Islington or London Spaw ;
> Some go but just to drink the water,
> Some for the ale which they like better.

The annual Welsh fair, held in the Spa Field hard by, must have brought additional custom to the tavern, and in 1754 the proprietor, George Dodswell, informed the public that they would meet with the most inviting usage at his hands, and that during the fair there would be the " usual entertainment of roast pork with the oft-famed flavoured Spaw ale." From this date onwards the London Spa would appear to have been merely frequented as a tavern. [2] The present public-house was built on the old site in 1835.

[1] *May Day, or the Origin of Garlands*, a poem published in 1720. *The Field Spy*, published in 1714 (Rogers, *Views of Pleasure Gardens of London*, p. 46), speaks of the spring and garden as if a good deal frequented in 1714.

[2] A rare bronze ticket of oblong form, incised with the words, " London Spaw No. 19," is in the possession of Mr. W. T. Ready, the London coin dealer. It may belong to about the middle of the last century.

MAY DAY AT THE LONDON SPA. 1720.

[The London Spaw, an advertisement, August 1685, folio sheet in British Museum ; Pinks's *Clerkenwell*.]

VIEWS.

1. A view of the London Spa in Lempriere's set of views, 1731; Crace, *Cat.* p. 588, No. 41. Cp. Pinks's *Clerkenwell*, p. 168.

2. Engraving of the Spa garden, T. Badeslade, inv. ; S. Parker, sculp.; frontispiece to *May Day, or the Origin of Garlands*, 1720.

THE NEW WELLS, NEAR THE LONDON SPA

Houses in Lower Rosoman Street,[1] Clerkenwell, west side, about one hundred yards from the London Spaw public-house, now occupy the site of this place of amusement.

The New Wells commanded a pleasant prospect of the fields and country beyond ; but nothing is known of the medicinal waters, and the prominent feature of the place was a theatre, probably intended to rival Sadler's Wells, in which entertainments, consisting of dancing, tumbling, music and pantomime were given from 1737 (or earlier[2]) till 1750. The purchase of a pint of wine or punch was generally the passport necessary for admission, and the gardens were open on Sunday as well as on week-day evenings. The entertainments usually began at five o'clock, and concluded about ten. In 1738, there were comic songs and dancing, an exhibition

[1] Rosoman Street was called after Mr. Rosoman, who about 1756 built the west side, which was then called Rosoman Row. Rosoman, who acted at the New Wells in 1744, was the well-known proprietor of Sadler's Wells. Pinks (*Clerkenwell*) states that the houses numbered (in his time) 5 to 8 occupied the site of the Wells.

[2] The New Wells seem to have been already established in 1737. The earliest advertisement quoted in Pinks is of 1738, but there are earlier advertisements (W. Coll.), May to August 1737, in one of which reference is made to the alterations in the theatre that season.

of views of Vauxhall, and a whimsical, chymical and pantomimical entertainment called the *Sequel.*

During the next year (1739) similar entertainments were given, and Mr. Blogg sang the " Early Horn," and " Mad Tom " with a preamble on the kettledrums by Mr. Baker.   At this time the place possessed a kind of Zoological Gardens, for there was then to be seen a fine collection of large rattlesnakes, one having nineteen rattles and " seven young ones," a young crocodile imported from Georgia, American darting and flying squirrels, " which may be handled as any of our own," and a cat between the tiger and leopard, perfectly tame, and one of the most beautiful creatures that ever was in England. This show could be seen for a shilling.

In 1740 a Merlin's Cave was added to the attractions of the gardens (cp. " Merlin's Cave," *infra*), and there was displayed a firework representation of the siege of Portobello by Admiral Vernon.   On 3 July, 1742,[1] Monsieur and Madame Brila from Paris and their little son, three years old, exhibited several curiosities of balancing, and the two Miss Rayners, rope-dancing.   There were songs and dancing ; a hornpipe by Mr. Jones of Bath, who played the fiddle as he danced, and an exhibition of views of the newly opened Rotunda at Ranelagh.   In June 1744 there was a pantomime, *The Sorceress, or Harlequin Savoyard ;* the part of Harlequin being sustained by Mr. Rosoman.   A dance of Indians in character concluded an entertainment witnessed by a crowded and " polite " audience of over seven hundred persons.   In August of the same year a Mr. Dominique jumped over the heads of twenty-four men with drawn swords ; Madam Kerman performed on the tight-rope, danced on stilts, and (according to the advertisements) jumped over a garter ten feet high.

[1] *Daily Post,* 3 July, 1742 (quoted in *Gent. Mag.* 1813, pt. ii. p. 561).

Next came to the Wells (1745) a youthful giant seven feet four inches high, though under sixteen years of age, who occasionally exhibited his proportions on the rope. In 1746 there appeared a Saxon Lady Giantess seven feet high, and the wonderful little Polander, a dwarf two feet ten inches in height, of the mature age of sixty, "in every way proportionable, and wears his beard after his own country's fashion." During this year Miss Rayner performed the feat of walking up an inclined rope, one hundred yards long, extending from the stage to the upper gallery, having two lighted flambeaux in her hands.

The same year (1746) witnessed the celebration at Sadler's Wells and other places of entertainment in London of the victory of the Duke of Cumberland at Culloden. At the New Wells were given representations of the battle, and the storming of Culloden House. Mr. Yeates [1] (or Yates), the manager at this time, in acknowledging his gratification at the applause manifested, regretted that on the appearance of Courage (the character symbolising the Duke of Cumberland) several hearty Britons exerted their canes in such a torrent of satisfaction as to cause considerable damage to his benches. About this period Mrs. Charlotte Charke (the youngest daughter of Colley Cibber the dramatist) appeared at the Wells as Mercury in the play of *Jupiter and Alcmena*.

From 1747 to 1750 the theatre and gardens remained closed, but after having been considerably improved they were re-opened on 16 April, 1750. Towards the close of this year, Hannah Snell made her appearance and went through a number of military exercises in her regimentals. This warlike lady, who had served under the name of James Gray as a marine at the siege of Pondicherry, and who had been several times wounded in action, was one of the first party

---

[1] Doran's *London in Jacobite Times*, ii. pp. 148, 149.

that forded the river, breast high, under the enemy's fire. She worked laboriously in the trenches, and performed picket duty for seven nights in succession.

The entertainments at the New Wells appear to have ceased about 1750. In 1752 the proprietor, Yeates, let the theatre to the Rev. John Wesley, and in May of that year, it was converted into a Methodist tabernacle. A few years later the theatre was removed, probably in 1756, when Rosoman Row (now Rosoman Street) was formed.

[Cromwell's *Clerkenwell*, p. 254 ; Pinks's *Clerkenwell;* newspaper advertisements, W. Coll.].

THE ENGLISH GROTTO, OR GROTTO GARDEN, ROSOMAN STREET

The English Grotto was in existence in 1760, and is described as standing in the fields, near the New River Head. A view of that date [1] represents it as a small wooden building resembling the London Spa. A flag is flying from the roof, and some well-dressed people are seen walking near it. A garden, with a curious grotto and water-works, were probably its only attractions.

It may be conjectured that this English Grotto is identical with the Grotto Garden in Rosoman Street, which was kept in (or before) 1769 [2] by a man named

[1] The English Grotto has escaped the minute research of Mr. Pinks, and his continuator Mr. Woods (cp. however, Daniel, *Merrie England*, i. chap. ii. p. 33). It is practically known only from the following views :—

    (1) A view of the English Grotto, near the New River Head. Chatelain del. et sculp. 1760. Crace, *Cat.* p. 591, No. 60 (cp. engraving (*circ.* 1760), without artist's name, in W. Coll.).

    (2) The Grotto, near the New River Head, 1760. A drawing in Indian ink. Crace, *Cat.* p. 590, No. 59.

    (3) A water-colour copy of No. 1 by R. B. Schnebellie. Crace, *Cat.* p. 591, No. 61.

[2] The continuator of Pinks (p. 740) quotes advertisements of 1769, without, however, specifying the newspapers referred to. J. T. Smith, *Book for a Rainy Day*, p. 70, refers to the Grotto Garden as being kept by Jackson in 1779. Pinks (p. 169) mentions the fountain and Grotto in 1780, and describes the site.

Jackson, a successful constructor of grottoes, and contrivances of water-works. In 1769 he advertised the place as his Grand Grotto Garden, and gold and silver fish Repository. In the garden was a wonderful grotto ; an enchanted fountain ; and a water-mill, invented by the proprietor, which when set to work represented fireworks, and formed a beautiful rainbow. A variety of gold and silver fish, " which afford pleasing ideas

A VIEW OF THE ENGLISH GROTTO NEAR THE NEW RIVER HEAD.
Circ. 1760.

to every spectator " might be purchased at this repository. Sixpence was sometimes charged for admission, and a number of people are said to have resorted there daily. The place was still in Jackson's possession in 1780.

The house and Grotto Garden were at the north-east corner of Lower Rosoman Street (originally Rosoman Row), almost facing the London Spa. About 1800 the house, or its later representative, was No. 35, Lower

Rosoman Street, and in its garden were some remains of the wonderful grotto.   From the windows there was still a pleasing prospect of the country for many miles. In this house Mr. Pickburn, the printer, first published *The Clerkenwell News* in 1855, and continued to print the newspaper there until 1862.

[For authorities and views, see notes.]

THE Mulberry Garden in Clerkenwell, the site of which was afterwards occupied by the House of Detention, was open in 1742, but contrary to the usual practice, the proprietor (W. Body) made no charge for admission, relying for profit on the sale of refreshments.

It was a somewhat extensive garden with a large pond, gravelled walks, and avenues of trees. From the seats placed beneath the shade of a great mulberry tree, probably one of those introduced into England in the reign of James I., the players in the skittle-alley might often be watched at their game. The garden was open from 6 p.m. in the spring and summer, and, especially between 1742 and 1745, was advertised in the newspapers with extravagant eulogy. " Rockhoutt [1] (the proprietor declared) has found one day and night's Al Fresco in the week to be inconvenient; Ranelagh House, supported by a giant whose legs will scarcely support him [2]; Mary le Bon Gardens, down on their marrow-bones; New wells [3] at low water; at Cuper's [4] the fire almost out." The attractions offered were a band of wind and string instruments in an orchestra in

[1] Rockhoutt = Rockholt House in Essex.
[2] The legs referred to are those of Sir Thomas Robinson, the principal proprietor of Ranelagh, nicknamed Long Sir Thomas.
[3] The New Wells, Clerkenwell.
[4] Cuper's Gardens, Lambeth.

the garden and occasional displays of fireworks and illuminations. The proprietor professed (6 April, 1743) to engage British musicians only, maintaining that "the manly vigour of our own native music is more suitable to the ear and heart of a Briton than the effeminate softness of the Italian." On cold evenings the band performed in the long room. On 2 September, 1742, the proprietor excused himself from a pyrotechnic display on the ground that it was the doleful commemoration of the Fire of London. On 9 August, 1744, there was a special display of fireworks helped out by the instrumental music of the "celebrated Mr. Bennet." At this fête "honest Jo Baker" beat a Trevally on his side drum as he did before the great Duke of Marlborough when he defeated the French at the Battle of Malplaquet. This entertainment must have been popular, for beyond the sixteen hundred visitors who were able to gain admission, some five hundred others are said to have been turned away. On 25 August, in the same year, another firework display was given, and on this occasion the proprietor condescended to make a charge of twopence per head for admission.

The gardens do not appear to have been advertised between 1745 and 1752, during which period they were probably kept by a Mrs. Bray, who died on 1 March, 1752, "with an excellent good character." Beyond this, her obituary only records that she "is thought to have been one of the fattest women in London." In 1752 the gardens were in the hands of Clanfield, the firework engineer of Cuper's Gardens, who every summer evening provided vocal and instrumental music, from six o'clock, and fireworks at nine.[1] The admission was sixpence with a return of threepence in refreshments.

[1] Newspaper advertisement in "Public Gardens" collection in Guildhall Library, London.

Fashionable gentlemen appear to have played an occasional game of ninepins or skittles in the Mulberry Garden, but on the whole the place enjoyed only a local celebrity among tradesmen and artisans, and its proprietor, in elegant language,[1] made his appeal to " the honest Sons of trade and industry after the fatigues of a well-spent day," and invited the Lover and the jolly Bacchanalian to sit beneath the verdant branches in his garden.

Nothing is known of the garden subsequent to 1752. The site was used about 1797 as the exercising ground of the Clerkenwell Association of Volunteers, and the House of Detention (now replaced by a Board School) was subsequently built on it.

[Pinks's *Clerkenwell.*]

VIEWS.

Two engravings, probably contemporary, showing well-dressed gentlemen playing at ninepins near the mulberry tree : Guildhall Library, London (*Catal.* p. 210). One of these views is engraved in Pinks, p. 128.

[1] Advertisement in *Daily Advertiser*, 8 July, 1745.

SADLER'S WELLS

Towards the close of the seventeenth century there stood on the site of the present Sadler's Wells Theatre (Rosebery Avenue, Clerkenwell), a wooden building of a single story erected by Sadler, a surveyor of the highways, as a Music House. The house stood in its own grounds, and the New River flowed past its southern side.

It was in the garden of this house that in 1683 some workmen in Sadler's employ accidentally unearthed an ancient well, arched over and curiously carved. Sadler, suspecting the water to have medicinal properties, submitted it for analysis to a doctor, who advised him to brew ale with it. This he did with such excellent results that the ale of Sadler's Wells became, and long remained, famous. In 1684, Dr. Thomas Guidot issued a pamphlet setting forth the virtues of the water which he described as a ferruginous chalybeate, akin to the waters of Tunbridge Wells, though not tasting so strongly of steel and having more of a nitrous sulphur about it. Being neither offensive nor unpleasant to taste, a man was able to drink more of it than of any other liquor. It might be taken with a few carraway comfits, some elecampane, or a little preserved angelica to comfort the stomach. A glass of Rhenish or white wine might also accompany the tonic, and habitual smokers would find it very convenient to take a pipe after drinking.

Sadler lost no time in advertising his Wells,[1] and in preparing for the reception of the water-drinkers. He laid out his garden with flowers and shrubs, and constructed in the centre a marble basin to receive the medicinal water. Posturers, tumblers and rope-dancers, performing at first in the open-air, were engaged. A Mrs. Pearson played on the dulcimer on summer evenings at the end of the Long Walk, and visitors danced to the strains of a band stationed on a rock of shellwork construction. The place soon became popular, and hundreds of people came daily to drink the water.

Epsom and Tunbridge Wells (in Kent) saw in Sadler's Wells a serious rival to their own spas, and in 1684 a tract was issued protesting against this " horrid plot " laid to persuade people that " Sadler's Musick House is South-Borrow and Clarkenwell Green Caverley Plain." Was it possible for water from such a source to " bee effectual as our wonder-working fountains that tast of cold iron, and breathe pure nitre and sulphur " ? Audacious and unconscionable Islington should surely be content with its monopoly from time immemorial of the sale of cakes, milk, custards, stewed prunes, and bottled ale. But even if the waters " could be conceited somewhat comparable, where is the air ? Where the diversions ? Where the conveniences ? "

Possibly this tirade was not ineffectual ; at any rate, about 1687 the place was comparatively deserted and the well fell into disuse. " Sadler's excellent steel waters " were, however, again advertised in 1697 as being as full of vigour, strength and virtue as ever they were and very effectual for curing all hectic and hypochondriacal heat, for beginning consumptions and for melancholy distempers. The water-drinking appears to have finally

---

[1] Sadler originally advertised the place as " Sadler's New Tunbridge Wells," but it soon became known simply as Sadler's Wells. On the confusion with the neighbouring New Tunbridge Wells (Islington Spa), see Islington Spa, supra, note 3.

ceased early in the eighteenth century ; [1] though the
place, surrounded by fields till quite late in the century,
remained a pleasant resort for Londoners.

> There you may sit under the shady trees
> And drink and smoke fann'd by a gentle breeze.[2]
>
> There pleasant streams of Middleton
> In gentle murmurs glide along
> In which the sporting fishes play
> To close each wearied Summer's day.
> And Musick's charms in lulling sounds
> Of mirth and harmony abounds ;
> While nymphs and swains with beaux and belles
> All praise the joys of Sadler's Wells.
> The herds around o'er herbage green
> And bleating flocks are sporting seen
> While Phœbus with its brightest rays
> The fertile soil doth seem to praise.[3]

As late as 1803 mention is made of the tall poplars,
graceful willows, sloping banks and flowers of Sadler's
Wells ; and the patient London fisherman, like his
brethren of the angle of the eighteenth century, still
stood by the stream.[4]

From about 1698 the gardens ceased to be a prominent feature of Sadler's Wells, and the fortunes of the
place from that time to the present day mainly concern
the historian of the Theatre and the Variety Stage, and
can only be dealt with briefly in the present work.

In 1698 (23 May) a vocal and instrumental concert
was given, and the company enjoyed such harmony as
can be produced by an orchestra composed of violins,

[1] About 1800 the forgotten well was accidentally re-discovered
between the stage door and the New River.

[2] A poem by William Garbott, entitled the *New River*, published
probably about 1725.

[3] *A new song on Sadler's Wells*, set by Mr. Brett, 1740.

[4] The Sadler's Wells anglers are mentioned in the *Field Spy*, a
poem of 1714. The New River remained open until 1861–62
when it was covered in.

hautboys, trumpets and kettle-drums. This was one of the concerts given in the Music House twice a week throughout the season and lasting from ten o'clock to one. In 1699 James Miles and Francis Forcer (*d.* 1705 ?), a musician, appear to have been joint proprietors of Sadler's Wells, which was for some years styled Miles's Music House. In this year (1699) there was an exhibition of an " ingurgitating monster," a man, who, for

SADLER'S WELLS ANGLERS. 1796.

a stake of five guineas, performed the hardly credible feat of eating a live cock. This disgusting scene was witnessed by a very rough audience, including however some beaux from the Inns of Court. A brightly painted gallery in the saloon used for the entertainments appears to have been occupied by the quieter portion of the audience, who were able from thence to survey the pit below, which was filled, according to Ned Ward (*circ.* 1699), with butchers, bailiffs, prize-fighters, and housebreakers. The audience smoked and regaled themselves with ale and cheese-cakes ; while the organ played, a scarlet-clad fiddler performed, and a girl of eleven gave a sword dance.

In 1712, Miles's Music House was the scene of a fatal brawl in which Waite, a lieutenant in the Navy, was killed by a lawyer named French, " near the organ-loft." In 1718 it is mentioned as the resort of " strolling damsels, half-pay officers, peripatetic tradesmen, tars, butchers and others musically inclined."

Miles died in 1724 and probably about that time Forcer's son, Francis Forcer, junior (d. 1743), an educated man of good presence, became proprietor and improved the entertainments of rope-dancing and tumbling. The neighbourhood of Sadler's Wells about this period was infested by foot-pads. It was consequently a common sight to see link-boys with their flaming torches standing outside the theatre, and horse patrols were often advertised (circ. 1733–1783) as escorts to the City and the West End. Occasionally the play-bills announced :—" It will be moonlight."

In 1746 Rosoman was proprietor, and introduced the system of admitting the pit and gallery free, on the purchase of a pint of wine. A charge of half-a-crown was made for the boxes. The audience smoked and toasted one another. The man-servant by day became a beau at night ; and with the lady's-maid, decked out in colours filched from her mistress, gazed open-mouthed at the wonderful sights. Winifred Jenkins describes her experiences, in *Humphry Clinker* (1771) :—" I was afterwards of a party at Sadler's Well, where I saw such tumbling and dancing on ropes and wires that I was frightened and ready to go into a fit. I tho't it was all enchantment, and believing myself bewitched, began for to cry. You knows as how the witches in Wales fly on broom-sticks ; but here was flying without any broom-stick or thing in the varsal world, and firing of pistols in the air and blowing of trumpets and singing, and rolling of wheelbarrows on a wire (God bliss us!) no thicker than a sewing thread; that to be sure they must deal with the Devil. A fine gentleman with a pig's tail and a golden sord by his side, came to comfit me and offered for to treat me with a pint of wind; but I would not stay; and so in going through the dark passage he began to show his cloven futt and went for to be rude; my fellow sarvant Umphry Klinker bid him be sivil, and he gave the young man a dous in the chops; but i' fackins Mr. Klinker warn't long in his debt; with a good oaken sapling he dusted his doublet, for all his golden cheese-toaster; and fipping me under his arm carried me huom, I nose not how, being I was in such a flustration."

Between 1752 and 1757 Michael Maddox exhibited his wire-dancing and his tricks with a long straw, which he manipulated while keeping his balance on the wire. In 1755 (and for many years afterwards) Miss Wilkinson, the graceful wire-dancer and player of the musical glasses, was a principal performer.

Giuseppe Grimaldi ("Iron Legs") the father of the famous clown, was the ballet-master and chief dancer in 1763 and 1764; and remained at the Wells till 1767. Harlequinades and similar entertainments were from this time added to the ordinary amusements of tumbling and rope-dancing.

In 1765 Rosoman pulled down the old wooden house and erected in its place a new theatre which in part survives in the building of the present day. The seats now had backs with ledges, as in our music-halls, to hold the bottles and glasses of the audience. About this time, or a few years later, the charge for a box was three shillings including a pint of wine (port, Mountain, Lisbon or punch), and eighteen pence and one shilling for the pit and gallery; an extra sixpence

SOUTH WEST VIEW of

from a Drawing by

London, Published 1 June 1812.

SADLER'S WELLS,
R. C. Andrews 1792

by Robert Wilkinson, N.º 58 Cornhill

VIEW OF THE THEATRE IN ITS FORMER STATE.

SADLER'S WELLS IN 1792, AND AS IT WAS BEFORE 1765.

E

entitling the ticket-holder to a pint of the wine allowed to the box-holders. Angelo, at a later time, refers in his *Reminiscences* to the Cream of Tartar Punch and the wine of the Sloe Vintage usually drunk at Sadler's Wells.

Among the vocalists were Mrs. Lampe (1766-1767) and the famous Thomas Lowe (1771 and later). In 1768 Spinacuti exhibited his wonderful monkey which performed on the tight-rope feats resembling Blondin's. Jemmy Warner, the clown, appeared in 1769, and Richer, the wire and ladder dancer, in 1773; and the years 1775 and 1776 were noticeable for the appearance of James Byrne, the harlequin, father of Oscar Byrne. In 1778 the interior of the theatre was entirely altered and the roof considerably raised. The audience now often included people of rank, such as the Duke and Duchess of York and the Duke and Duchess of Gloucester.

In 1781 Joseph Grimaldi (*b.* 1779, *d.* 1837) made his first appearance at Sadler's in the guise of a monkey, and appeared there year by year till within a few years of his retirement. On 17 March, 1828, he took a farewell benefit there, playing " Hock," the drunken prisoner in " Sixes, or the Fiend." His final appearance was at Drury Lane on 27 June, 1828, when, prematurely broken down in health, he sang, seated, his last song, and made his farewell speech.

The Dibdins, Charles the elder in 1772 and Charles the younger, 1801 to 1814, wrote many plays and songs for Sadler's Wells. Charles the younger and Thomas Dibdin were also proprietors and managers.

Among the performers who appeared between the years 1780 and 1801 were Miss Romanzini, the ballad-vocalist, afterwards Mrs. Bland. Braham (then Master Abrahams) the singer; Paul Redigé the clever tumbler, called " the little Devil " ; La Belle Espagnole, his wife ; Dighton and " Jew " Davis, pantomimists ;

Bologna and his sons in their exhibitions of postures
and feats of strength ; Placido the tumbler, Dubois the
clown, and Costello (1783), whose wonderful dogs
enacted a play called *The Deserter*. Edmund Kean,
the tragedian, appeared in June 1801 as " Master
Carey, the pupil of Nature," and recited Rollo's address
from *Pizarro*.

SPINACUTI'S MONKEY AT SADLER'S WELLS, 1768.

Among the varied entertainments at Sadler's may be
mentioned the pony-races in 1802 (July) and 1822
(April and June). A course was formed by means of a
platform carried from the stage round the back of
the pit. In 1806 and 1826 a racecourse was formed
outside in the ground to the east of the theatre ;
booths, stands, and a judge's box were erected, and
many of the most celebrated full-sized ponies with a
number of jockeys of "great celebrity" and light-

weight were, at least according to the bills, engaged.
In 1826 (June) a balloon ascent from the grounds was
made by Mrs. Graham, and in 1838 her husband also
ascended. Belzoni, the famous excavator, exhibited
his feats of strength in 1803. In 1804 Sadler's Wells
was known as the "Aquatic Theatre." A large tank
filled with water from the New River occupied nearly
the whole of the stage, and plays were produced with
cascades and other "real water" effects.

Our rapid survey, omitting many years, now passes
on to 1844, when Samuel Phelps became one of the
proprietors of Sadler's Wells. During Phelps's memorable management (1844–1862) there were produced
some thirty of Shakespeare's plays, occupying about
four thousand nights — *Hamlet* being played four
hundred times.

In 1879 Sadler's Wells was taken by Mrs. Bateman
(from the Lyceum Theatre), and under her management the whole of the interior was reconstructed. At
the present time it is a music-hall with two houses
nightly. It is curious to note that Macklin, describing
Sadler's Wells as he remembered it some years before
Rosoman's time, says that several entertainments of
unequal duration took place throughout the day, and
were terminated by the door-keeper calling out "Is
Hiram Fisteman here?" Fisteman being a mythical
personage whose name signified to the performers that
another audience was waiting outside. The price of
admission at that time was threepence and sixpence ;
to-day the charge is twopence, a box being procurable
for a shilling.

[The authorities are numerous. The Percival collection relating
to Sadler's Wells (in Brit. Mus.) contains a great mass of material
bound in fourteen volumes. Useful summaries are given in Pinks's
Clerkenwell, 409, ff ; in the *Era Almanack*, 1872, p. 1, ff ; in
M. Williams's *Some London Theatres ;* and in H. Barton Baker's
London Stage, ii. p. 187, ff]

VIEWS.

The views, especially those of the 19th century, are abundant. The following are of the 18th century :—

1. A view of Sadler's Wells.   C. Lempriere, sculp., 1731. Crace, *Cat.*, p. 593, No. 77 ; cp. *ib.* p. 592, No. 76.

2. Hogarth's Evening, showing old Sadler's Wells and the Sir Hugh Middleton tavern.

3. South-west view of Sadler's Wells, from a drawing by R. C. Andrews, 1792 ; with a smaller view of the same in its former state.   Wise, sc., published in Wilkinson's *Londina Illustrata.*

Many others may be seen in the Percival and Crace collections.

THE Merlin's Cave, a tavern standing in the fields near the New River Head, close to the present Merlin's Place, possessed extensive gardens and a skittle-ground, which were frequented by Londoners especially on Sundays.

It was probably built in 1735 or not long afterwards[1] and derived its name from the Merlin's Cave constructed in 1735 by Queen Charlotte in the Royal Gardens at Richmond. The Richmond Cave was adorned by astrological symbols, and contained wax-work figures, of which the wizard Merlin was the chief. By the end of 1735 humble imitations of the Cave were established in various parts of the Kingdom, and it is highly probable that the Merlin's Cave tavern had an exhibition of this kind. The New Wells in Lower Rosoman Street, Clerkenwell, possessed a Merlin's Cave in 1740.[2]

About 1833 the gardens of the Merlin's Cave were built over. The New Merlin's Cave, a public-house

[1] A newspaper cutting in "Public Gardens" collection in Guildhall Library, records the death on 2 February, 1786, of Mrs. Bennet, of Merlin's Cave, Spa Fields, who was the successor of her uncle, Mr. Hood.

[2] A view of the Merlin's Cave at Richmond forms the frontispiece of *Gent. Mag.* 1735; on the cave, *see* Walford's *Greater London*, ii. 345, ff

now numbered 131 Rosoman Street, stands a little north of the old site.

[Pinks's *Clerkenwell*, 580, 581 ; Wheatley's *London*, s.v.]

VIEWS.

1. A view of the skittle-ground, Merlin's Cave, New River Head, with rules and instructions for playing. A print published by G. Kearsley, 1786. Crace, *Cat.* p. 592, No. 71.

2. Old Merlin's Cave near the New River Head, Rosoman Street. A drawing by C. H. Matthews, 1833. Crace, *Cat.* p. 592, No. 70.

BAGNIGGE WELLS

A MODERN public-house, " Ye olde Bagnigge Wells," standing on the west side of the King's Cross Road (formerly Bagnigge Wells Road), and the building yard of Messrs. Cubitt, behind it, now occupy part of the site of these famous Wells.

Bagnigge House, the building which formed the nucleus of the place of entertainment called Bagnigge Wells, is believed to have been a summer residence of Nell Gwynne. It fronted Bagnigge Wells Road, and was pleasantly situated, lying in a hollow called Bagnigge Wash (or Vale) ; and being well sheltered on all sides, except the south, by the rising grounds of Primrose Hill, Hampstead and Islington.[1]

[1] A square stone bearing the inscription given below was, about 1760, over an old gateway in the wall to the north of the Long Room, and was still there in 1843. In 1850 it was to be seen in Coppice Row, now Farringdon Road.

S T

THIS IS BAGNIGGE

HOUSE NEARE

THE PINDER A

WAKEFEILDE

1680.

The Pinder a Wakefielde (the modern representative of which stands near the old site in Gray's Inn Road) was a tavern ; and some writers have inferred from the above inscription that Bagnigge Wells itself was a place of entertainment as early as 1680.

In 1757 a Mr. Hughes, described as a man curious in gardening, and apparently the tenant of Bagnigge House, found that the more he watered his plants with the water drawn from a well in the garden, the less they seemed to thrive. He asked the opinion of a doctor, John Bevis, who analysed the water, and pronounced it a valuable chalybeate. At the same time the water of another well, sunk in the ground adjoining Bagnigge House, was discovered to possess cathartic properties. Hughes, realising the commercial possibilities of these wells, opened the house and gardens to the public, at least as early as April 1759. The place was open daily, including Sundays, and in 1760 Bevis published a pamphlet, setting forth the virtues of the waters.

The chalybeate well was situated just behind the house, and the cathartic well about forty yards north of the chalybeate. The water of the two wells, which were each some twenty feet in depth, was, however, brought to one point, and thence drawn from a double pump placed within a small circular edifice consisting of pillars supporting a dome, erected behind the house. This was commonly called the Temple. The chalybeate was of a ferruginous character having "an agreeable and sprightly sub-acid tartness," and was, according to Bevis, "apt to communicate a kind of giddiness with an amazing flow of spirits and afterwards a propensity to sleep if exercise be not interposed." The purging water left a "distinguishable brackish bitterness on the palate," and three half-pints were "sufficient for most people," without the addition of salts to quicken their virtue.

The charge for drinking the water at the pump was threepence : half a guinea entitled the visitor to its use throughout the season. At a later date when Bagnigge Wells was mainly frequented for its tea-gardens, a general charge of sixpence was made for admission.

The Long Room,[1] the old banqueting hall of Bagnigge House, was about seventy-eight feet by twenty-eight feet with a rather low ceiling and panelled walls. At one end of the room was a distorting mirror, a source of considerable amusement, which, for instance, revealed to Captain Tommy Slender of the Middlesex Militia, so odd a figure, that he was almost "hyp'd to death." Filled with apprehension he consulted a physician, who understanding the use of the concave and convex mirror made his patient take copious draughts of the water, and, after pocketing his fee, led him to another panel of the glass, where the Captain beheld a portly well-conditioned man. Vastly pleased he went home convinced of the virtues of the wells. At the other end of the room was a good organ[2] which provided music for the company. A water organ was also to be heard in the grounds. The organ performances were prohibited on Sundays by the magistrates from about 1772, apparently with the idea of rendering the attractions of Bagnigge Wells less dangerously seductive. The organ was, however, played regularly on the week-day afternoons.[3]

From about 1760 till near the end of the eighteenth century Bagnigge Wells was a popular resort. Some hundreds of visitors were sometimes to be found in the morning for the water-drinking, and early breakfasts

[1] Over one of the chimney-pieces of the room was the garter of the order of St. George, in relief, and over another the bust of a woman in Roman dress, popularly supposed to represent Nell Gwynne. This bust was let into a circular cavity of the wall, bordered with festoons of fruit and flowers moulded in delf earth and coloured after nature. Owing to the number of visitors promenading in the Long Room to the hindrance of the waiters, the room was, before 1797, divided into two, though we are told that the "former elegance" remained.

[2] The organ and its organist (under Davis), Charley Griffith, are shown in an engraving "The Bagnigge Organfist" (undated). "Published for the benefit of decayed musicians."

[3] *Picture of London*, 1802.

"THE BREAD AND BUTTER MANUFACTORY, OR THE HUMORS OF BAGNIGGE WELLS," 1772.
(INTERIOR OF LONG ROOM.)

were provided. In the afternoon the Long Room and the gardens were thronged by tea-drinkers, especially on Sundays. Stronger beverages were not unknown, and a bowl of good negus was a feature here. The lawyer, the man about town, and the active city merchant, no less than the gouty, and the hypochondriac, came to while away an hour or two :—

> Ye gouty old souls and rheumaticks crawl on,
> Here taste these blest springs, and your tortures are gone ;
> Ye wretches asthmatick, who pant for your breath,
> Come drink your relief, and think not of death.
> Obey the glad summons, to Bagnigge repair,
> Drink deep of its streams, and forget all your care.
>
> The distemper'd shall drink and forget all his pain,
> When his blood flows more briskly through every vein ;
> The headache shall vanish, the heartache shall cease,
> And your lives be enjoyed in more pleasure and peace.
> Obey then the summons, to Bagnigge repair,
> And drink an oblivion to pain and to care.[1]

The city matron deemed it the very home of fashion : —

> Bon Ton's the space 'twixt Saturday and Monday,
> And riding in a one-horse chair on Sunday :
> 'Tis drinking tea on summer afternoons
> At Bagnigge Wells with china and gilt spoons.[2]

With " genteel females " there mingled others of decidedly bad reputation.[3] Even a feminine pickpocket [4] was not unknown. The notorious John Rann,[5] who,

---

[1] " Bagnigge Wells," a song in the *London Magazine*, June, 1759.

[2] Colman's prologue to Garrick's *Bon Ton*, 1775.

[3] This is made sufficiently clear in the *Sunday Ramble* (1774, &c.) ; in the poem cited in the next note, and in Trusler's *London Adviser* (1786).

[4] *Bagnigge Wells*, an anonymous poem (1779).

[5] *The life of John Rann, otherwise Sixteen Strings Jack*, reprinted London, 1884 ; C. Whibley in *The New Review*, 1896, p. 222 ; cp. also the print " The Road to Ruin."

as Dr. Johnson observed, towered above the common
mark as a highwayman, was a visitor at Bagnigge
Wells, and a favourite with some of the ladies there.
On 27 July, 1774, Rann was brought before Sir John
Fielding after one of his escapades, but was acquitted,
the magistrate exhorting him in a pathetic manner
to forsake his evil ways. On the Sunday following
(31 July), he appeared at Bagnigge Wells with all his
old assurance, attired in a scarlet coat, tambour waistcoat, white silk stockings, and a laced hat. On each knee
he wore the bunch of eight ribbons, which had gained
him his sobriquet of Sixteen Strings Jack. On this
occasion his behaviour gave such offence to the company
that he was thrown out of one of the windows of the
Long Room. About four months later, 30 November,
1774, he was hanged at Tyburn for robbing Dr. Bell,
chaplain to the Princess Amelia.

The grounds of Bagnigge Wells were behind the
Long Room, and were laid out in formal walks,
with hedges of box and holly. There were a
number of fine trees, some curiously trimmed, and
a pretty flower garden. Ponds containing gold
and silver fish, at that time a novelty, were in the
gardens ; and the pond in the centre had a fountain
in the form of a Cupid bestriding a swan from whose
beak issued streams of water.

Parallel with the Long Room, and separating the
eastern part of the grounds from the western (and by
far the larger) portion, ran the river Fleet, with seats
on its banks, for such as "chuse to smoke or drink
cyder, ale, etc., which are not permitted in other parts
of the garden." Willows, large docks and coarse
plants, elder bushes and other shrubs in luxurious
profusion, fringed the banks ; and we hear of Luke
Clennell, the artist, making studies of the foliage.

Three rustic bridges spanned the stream, and amid
the trees were two tall leaden figures ; one a rustic

with a scythe, the other a Phyllis of the hay-fields, rake in hand.

Arbours for tea-drinking, covered with honeysuckle and sweetbriar, surrounded the gardens ; and there was a rustic cottage and a grotto. The last named, a small castellated building of two apartments open to the gardens, was brightly decorated in cockney fashion with shells, fossils, and fragments of broken glass. A bowl-ing-green and skittle-alley were among the attractions of the Wells, and a bun-house or bake-house was erected (before 1791) on the south side of the house, but not immediately contiguous to it.

Hughes, the original proprietor, appears to have remained at the Wells till about 1775 ; and a Mr. John Davis was subsequently the lessee till his death in 1793. During the last twenty years of the eighteenth century the company, for the most part, seems to have con-sisted of persons of lower rank than formerly :—

> Cits to Bagnigge Wells repair
> To swallow dust and call it air.

Prentices and their sweethearts, and city matrons with their husbands, frequented the place ; while unfledged Templars paraded as fops, and young ensigns sported their new cockades. The morning water-drinking was not neglected, but the full tide of life at Bagnigge was from five to eight p.m. on Sundays, when the gardens were crowded with tea-drinkers. A prentice-song sets forth the delights of the Wells :—

> Come prithee make it up, Miss, and be as lovers be
> We'll go to Bagnigge Wells, Miss, and there we'll have some tea ;
> It's there you'll see the lady-birds perched on the stinging nettles,
> The crystal water fountain, and the copper shining kettles.
> It's there you'll see the fishes, more curious they than whales,

Frontispiece *for the* Sunday Ramble;
Being a View in Bagnigge Wells Garden, drawn on ye Spot.

Page sculp

Salubrious Waters, Tea, and Wine;
Here you may have, and also dine;
But, as ye, through the Garden rove,
Beware, fond Youths, the Darts of Love.

And they're made of gold and silver, Miss, and wags their little
   tails ;
They wags their little tails, they wags their little tails.

About 1810 the place became more exclusively the
resort of the lower classes, though the situation
was still somewhat picturesque.   In 1813 Thomas
Salter, the lessee, became bankrupt, and Bagnigge Wells
was put up for sale by auction[1] on four days in the
month of December.   Not a bench or shrub was
omitted :   the "excellent fine-toned organ," the
water-organ, the chandeliers from the Long Room,
dinner and tea services of Worcester china ; the tea-
boxes, two hundred drinking tables, four hundred tea-
boards, and some four hundred dozen of ale and stout.
The various rooms and buildings were also offered for
sale, including " Nell Gwyn's house," the summer-
house, the bake-house, the grotto, temple, bridges ; the
two leaden rustics,[2] the fountains and all the gold and
silver fish.   Also the pleasure and flower gardens with
their greenhouses, all the trees, including a " fine variegated holly tree," the gooseberry and currant bushes,
the hedges, shrubs and flowers.

In the year following, however, the place was re-
opened under W. Stock's management, and though
the gardens[3] were now curtailed of all the ground
west of the Fleet (at this time a ditch-like, and,
on warm evenings, malodorous stream), an attempt
was made to revive their popularity.   The proprietor's efforts were not very successful, and during

[1] Sale Catalogue, 1813. (Copy in Brit. Mus.)

[2] A few years before 1891, these figures were in the possession
of Dr. Lonsdale of Carlisle (Wheatley's *London P. and P.*).

[3] The temple (behind the Long Room) and the grotto to the
north of it, were, as formerly, in the garden east of the Fleet.   The
western garden, previous to its curtailment, contained the rustic
cottage nearly opposite the grotto, and the pond with its swan and
Cupid fountain about the middle of the garden.

the next few years the premises frequently changed hands. In 1818 the lessee of Bagnigge Wells was Mr. Thorogood, who let it to Mr. Monkhouse (from White Conduit House) about 1831. In April 1831 Monkhouse advertised the Concert Room as being open every evening for musical entertainments, which continued to be the main feature of Bagnigge Wells until its close. In, or before, 1833 Richard Chapman was the proprietor, and John Hamilton in 1834.

In 1838 (August 14th), the lessees, Mr. and Miss Foster, announced for their benefit night an array of concert-room talent :—Le Mœurs of Bagnigge Wells, Mr. Darking (of the London concerts), Miss Anderson (from the Mogul Concert Room), Messrs. Sutton and Gibson (Sadler's Wells), Master Clifford (Yorkshire Stingo), Mr. H. Smith (Royal Union Saloon), Mr. Boyan (Queen's Head Rooms), Mr. Roberts (White Conduit); and the songs included "Tell me, my heart," "Billy the Snob" (in character), "Pat was a darling boy." A scene was given from *Julius Cæsar* ; a soliloquy from *Hamlet* ; and one Simpson exhibited classical delineations of the Grecian statues. The concert was followed by a ball, in which were danced a Highland fling (by a Mr. McDougal), a double comic medley dance, a waterman's hornpipe, and a hornpipe in real fetters and chains. During the evening a balloon was sent up from the grounds ; and sixpence procured admission to the whole. On other concert nights the admission was as low as threepence. Among the singers in the latest days of Bagnigge Wells were the well-known Paddy O'Rourke, Alford, Ozealey, Prynn, Box, Sloman, Booth, Gibbs and Dickie. Besides the songs and duets, portions of plays were acted, though without scenery or special dresses.

The year 1841 witnessed the last entertainment at Bagnigge Wells, when on 26 March there was an evening performance (admission sixpence) of glees, farces

F

and comic songs. The dismantling of the place was now begun. The grotto, which was already in a very dilapidated condition, was destroyed by some passers by in the early morning of 6 April, 1841.

In 1843 all that remained was the north end of the Long Room, and, according to a representative of *Punch*, who visited the spot in September of that year, the old well was filled up with rubbish and mosaics of oyster shells. Shortly afterwards, the present tavern was built ; Mr. Negus, a name suggestive of other days, being the tenant in 1850.

[Pinks's *Clerkenwell;* Walford's *O. & N. London;* Palmer's *St. Pancras*, p. 77, ff.; Wheatley's *London P. & P.*; Kearsley's *Strangers' Guide;* Noorthouck's *London*, p. 752, ff. ; Clinch's *Marylebone and St. Pancras*, p. 148, ff. ; Malcolm's *Lond. Rediv.* (1803), p. 237 ; *Sunday Ramble* (various editions) ; Rimbault in *Notes and Queries*, 1st ser. ii. 228 ; 4th ser. xi. 24 ; *Era Almanack*, 1871 (account of Bagnigge Wells by Blanchard).]

VIEWS.

The following views may be noted :—

1. "Ancient stone from Bagnigge Wells," engraved in Pinks, p. 558.

2. "The Bread and Butter Manufactory, or the Humors of Bagnigge Wells," a mezzotint published by Carrington Bowles, 1772 ; cp. an aquatint print from a painting by Sanders, published by J. R. Smith in 1772.

3. Mr. Deputy Dumpling and Family enjoying a summer afternoon, a print (1780) published by Carrington Bowles. Crace, *Cat.* p. 583, No. 84.

4. Bagnigge Wells, near Battle Bridge, a print (1777). Crace, *Cat.*, p. 583, No. 82 ; engraved in Walford's *O. & N. London*, ii. p. 294.

5. Bagnigge Wells Garden, frontispiece engraved for the *Sunday Ramble*, "drawn on ye spot," Page sculp. (*circ.* 1774 ?) (W. Coll.); engraved in Pinks, p. 563.

6. "A Bagnigge Wells scene : or, No resisting temptation." An engraving published by Carrington Bowles, 1780. Crace, *Cat.*, p. 583, No. 85 ; a hand-coloured mezzotint in Brit. Mus. *Catal. of Prints*, vol. iv., No. 4,545.

7. View of the Tea-gardens and Bun-house, from a drawing, taken in 1790 (?) ; copy in sepia in W. Coll.; an almost identical view is reproduced in Rogers's *Views of Pleasure Gardens of London*, p. 23, "from a drawing made in 1827."

8. "The Road to Ruin" (with figure of John Rann). Crace, *Cat.*, p. 583, No. 86.

9. A view taken from the centre bridge in the gardens of Bagnigge Wells. An example in Crosby Coll.; also reproduced in Ashton's *The Fleet*.

10. The original garden entrance to Bagnigge Wells (*circ.* 1800 ?) J. T. Smith del. Etched in Rogers's *Views of Pleasure Gardens of London*, p. 26.

11. View of Bagnigge Wells Gardens, 1828, engraving in Cromwell's *Clerkenwell*, p. 414 ; reproduced in Pinks, p. 567.

12. A collection of manuscript notes, sketches and drawings, relating to Bagnigge Wells in its later days, made by Anthony Crosby. (Guildhall Library, London.)

13. "Residence of Nell Gwynne, Bagnigge Wells." An engraving, C. J. Smith, sc. 1844 ; Crace, *Cat.*, p. 583, No. 88 ; Pinks, p. 559.

"LORD COBHAM'S HEAD."

THE Lord Cobham's (or Cobham's) Head, named after Sir John Oldcastle "the good Lord Cobham," was situated in Cold Bath Fields, and on the west side of Coppice Row, now Farringdon Road, at the point where it was joined by Cobham Row.

It was first opened in 1728 (about April), and in its garden there was then "a fine canal stocked with very good carp and tench fit to kill," and anglers were invited to board at the house. It was advertised to be let or sold in 1729, and little is heard of it till 1742 when it possessed a large garden with a "handsome grove of trees," and gravel walks, and claimed to sell the finest, strongest and most pleasant beer in London at threepence a tankard. Some vocal and instrumental music was at this time provided in the evening, and the walks were illuminated.

In 1744 a good organ was erected in the chief room of the inn and the landlord, Robert Leeming, for one of his concerts in 1744, announced Mr. Blogg and others to sing selections from the Oratorios of "Saul" and "Samson"; a concerto on the organ by Master Strologer and the Coronation Anthem of Mr. Handel. After the concert came a ball, the price of admission to the whole entertainment being half-a-crown. For July 20th of the same year there was announced "a concert of musick by the best Masters," for the benefit of a reduced citizen, followed by the display of a

" set of fireworks by several gentlemen lovers of that
curious art—Rockets, line ditto, Katherine wheels, and
many other things ; likewise will be shewn the manner
of Prince Charles's distressing the French after he
passed the Rhine." The concerts do not appear to
have been given after this period but the Cobham's
Head long continued to exist as a tavern, and is marked
in Horwood's Plan of 1799.

Printed for & Sold by BOWLES & CARVER. SUMMER AMUSEMENT. Nᵒ 69 in Sᵗ Pauls Church Yard LONDON

In December 1811 it was sold by auction, being
described at that time as a roomy brick building with a
large yard behind, probably all that was left of the
gardens. About 1860 during the operations for the
Metropolitan Railway the Cobham's Head was inun-
dated by the bursting of a New River Main, and was
so much injured by the undermining for the Railway
that it had to be vacated.

[Pinks's *Clerkenwell;* Wheatley's *London P. and P.*, "Coppice
Row."]

"SIR JOHN OLDCASTLE" TAVERN AND GARDENS.

THE Sir John Oldcastle Tavern was situated in Cold Bath Fields on the west side of Coppice Row, and was on the same side of the road as the Lord Cobham's Head, but rather nearer to Bagnigge Wells. It was originally a way-side inn, but during the first half of the eighteenth century became a well-known tavern. In 1707 (July 18th) the Clerkenwell Archers held their annual dinner there, and frequented it for some years.

In the rear of the house were extensive gardens, well planted with trees ; and from 1744 to 1746 these were open during the summer for evening entertainments. A band " of the best Masters " played from five o'clock till nine ; the walks were lit with lamps, and fireworks were displayed at the close of the evening. The admission was sixpence, including refreshments. In July 1746 concerts of vocal and instrumental music were announced, at which the chief vocalist, Mr. Blogg, sang such songs as " Come, Rosalind," " Observe the fragrant blushing Rose " and " The Happy Pair."[1]

In 1753 a Smallpox Hospital was erected on part of

[1] For New Year's day 1751, new fireworks in the Chinese manner were announced to take place at the Sir John Oldcastle (Pinks, p. 738). This was a special subscription entertainment. The regular open-air amusements appear to have come to an end in 1746.

the Oldcastle estate, but the Sir John Oldcastle, immediately adjacent, was left standing till 1762 when, being in a ruinous condition, it was pulled down.

[Pinks's *Clerkenwell;* Larwood and Hotten, *History of Signboards,* p. 97 ; Tomlins's *Perambulation of Islington,* p. 172 ; *Low Life* (1764), p. 81 ; *The Field Spy* (London, 1714) ; Ashton's *The Fleet,* p. 117.]

VIEWS.

South view of the Sir John Oldcastle in Lempriere's Set of Views, 1731.

ST. CHAD'S WELL, BATTLE BRIDGE.

THE site of St. Chad's Well, a mineral spring and garden at Battle Bridge, is now partly occupied by St. Chad's Place, a small street turning out of the Gray's Inn Road (east side) and lying between the King's Cross Station (Metropolitan Railway) and the Home and Colonial Schools.

About the middle of the eighteenth century the Well was in considerable repute, at least in the neighbourhood, and is said to have been visited in the morning by hundreds of people who paid threepence for the privilege of drinking. A hamper of two dozen bottles could be bought for £1. At that time the gardens attached to the Well were very extensive, and abounded with fruit trees, shrubs, and flowers.

During the last ten or twenty years of the eighteenth century few visitors frequented the Well ; [1] though we hear of it again about 1809, as being much resorted to by the lower classes of tradesmen on Sundays.

In the early part of the nineteenth century it had a few visitors of note. Sir Allan Chambré, the judge, used to visit the Well, and Munden, the comedian,

---

[1] The Well at Battle Bridge (*i.e.* St. Chad's) is mentioned with four other London Wells in the *Macaroni and Theatrical Magazine* for January 1773, p. 162. A Mr. Salter was part proprietor of the Well for many years previous to 1798. His mind became deranged and on 17 July, 1798, he was found drowned in a pond in the garden of St. Chad's (*The Courier* for 18 July, 1798).

when living at Kentish Town, drank the water three times a week. Mr. Mensall, the master of the Gordon House Academy at Kentish Town, used to march his young gentlemen to St. Chad's once a week in order to save in doctor's bills. John Abernethy, the surgeon, was also a visitor. When Hone visited the place in 1825, the Spring of St. Chad was once more almost deserted. Hone found a faded inscription "St. Chad's Well," placed over a pair of wooden gates, one of which (to quote his description) "opens on a scene which the unaccustomed eye may take for the pleasure-ground of Giant Despair. Trees stand as if made not to vegetate, clipped hedges seem willing to decline, and nameless weeds straggle weakly upon unlimited borders." "On pacing the garden alleys, and peeping at the places of retirement, you imagine the whole may have been improved and beautified for the last time by some countryman of William III." "If you look upwards you perceive painted on an octagon board 'Health Restored and Preserved.' Further on, towards the left stands a low, old-fashioned, comfortable-looking large-windowed dwelling, and ten to one but there also stands at the open door an ancient, ailing female in a black bonnet, a clean. coloured cotton gown, and a check apron ; . . . . this is the Lady of the Well."

In September 1837 the dwelling-house, spring and garden were put up to auction by their proprietor, a Mr. Salter. The next proprietor, William Lucas, finding that the celebrity of the waters had for a number of years past been confined chiefly to the neighbourhood, issued in 1840 a pamphlet and hand-bills in which the water was described as perfectly clear when fresh drawn, with a slightly bitter taste. It was composed of sulphate of soda and magnesia in large quantities, and of a little iron held in solution by carbonic acid. The waters were recommended as a universal medicine, being "actively purgative, mildly tonic and powerfully diuretic." The Pump-room was opened at 5 a.m., and the price of admission was threepence, or one guinea a year. By this time the old garden had been considerably curtailed by the formation of St. Chad's Place, and by letting out (1830) a portion as a timber yard. But it was more carefully kept, and a new and larger pump-room had been built in 1832. A fore-court adjoined the Gray's Inn Road, and next to it were the dwelling-house and pump-room. Beyond them was the garden which on the north was joined by the backs of the houses in Cumberland Row, and on the south by the timber-yard.

The pump-room was still in existence in 1860,[1] but was removed about that time during the operations for the new Metropolitan Railway.

[Pinks's *Clerkenwell*, pp. 504-506; Kearsley's *Strangers' Guide* s.v. "Battlebridge"; Lysons's *Environs*, iii. (1795), p. 381; Lambert's *London*, iv. 295; Hughson's *London*, vi. p. 366; *Gent. Mag.* 1813, pt. 2, p. 557; Cromwell's *Islington*, p. 156, ff.; Hone's *Every Day Book*, i. 322, ff.; E. Roffe's *Perambulating Survey of St. Pancras*, p. 13; Palmer's *St. Pancras*, p. 75; Clinch's *Marylebone, and St. Pancras*; Ashton's *The Fleet*, p. 49.]

VIEWS.

1. St. Chad's Well, a view from the garden. Water colour drawing by T. H. Shepherd, 1850. Crace, *Cat.* 583, No. 81.

2. Plan annexed to the auctioneer's particulars and conditions of sale of St. Chad's Well, 1837 (*see* Pinks, p. 506).

[1] Coull's *St. Pancras*, p. 22.

BOWLING GREEN HOUSE, NEAR THE FOUNDLING HOSPITAL

THE Bowling Green House, a tavern with a large bowling green attached to it on the south, was situated at the back of the Foundling Hospital, and south of the New Road. A lane turning out of Gray's Inn Lane led to it. It is first mentioned in 1676,[1] and it afterwards gained notoriety as a resort of gamesters. On a day in March, 1696, the house was suddenly surrounded by soldiers and constables, who seized and conveyed before a Justice of the Peace every person found on the premises. Some of the offenders had to pay a fine of forty shillings apiece.[2]

In the course of years, the character of the place changed, and in 1756 the proprietor, Joseph Barras,[3] announced that he had greatly altered and fitted up the Bowling Green House [4] in a " genteel manner." The

---

[1] In the minutes of a Vestry Meeting in St. Giles's parish, held in 1676, it is recorded that a meeting is appointed with the parishioners in St. Andrew's, Holborn, about the Bowling Green in Gray's Inn Fields and the houses near thereabouts built (F. Miller's *St. Pancras*, p. 77).

[2] Malcolm's *Manners and Customs of London* (1811), p. 209.

[3] Barras's advertisement is quoted in Palmer's *St. Pancras*, p. 310.

[4] It was generally known as the Bowling Green House, but the sign of the inn appears to have been the Three Tuns, for in a plan of the new road from Paddington to Islington (*London Mag.* 1756), the place is marked as the Three Tuns Ale House and the Three Tuns Bowling Green.

Bowling Green was declared to be in exceeding fine order, and coffee, tea, and hot loaves were to be had every day.   J. P. Malcolm [1] says that the Bowling Green House was for many years a quiet country retreat, but shortly before 1811 it was removed, and Judd Street, Tonbridge Street, &c., began to cover the space south of New Road.   Hastings Street and part of Tonbridge Street appear to be on the site.

[Authorities cited in the notes.]

---

[1] Malcolm in *Gent. Mag.* 1813, pt. 2, pp. 427–429.   The Bowling Green House is marked in Horwood's Plan C, 1799 ; in a map of 1806 in Lambert's *London*, vol. iv., and in Wallis's plan of 1808.

ADAM AND EVE TEA GARDENS, TOTTENHAM COURT ROAD

THE premises of the Adam and Eve stood at the north-west extremity of Tottenham Court Road, at the lower end of the road leading to Hampstead, and occupied the site of the manor-house of the ancient manor of Tottenhall or Tottenham.

The Adam and Eve Tavern is known to have been in existence under that sign in 1718.[1] Already in the seventeenth century Tottenham Court is mentioned as a place of popular resort, one of "the City out-leaps" (Broome, *New Academy*, 1658). George Wither (*Britain's Remembrancer*, 1628) speaks of the London holiday-makers who frequented it :—

> "And Hogsdone, Islington and Tottenham Court,
> For cakes and cream had then no small resort."

In 1645 Mrs. Stacye's maid and two others (as the Parish books of St. Giles in the Fields record) were fined one shilling apiece for the enormity of " drinking at Tottenhall Court on the Sabbath daie."[2] In

---

[1] Walford, v. 304, cites a newspaper advertisement of September 1718, announcing that "there is a strange and wonderful fruit growing at the Adam and Eve at Tottenham Court, called a Calabath, which is five feet and a half round, where any person may see the same gratis."

[2] Cunningham's *Handbook of London* (1850), "Tottenham Court Road"; *see also* Paxton's *History of St. Giles' Hospital and Parish* (cited in F. Miller's *St. Pancras*, p. 161), where similar fines for drinking at Tottenham Court are recorded for the year 1644.

Wycherley's *Gentleman Dancing-master* (1673) a ramble to Totnam Court is mentioned together with such fashionable diversions as a visit to the Park, the Mulberry Garden, and the New Spring Garden (*i.e.* Vauxhall).

In the succeeding century Tottenham Court Fair and the "Gooseberry Fair" doubtless brought many a customer to the Adam and Eve, and in the spring-time, as Gay expresses it, "Tottenham fields with roving beauty swarm." The Adam and Eve then possessed a long room, with an organ, and in its spacious gardens in the rear and at the side of the house were fruit-trees and arbours for tea-drinking parties. There were grounds for skittles and Dutch-pins, and in the fore-court which was shadowed by large trees, tables and benches were placed for the visitors. At one time it could boast the possession of a monkey, a heron, some wild fowl, some parrots, and a small pond for gold fish.

Vincent Lunardi, the first man in England to make a balloon ascent,[1] made an unexpected appearance at the Adam and Eve Gardens on 13 May, 1785. He had ascended from the Artillery Ground about one o'clock, but the balloon, being overcharged with vapour, descended in about twenty minutes in the Adam and Eve Gardens. " He was immediately surrounded by great numbers of the populace, and though he proposed re-ascending, they were not to be dissuaded from bearing him in triumph on their shoulders." [2]

Towards the end of the eighteenth century [3] the Adam and Eve began to be hemmed in by buildings ; by Brook Street (now Stanhope Street) on the west, and

---

[1] His first ascent was on 15 September, 1784. This was the first ascent in England, but it may be noted that Mr. J. Tytler had made an ascent from Edinburgh on 27 August, 1784.

[2] The *Morning Herald and Daily Advertiser*, Saturday, 14 May, 1785.

[3] See Horwood's *Plan*, 1793.

R.^d Cosway delineavi.   F. Bartolozzi Sculp.^t

·· et sc

Protinus æthereà tollit in astra via.

VINCENT LUNARDI ESQ.^r

Secretary to the Neapolitan Ambassador
and the first aerial Traveller in the
English Atmosphere
Septr 15. 1784.

Published Octr 5.th 1784 by John Bell British Library Strand

by Charles Street (now Drummond Street, western end)
on the north. The gardens however appear to have
retained their old dimensions,[1] and at that time extended as far north as Charles Street.[2]

The thousands of honest holiday-makers who visited
the gardens had, however, towards the end of the
eighteenth century, been replaced by a motley crew of
highwaymen, footpads and low women,[3] and in the
early years of the present century (before 1811) the
magistrates interfered : " the organ was banished, the
skittle grounds destroyed, and the gardens dug up for
the foundation of Eden Street."

About 1813 the Adam and Eve Tavern and Coffee
House, once more respectably conducted, was a one-
storied building. Part of it fronted the New (Euston)
Road, while an archway in the Hampstead Road led to
the other parts of the premises. A detached gabled
building, originally part of the domestic offices of the
old Tottenhall Manor House, was still standing at
this time and was used as a drinking parlour in connection with the Adam and Eve. Six small houses and
shops also adjoined the tavern and brought the proprietor about £25 each a year in rent, though they are
said to have been partly constructed out of the boxes in
the old tea-gardens.

The large public-house called the Adam and Eve,
which now stands on the old site at the corner of the
Euston and Hampstead Roads, was built in 1869.

Near the Adam and Eve was the Cold Bath in the

---

[1] See Wallis's *Plan*, 1808.

[2] Thus the grounds must at that time have covered the space
now occupied by Eden Street and Seaton (formerly Henry) Street.

[3] There may be some exaggeration in this description (based on
Wilkinson), for in the *Picture of London*, 1802, p. 370, the Adam
and Eve is enumerated among the tea-gardens frequented by the
middle classes, and is described as somewhat similar to the Jew's
Harp, with a small organ in the room upstairs where tea, wine and
punch are served.

New Road. It was in existence in 1785, when it was advertised [1] as in fine order for the reception of ladies and gentlemen. The bath was situated in the midst of a pleasant garden, and was constantly supplied by a spring running through it. The water was described as serviceable to persons suffering from nervous disorders and dejected spirits.

[Wilkinson's *Londina illust.*, i. "Tottenhall," Nos. 92, 93; Hone's *Year Book*, p. 47, cp. p. 317; Walford, iv. 477; v. 303 ff.; Palmer's *St. Pancras*, p. 204, ff.; Larwood and Hotten, *Signboards*, 257, 258; Brayley's *Londiniana*, ii. p. 165; Cunningham's *London* (1850), "Tottenham Court Road"; F. Miller's *St. Pancras*, p. 161; Wheatley's *London*, "Tottenham Court Road" and "Adam and Eve."]

VIEWS.

1. The scene of Hogarth's March to Finchley (see Nichols's *Hogarth*, i. 155, ff.) is laid at the Tottenham Court Turnpike, at the south end of the Hampstead Road. On the right is the King's Head tavern, and on the left the Adam and Eve. The sign of Adam and Eve appears on a post in the road, and Hogarth has inscribed it "Tottenham Court Nursery," in allusion to Broughton's amphitheatre for boxing that existed here (*see* Walford, v. 304).

2. Two views in Wilkinson's *Londina*, i. "Remains of the Manor House denominated the lordship of Toten-hall, now vulgarly called Tottenham Court, and occupied by the Adam and Eve Tea House and Gardens." Shepherd del., Wise sculp. (published 1813). Beneath this is a plan of the vicinity marking Eden Street. ii. Part of the Adam and Eve coffee rooms, Hampstead Road, J. Carter del., Wise sculp. (published 1811).

3. A woodcut in Hone's *Year Book*, p. 47, of the Adam and Eve (before 1825), substantially the same as Wilkinson's second view. The views in Wilkinson and Hone show the Adam and Eve in its altered condition after the proprietor Greatorex (end of eighteenth century?) had made an addition to the tavern, fronting the New Road.

---

[1] Walford, v. 305.

THE Peerless Pool should, in strictness, be described in a history of sports and pastimes, but as a pleasant summer resort, an oasis in the regions of Old Street and the City Road, it must be allowed a place in the present volume.

In ground immediately behind St. Luke's Hospital (built 1782–84), Old Street, was one of the ancient London springs which had formed, by its overflowings, a dangerous pond, referred to,[1] as early as 1598, as the "clear water called Perillous Pond, because divers youths by swimming therein have been drowned."

In the seventeenth century it was apparently resorted to for the favourite amusement of duck-hunting : "Push, let your boy lead his water spaniel along, and we'll show you the bravest sport at Parlous Pond" (Middleton's *Roaring Girl*, 1611).

In 1743, William Kemp, a London jeweller, who had derived benefit from his plunges in its water, took the Parlous Pond in hand. He embanked it, raised the bottom, changed its name to Peerless Pool, and opened it to subscribers as a pleasure bath. In the adjacent ground, of which he held the lease, he introduced other attractions : in particular he constructed a fish-pond, 320 feet long, 90 feet broad, and 11 feet deep, and stocked it with carp, tench, and other fish. The

---

[1] Stow's *Survey*, p. 7 (ed. Thoms).

G

high banks of this were thickly covered with shrubs, and on the top were walks shaded by lime trees. To the east of the fish-pond was a Cold Bath (distinct from the Pool) 36 feet long and 18 feet broad,[1] supplied by a spring. The Peerless Pool itself as contrived by Kemp was an open-air swimming-bath, 170 feet long, more than 100 feet broad, and from 3 to 5 feet deep. It was nearly surrounded by trees, and the descent was by marble steps to a fine gravel bottom, through which the springs that supplied the pool came bubbling up. The entrance was from a bowling-green on the south side, through a marble saloon (30 feet long) which contained a small collection of light literature for the benefit of subscribers to the Pool. Adjoining this were the dressing boxes.

The place became, from about the middle of the eighteenth century, a favourite resort of London anglers and swimmers, and many London merchants and persons of good position were among the subscribers. An annual payment of one guinea entitled subscribers to the use of the baths, and to the diversion of "angling and skating at proper seasons." Occasional visitors paid two shillings each time of bathing.

About 1805 Mr. Joseph Watts (father of Thomas Watts, the well-known Keeper of Printed Books at the British Museum) obtained a lease of the place from St. Bartholomew's Hospital at a rental of £600 per annum, and eventually saw his way to a profit by building on part of the ground. He drained the fish-pond which lay due east and west, and built the present Baldwin Street on the site. The old-fashioned house inhabited by Kemp, which stood in a garden and orchard of apple and pear trees overlooking the west end of the fish-pond, Watts pulled down, erecting Bath Buildings

---

[1] At a depth of four feet was a bottom of " lettice " work under which the water was five feet deep.

THE PLEASURE BATH,
PEERLESS POOL, CITY ROAD.

TERMS OF

PLEASURE BATH

	£. s. d
Month	0 9 0
Two Months	0 16 0
Year	1 1 0

| Single Baths with Towels and Box ... | 0 1 0 |
| Ditto without | 0 0 6 |

SUBSCRIPTION.

COLD BATH

	£. s. d.
Month.....	0 10 0
Two Months	0 17 0
Year	1 10 0

| Single Baths | 0 1 0 |

THE PLEASURE BATH
OF PEERLESS POOL,

THE largest in England, is situated in the immediate neighbourhood of the heart of the City, within Ten minutes' direct walk of the Bank and Exchange. (vide plan.) Surrounded by trees and shrubberies, open to the air, although entirely screened from observation, and most ample in its dimensions—**170** FEET in length, by **108** in breadth—it offers to the Bather the very advantages he would least expect to find at so short a distance from the centre of the metropolis. Its depth, which increases gradually from 3 feet 6 inches to 4 feet 8 inches, is such as to afford free scope to the Swimmer, while it precludes all fear of accident to any . and the temperature of the water rises to a height sufficient to ensure all the comfort and luxury of Bathing, without the risk of injury to health, from a too violent contrast with the external air.

THE COLD BATH,

THIRTY-SIX feet by EIGHTEEN, is the largest of its kind in London, and both Baths are entirely supplied by Springs, which are constantly overflowing.

The City Road is the line from all parts of the WEST END to the City. Omnibuses pass both ways nearly every minute throughout the day.

BILL OF PEERLESS POOL.   *Circ.* 1846.

on the spot.[1]   The pleasure bath and the cold bath he, however, continued to open to the public at a charge of one shilling, and Hone gives a pleasant description of it as it was (still in Watts's proprietorship) in 1826. "Its size," he says, "is the same as in Kemp's time, and trees enough remain to shade the visitor from the heat of the sun while on the brink."   "On a summer evening it is amusing to survey the conduct of the bathers; some boldly dive, others 'timorous stand,' and then descend, step by step, 'unwilling and slow'; choice swimmers attract attention by divings and somersets, and the whole sheet of water sometimes rings with merriment.   Every fine Thursday and Saturday afternoon in the summer, columns of blue-coat boys, more than three score in each, headed by their respective beadles, arrive, and some half strip themselves ere they reach their destination; the rapid plunges they make into the Pool, and their hilarity in the bath, testify their enjoyment of the tepid fluid."

The Pool was still frequented in 1850,[2] but at a later time was built over.   Its name is kept locally in remembrance by Peerless Street, the second main turning on the left of the City Road, just beyond Old Street, in coming from the City.   This street was

---

[1] Watts's building operations do not appear to have been completed till about 1811 or later (cp. Hughson's *London*, iv. (1811), p. 414).

[2] Peerless Pool is mentioned in *The Picture of London*, 1829 (p. 370), as one of the principal public baths of London. Cunningham, *Handbook of London*, 1850, speaks of it as a then existing public bath.   Mr. Hyde Clark writing in *Notes and Queries* (7th Series, viii. 214, 215) for 14 September, 1889, says that "it continued to be used as a bath until comparatively late years."   I am informed that after the death of Joseph Watts, the Bath was carried on by his widow, Mrs. Watts, and by the sons, Thomas Watts of the British Museum and his brother.   It seems to have been built over at some time between 1850 and 1860.

formerly called Peerless Row, and formed the northern
boundary of the ground laid out by Kemp.[1]

[Maitland's *Hist. of London*, i. p. 84, ff.; Dodsley's *London*, "Peerless Pool"; Noorthouck's *London*, p. 756, ff.; Trusler's *London
Adviser* (1786), p. 124; Hone's *Every Day Book*, i. p. 970, ff.;
Pennant's *London*, p. 268; Wheatley's *London P. and P.* iii. s.v.;
newspaper cuttings, &c., W. Coll.]

VIEWS.

1. Two woodcuts (pleasure bath and fish-pond) from drawings,
circ. 1826, by John Cleghorn in Hone's *Every Day Book* (cited
above).

2. View of Peerless Pool Bath and Gardens in 1848; coloured
drawing by Read. Crace, *Cat.* p. 608, No. 9.

3. The Pleasure Bath, Peerless Pool. An advertisement bill
with woodcut of the bath, surrounded by trees and shrubberies, and
a plan of the vicinity (1846?), W. Coll.; cp. Crace, *Cat.* p. 608,
No. 8.

---

[1] The grounds originally extended on the north-east to a tavern
called The Fountain, which was frequented by tea-parties :—

> And there they sit so pleasant and cool,
> And see in and out the folks walk about,
> And gentlemen angling in Peerless Pool.

(Lines in Hone, *loc. cit.*). There is now a public house called
The Old Fountain at the east end of Baldwin Street. The Shep-
herd and Shepherdess (*q.v.*) was close by on the other side of the
City Road.

THE SHEPHERD AND SHEPHERDESS,
CITY ROAD

THE Shepherd and Shepherdess ale-house stood on or near the site afterwards occupied by the well-known Eagle Tavern in the City Road and Shepherdess Walk.

It was built at some time before 1745, and its gardens were frequented in the last century by visitors, who regaled themselves with cream, cakes and furmity. Invalids sometimes stayed at the Shepherd and Shepherdess[1] to benefit by the pure air of the neighbourhood. The City Road (opened in 1761) was cut through the meadow-grounds that surrounded the inn. The place gradually lost its rural isolation, but it is found enumerated among the tea-gardens resorted to by Londoners of the " middling classes " in the first quarter of the nineteenth century.

The Shepherd and Shepherdess appears to have been pulled down about 1825, at which time Thomas Rouse built on or near its site the Eagle Tavern (rebuilt 1838) which formed the nucleus of the famous Eagle establishment with its Grecian saloon and theatre, its gardens and dancing pavilion. The tavern, grounds and theatre were purchased by " General " Booth in 1882, and have since been occupied by the Salvation Army.[2]

[1] Cp. Lewis's *Islington*, p. 31, note 6, referring to August 1758.

[2] For the connexion of the Salvation Army with the Eagle, and for some details as to the history of the Eagle tavern and gardens see *The Times* for 1882 (Palmer's *Index*, under " Salvation Army,"

[Larwood and Hotten, *Signboards*, 352, 353 ; *Picture of London*, 1802 and 1823 ; Walford, ii. 227, 274.]

June to September). On the Eagle *see also* Dickens, *Sketches by Box* (Miss Evans and the Eagle) ; Hollingshead's *My Lifetime*, i. p. 25, ff.; Ritchie's *Night-side of London* (1858) ; Stuart and Park, *The Variety Stage*, p. 35, ff. &c. ; *Era Almanack*, 1869, p. 80 ; H. Barton Baker's *The London Stage*, ii. p. 254, ff. ; and a view of the garden in Rogers's *Views of Pleasure Gardens of London*, p. 57.

THE SPRING GARDEN, STEPNEY

This Spring Garden was situated a little distance to the north of the Mile End Road and its eastern side abutted on what is now Globe Road.

It was in existence at least as early as 1702, and at that period seems to have been sometimes known as the Jews' Spring Garden,[1] probably because it was owned or frequented by some of the wealthy Jews who at that time and long afterwards resided in Goodman's Fields and the neighbourhood. There was a tavern attached to the gardens, the keeper of which, in 1743, was a Mr. Dove Rayner,[2] described as a man of " agreeable mirth and good humour."

The garden continued to exist till 1764 when we hear of it as a Sunday evening resort of holiday-makers,[3] but it does not appear to be mentioned at a later date.

In Horwood's Plan (G) of 1799 the garden (or its site), together with a few buildings, is marked as Spring Garden Court. Later on, in the present century, the

---

[1] *The Post Man*, Oct. 3 to 6, 1702, has the advertisement " At Milend the garden and house called *the Jews Spring Garden* is to be let. Enquire at Capt. Bendal's at Milend " (*Notes and Queries*, 1st ser. ii. 463). Mr. Alexander Andrews (*ib.* 2nd ser. viii. 422) has shown that this Jews' Spring Garden is in all probability to be identified with the Spring Garden marked in a map of Stepney parish of 1702.

[2] Rayner, Master of the Spring Garden at Stepney, died April 3, 1743, aged 70 (*London Daily Post* for 6 April, 1743).

[3] *Low Life* (1764), " Stepney Spring Gardens."

ground was known as Spring Grove.   Nicholas Street
and Willow Street, between Globe Road and St. Peter's
Road on the west, now appear to occupy part of the site.

About the middle of the last century Stepney is
described as [1] a village consisting principally of houses
of entertainment to which vast crowds of people of both
sexes resorted on Sundays and at Easter and Whitsun-
tide, to eat Stepney buns and drink ale and cyder.

One of these inns was known as The Treat ; and
there is a print [2] of it, dated 1760, inscribed with the
couplet :—

> At Stepney now with cakes and ale,
> Our tars their mistresses regale.

---

[1] Dodsley's *London* (1761), s.v. "Stepney."   There are modern
streets known as Garden Street and Spring Garden Place, but
these are some distance *south* of the Mile End Road, not far from
St. Dunstan's, Stepney.

[2] See Crace, *Cat.* p. 616, No. 80.

I.

MARYLEBONE GROUP

§ 1. *Origin of Marylebone Gardens.*

THE principal entrance [1] to these well-known gardens was through The Rose (or Rose of Normandy), a tavern situated on the east side of the High Street, Marylebone, opposite (old) Marylebone Church. The gardens extended as far east as the present Harley Street ; and Beaumont Street, part of Devonshire Street, part of Devonshire Place, and Upper Wimpole Street now occupy their site. When enlarged (in 1753) to their fullest extent they comprised about eight acres, and were bounded on the south by Weymouth Street, formerly called Bowling Green Lane or Bowling Street.

As a place of amusement of the Vauxhall type, the gardens date, practically, from 1738, but the Marylebone garden and bowling-green came into existence at a much earlier period.

The gardens were originally those belonging to the old Marylebone Manor House,[2] and were detached from it in 1650. There were several bowling-greens in the immediate vicinity, the principal of which was a green appurtenant to the Rose, and situated in the gardens

---

[1] "The back entrance was from the fields, beyond which, north, was a narrow winding passage, with garden palings on each side, leading into High Street" (Smith's *Book for a Rainy Day*, p. 39).

[2] Pulled down in 1791. Devonshire Mews was built on the site.

behind this tavern. In 1659 the gardens of the
Rose, the nucleus of the later Marylebone Gardens,
consisted of gravel walks, a circular walk, and
the bowling-green which formed the central square.
The walks at that time were "double-set with quick-
set hedges, full grown and indented like town-
walls." On the outside of the whole was a brick wall,
with fruit trees.

Pepys records a visit in 1668 (7 May) :—"Then we
abroad to Marrowbone, and there walked in the garden :
the first time I ever was there, and a pretty place it is."

In 1691 the place was known as Long's Bowling
Green at the Rose, and for several years (*circ.* 1679-
1736) persons of quality might be seen bowling there
during the summer time :—

> At the Groom Porter's batter'd bullies play ;
> Some Dukes at Marybone bowl time away.[1]

Less innocent amusement was afforded by the tavern,
which, at the end of the seventeenth and in the
early part of the eighteenth century, was notorious as a
gaming-house. Sheffield, Duke of Buckingham (*d.*
1712) was wont at the end of the season to give a
dinner at the Rose to its chief frequenters, proposing as
the toast, "May as many of us as remain unhanged
next spring meet here again." "There will be deep
play to-night (says Macheath in the *Beggar's Opera*),
and consequently money may be pick'd up on the road.
Meet me there, and I'll give you the hint who is worth
setting."

Some special attractions were occasionally offered to
the quality who frequented the Bowling Green ; thus,
in 1718 there were illuminations there, and a consort of
musick to celebrate the King's birthday. In 1736 we

---

[1] These lines, often erroneously attributed to Lady Mary
Wortley Montagu, occur in Pope's *The Basset-table, an Eclogue.*
The allusion in the second line is to Sheffield, Duke of Buckingham.

hear of scaffolding, 135 feet high, that was erected
in the gardens for the Flying Man who was to fly
down it by a rope with a wheelbarrow before him.

§ 2. *Marylebone Gardens under Gough and Trusler.*
1738–1763.

Daniel Gough, who was proprietor of the Rose and
its gardens in 1737, first made a regular charge for
admission,[1] and in the summer of 1738 (July 12)
advertised and opened " Marybone[2] Gardens " as a
place of evening entertainment. He selected a band
from the Opera and the Theatres to play, from six to
ten, eighteen of the best concertos, overtures and airs ;
erected a substantial garden-orchestra, in which was
placed (1740) an organ by Bridge ; and built (1739–
1740) the House or Great Room for balls and suppers.
Gough was succeeded as manager (in 1751 ?) by John
Trusler,[3] who being by profession a cook paid attention
to the commissariat of the Gardens. The rich seed and
plum cakes, and the almond cheese-cakes made by his
daughter, Miss Trusler, became a spécialité of the place.

[1] Gough issued, 1738-9, silver tickets at 12*s*. each, admitting
two persons for the season. In 1740 the silver season-ticket,
admitting two, cost £1 1*s*. There are extant silver (or rather
base silver) season tickets of 1766 (Wilkinson, *Londina*, vol. ii., last
plate, No. 19) and of 1767 (Brit. Mus.). These later tickets,
admitting two, cost £1 11*s*. 6*d*., or two guineas. There are copper
tickets of 1770 (specimen in Brit. Mus.). In 1774 the ticket for
two cost two guineas.

[2] The use of the old spelling which occurs in all the advertisements and contemporary notices must be conceded.

[3] J. T. Smith and several modern writers state that Trusler was
proprietor in 1751. It would appear, however, from the newspapers that in 1754 John Sherratt was proprietor, and in May 1755
Mr. Beard was stated to have "lately taken the Gardens." Trusler
was undoubtedly manager from 1756–1763. He died before
October 1766.

Sir John Fielding, the magistrate, was of opinion that Londoners should not want Mrs. Cornelys's entertainments in Soho, when they had Ranelagh with its music and fireworks and Marybone Gardens with their music, wine and plum-cakes.

During this period (1738–1763) Marybone Gardens were opened in the morning for public breakfasting in the Great Room, and for a concert, beginning at twelve, to which the admission was two shillings, or one shilling.   The admission for the evening entertainment was the same, but was raised on exceptional nights to three shillings.

In August 1738, there were introduced " two Grand or Double Bassoons, made by Mr. Stanesby, junior, the greatness of whose sound surpass that of any other bass instrument whatsoever."   In 1741 a grand martial composition was performed by Mr. Lampe in honour of Admiral Vernon.   In 1744 Knerler, the violinist, was the principal executant ; and Mr. Ferrand performed on " the Pariton, an instrument never played on in publick before."

In 1747 Miss Falkner made her appearance and remained the principal female singer[1] till about 1752.

Mary Ann Falkner (or Faulkner),[2] was the niece of George Faulkner, the Dublin printer, and was a vocalist of celebrity in her day, though she never aspired beyond such songs as " Amoret and Phillis," " The Happy Couple," " Fair Bellinda," " Delia," and " The Faithful Lover."   She had many admirers, among whom were the Earl of Halifax (the second Earl), Lord Vane, and Sir George Saville ; but she behaved circumspectly, and bestowed her hand upon

---

[1] Cp. *Vocal Melody*, Book iii.   *A favourite collection of songs and dialogues sung by Master Arne and Miss Faulkner at Marybone Gardens, set by Mr. Arne.*   Published 15 August, 1751, by J. Walsh, Catherine Street, Strand.

[2] The name is variously spelt ; usually Falkner.

Wm Defesch.

a young man named Donaldson, the son of a linen-draper. Unfortunately, her husband, who had been brought up in what Dr. Trusler calls "the line of a gentleman," was extravagant and idle, and consented (about 1753) to a base arrangement by which his wife was taken under the protection of Lord Halifax.

The Earl built a house for Mrs. Donaldson at Hampton Court Green, where she seems to have lived quietly. At a later time when Halifax was contemplating marriage with the wealthy daughter of General Drury, she surprised him one evening in the walks at Vauxhall Gardens, and so exerted her influence that the Earl not only left his Vauxhall friends without an apology, but broke off his engagement with Miss Drury.[1]

Other vocalists of this period were Thomas Lowe (from 1750); Mr. Baker (1750); Master Michael Arne (1751); Madame Ramelio (1752–1753); Mrs. Chambers (1753); Champness (1757); Kear (1757); Thomas Glanville (1757); and Reinhold (from 1757). Defesch, the well-known musician, was engaged as first violin in 1748.

In 1758 "La Serva Padrona, or the Servant Mistress,"[2] the first Burletta ever given in the gardens, was performed and was often afterwards repeated. It was an adaptation of Pergolesi's composition by the elder Storace, and by Dr. Trusler, the proprietor's son. The younger Trusler subsequently became a clergyman and finally a bookseller. He distinguished himself by selling to his clerical brethren original sermons printed in script characters, and made in this way, as he told his Bishop, an income of £150 a year.

During this period of the Gardens' history the

---

[1] See Trusler's *Memoirs*, p. 63, ff.; cp. *Dict. Nat. Biog.*, art. "Dunk, George Montagu, second Earl of Halifax," 1716–1771.

[2] *The Servant Mistress*, a burletta translated from the Italian. Price 6*d.*, printed at Marybone Gardens.

evening entertainments were usually confined to concerts, though balls were given from time to time in the Great Room. Fireworks were not often displayed, but on 26 September, 1751, after a masquerade, they were introduced with a kind of apology :—" the playing-off the fireworks (which will begin at eleven o'clock) will not incommode the ladies." " A large collection " of fireworks was announced for display on the June evenings of 1753.

A view of Marybone Gardens in 1755 shows smartly-dressed people promenading in the Grand Walk, with the Orchestra and the Great Room on either hand. At this period families of good position had country houses in the High Street, Marylebone, and they probably availed themselves of the subscription tickets for the balls and concerts in the Gardens. Old Dr. John Fountayne, for instance, would stroll in from the Manor House School with his friend Mr. Handel. On one occasion the great composer begged for Fountayne's opinion on a new composition that the band was performing. They sat down together, and after a time the clergyman proposed that they should move. " It is not worth listening to—it's very poor stuff." " You are right, Mr. Fountayne," said Handel, " it *is* very poor stuff. I thought so myself when I had finished it." [1]

The Gardens appear to have been generally conducted in a respectable way, though the Duke of Cumberland, if Dr. Trusler [2] has not maligned him, used to behave in a scandalous manner when he visited the place. Probably, gentlemen did not always accede to the proprietor's humble request that they should not " smoak on the walks " ; and a scene occasionally occurred. One Saturday night in August 1751, an angry gentleman drew upon another who was un-

---

[1] Hone's *Year Book*, pp. 500–503.
[2] Trusler's *Memoirs*, p. 57.

MARYBONE GARDENS, 1755—1761.

armed, but had his sword struck out of his hand by a
" nobleman " standing by, so that the disputants were
reduced (we are told) to the use of cane and fist.
But on the whole, Marybone Gardens was a decent
and social place of amusement, and little parties
were to be seen chatting and laughing in its latticed
alcoves. In May 1753 when the Gardens had been
extended and improved, the place could boast (according to a contemporary account) of the largest and
politest assembly ever seen there.

A guard of soldiers and peace-officers conducted the
company (*circ.* 1741) to and from the Gardens, and at
eleven and twelve o'clock a special guard set off to take
people along the fields as far as the Foundling Hospital.
(*circ.* 1743). The neighbourhood of the Gardens was,
in fact, by no means safe. On a June night of 1751
when the entertainment was in full swing, some thieves
entered the house of Mr. William Coombs, a wine
merchant residing at the Gardens, and carried off his
plate and china. About three weeks later a gentleman
who was in the fields at the back of the Gardens,
listening to the strains of the band, had a pistol pointed
at him by a man who demanded his money and his
watch. On June 30, 1752, a servant going to
the Gardens was attacked in the fields and robbed
by two footpads.[1] At a later date (1764) the proprietor felt it necessary to offer " a premium of ten
guineas " for the apprehension of any highwayman
or footpad found on the road to the Gardens, and
a horse-patrol to and from the City was provided
at that time. It is said that Dick Turpin once
publicly kissed in the Gardens a beauty of the time
related to Dr. Fountayne. The lady expostulated, but
Turpin exclaimed " Be not alarmed, Madam, you can

---

[1] Two men were executed 15 June, 1763, at Tyburn for robbing, in Marybone Fields, the waiters belonging to Marybone
Gardens.

now boast that you have been kissed by Dick Turpin.
Good morning ! ''

§ 3. *The Gardens under Thomas Lowe.*   1763–1768.

In 1763 the Gardens and adjoining premises were
taken at a yearly rent of £170[1] by Thomas
(" Tommy ") Lowe, the favourite tenor of Vauxhall
Gardens, who had already appeared at Marybone Gardens in 1750. He engaged, among other singers,
Mrs. Vincent, Mrs. Lampe, and the beautiful Nan
Catley, then only eighteen. Lowe opened in May
(1763) with a " Musical address to the Town," in
which the singers (Lowe, Miss Catley and Miss Smith)
apologised for the absence of some of the attractions of
Ranelagh and Vauxhall :—

> Yet Nature some blessings has scatter'd around;
> And means to improve may hereafter be found.

The entertainments under Lowe's management consisted principally of concerts in which he himself took
a prominent part.[2] The Gardens were opened at
5 p.m. : the concert began at 6.30, and the admission
was one shilling. In 1765 the concerts included songs
from Dr. Boyce's "Solomon," and Mrs. Vincent sang

[1] Indenture between Robert Long and Thomas Lowe, dated
30 August, 1763. The lease was for fourteen years. Trusler
ceased to reside at the Gardens in 1764 when he went to Boyle
Street, Saville Row, and Miss Trusler carried on business as a
confectioner.

[2] The vocalists 1763–1767, besides Lowe, were—1763, Mrs.
Vincent, Mrs. Lampe, Miss Catley, Miss Hyat, Miss Smith, Miss
Plenius (1763?), and Mr. Squibb (Sig. Storace and Miss Catley
had benefits) ; 1764, Mrs. Vincent, Mrs. Lampe, Miss Moyse,
Miss Hyat, Mr. Squibb ; 1765, Mrs. Vincent, Mrs. Collett, Miss
Davis, Mrs. Taylor, Mr. Legg ; 1766, Mr. Taylor, Mr. Raworth,
Mrs. Vincent, Miss Davis ; 1767, Mrs. Gibbons.

"Let the merry bells go round" by Handel, accompanied by a new instrument called the Tintinnabula. There was a new Ode (August 31), called "The Soldier," "wrote and set to music by a person of distinction." In 1767 (August 28), Catches and Glees were performed.

THOMAS LOWE.

A wet season, combined, as would appear, with insufficient enterprise, involved the manager in difficulties, and by a Deed of 15 January, 1768, he assigned to his creditors all the receipts and profits arising from the Gardens. He retired in 1769, and was glad to accept an engagement at Finch's Grotto, though at

one period he had been making, it is said, £1,000
a year. He died 2 March, 1783. Dibdin says that
Lowe's voice was more mellow and even than that
of Beard, but that "Lowe lost himself beyond the
namby-pamby of Vauxhall"; while "Beard was at
home everywhere."

§ 4. *Later History of the Gardens.* 1768–1778.

During 1768,[1] the Gardens were carried on by Lowe's
creditors. The receipts for the season from season-
tickets (£1 11s. 6d. each) and money at the doors and
bars, were £2,085 1s. 7½d., but the result was a
deficit of £263 10s. 3d., though the salaries do not
appear to have been excessive. Miss Davis for six
nights got three guineas ; Mr. Phillips three guineas ;
Master Brown four guineas ; Werner, harpist for six
nights, two guineas. The Band cost £27 13s. a week.
Dr. Samuel Arnold, the musician, became proprietor
of the Gardens in 1769 ; and though he eventually
retired (in 1773?) a loser, the Gardens probably offered
more attractions under his management than at any
other period. The weather being wet and cold, the
opening of the season of 1769 was postponed till after
the middle of May. The proprietor sedulously advertised the "very effectual drains" that had been made in
the Gardens, "so that they become very dry and pleasant in a short time after heavy rains." A few light
showers, moreover, would not hinder the performances,
and when dancing took place there was a covered platform in the Garden.
The seasons of 1769 [2] and 1770 were sufficiently gay.

[1] The vocalists in 1768 were Reynoldson, Taylor, Phillips, Miss
Davis, Miss Froud.
[2] Performers in 1769 : Pinto, leader ; Hook ; Park, hautboy.
Vocalists, Mrs. Forbes, Miss Brent, Mr. Herryman, Mr. Reynoldson.

The ordinary admission at this time, and until the final
closing of the gardens was one shilling, raised to half-a-
crown, three shillings or three shillings and sixpence on
the best nights, when the performers had their benefits.
On such nights there were fireworks by Rossi and Clanfield ; the transparent Temple of Apollo was illuminated, and a ball concluded the entertainment. In
1769 nearly the whole staff took a benefit, in their turn.
Mrs. Forbes, Mr. Hook, Mr. Pinto, Piquenit the
treasurer, the doorkeepers, and finally the waiters.
Thomas Pinto was engaged as leader, James Hook,
father of Theodore Hook, as organist (1769–1772),
Mrs. Forbes and Miss Brent (afterwards Mrs. Pinto)
as singers. Hook's " Love and Innocence," a pastoral
serenata, was performed for the first time on 10 August
(1769), and there were Odes by Christopher Smart, set
to music by Arnold, and an " Ode to the Haymakers,"
by Dr. Arne.

In 1770[1] the leader was F. H. Barthelemon, one of
the best known violinists of his time, and distinguished
for his firmness of hand, and purity of tone. His
burletta, " The Noble Pedlar," was successfully pro-

---

[1] Performers, 1770 : Barthelemon (violin) ; Hook ; Reinhold,
Charles Bannister ; Mrs. Thompson ; Mrs. Barthelemon ; Mrs.
Dorman. It is well known that Thomas Chatterton the poet wrote
a burletta called *The Revenge*, which he sold to the management of
Marybone Gardens for five guineas. It was not published till 1795,
when it was issued as *The Revenge, a burletta acted at Marybone
Gardens, MDCCLXX.* In the Marybone Gardens' advertisements
of 1770 (and of later dates) no burletta bearing the name of *The
Revenge* appears, and the writer of the article " Chatterton " in
Dict. Nat. Biog. thinks that the burletta must have been performed
at some time subsequent to 1770, the year of Chatterton's death.
In *The Revenge* as published, the *dramatis personæ* are Jupiter, Mr.
Reinhold ; Bacchus, Mr. Bannister ; Cupid, Master Chency ;
Juno, Mrs. Thompson. Reinhold, Bannister, and Mrs. Thompson
sang at the Gardens 1770–1773, and Chency in 1770. I may add
that a burletta called *The Madman*, performed at the Gardens in
1770, has a plot quite distinct from that of *The Revenge*.

ANN CATLEY.

duced this year. "The Magic Girdle," and "The Madman," were also produced ; and the "Serva Padrona," was revived. On 4 September the Fourth Concerto of Corelli, with the additional parts for trumpets, French horns and kettledrums, was performed. In 1771 [1] "The Magnet" was performed (first time, 27 June) and Miss Catley, now principal singer at Covent Garden, made her re-appearance.

From 1772 to 1774 the productions of Torré [2] the fireworker made the gardens very popular. Residents in the neighbourhood thought the fireworks a nuisance, and attacked Torré in the newspapers. Mrs. Fountayne produced a rocket-case found in her own garden, and in 1772 Arnold, as proprietor, was summoned at Bow Street. He pleaded, however, a license from the Board of Ordnance, and the fires of Torré continued to burn bright. Torré's masterpiece, often repeated at the Gardens, was called the Forge of Vulcan. After the fireworks were over, a curtain rose, and discovered Vulcan and the "Cyclops" at the forge behind Mount Etna. The fire blazed, and Venus entered with Cupid, and begged them to make arrows for her son. On their assenting, the mountain appeared in eruption, and a stream of lava poured down its sides.

Numerous singers were engaged for 1772, [3] Charles Bannister, Reinhold, Mrs. Calvert and others, and the

[1] Performers, 1771 : Hook ; solo violin, Mons. Reeves ; Charles Bannister ; Mrs. Thompson ; Miss Esser ; Miss Harper (afterwards Mrs. John Bannister) ; Miss Thomas ; and Miss Catley who sang "The Soldier tired of War's Alarms " ; "Sweet Echo," from *Comus* (the echo "sung by a young gentleman "), &c.

[2] According to J. T. Smith (*Rainy Day*, p. 52, n.), Torré was a print-seller in partnership with Mr. Thane, and lived in Market Lane, Haymarket. Other fireworkers at the Gardens at this period were Clitherow (1772) ; Clanfield (1772 and 1773) ; Caillot of Ranelagh (1773, 1775, 1776).

[3] Performers, 1772 : Hook, organ ; Charles Bannister, Culver, Reinhold, Mrs. Calvert, Mrs. Forbes, Mrs. Foster, Mrs. Cartwright and Mrs. Thompson.

musical entertainments were " The Divorce," by Hook ;
" The Coquet," by Storace ; " The Magnet," and " La
Serva Padrona." Bannister gave his clever musical
imitations of well-known singers and of " the Italian,
French and German manner of singing." At Hook's
Annual Festival on 28 August (1772) " Il Dilettanti "
(by Hook) was given for the first time with choruses
by " the young gentlemen from St. Paul's Choir." The
pyrotechnic entertainments included a representation of
Cox's Museum, and a magnificent temple consisting of
" upwards of 10,000 cases of different fires all . . .
lighted at the same time." During the fireworks, martial
music was performed under Hook's direction in the
Temple of Apollo.[1]

In 1773 [2] the Gardens were open for three evenings
in the week. Handel's " Acis and Galatea " was performed (27 May), and Barthelemon's " The Wedding
Day," in which " Thyrsis, a gay young swain, is
beloved by Daphne, an antiquated damsel." Arne
conducted his catches and glees at a concert on 15
September.[3]

In 1774 [4] there was music every week-day evening.
Several novelties were introduced, but the fortunes of
the Gardens appear to have been waning. Dr. Arnold's
" Don Quixote " was performed for the first time on
30 June. The first Fête Champêtre took place in July,
but the newspapers attacked the management for charg-

[1] On his own benefit night in July 1772, Torré gave a representation of Hercules delivering Theseus from Hell, in addition to
the Forge of Vulcan.

[2] Performers, 1773 : Charles Bannister ; Reinhold ; Phillips ;
Barthelemon (leader) ; Miss Wilde ; Mrs. Thompson ; Mrs. Barthelemon. " Mr. Dibdin, of Drury Lane Theatre," was announced
to sing in Barthelemon's " La Zingara, or the Gipsy " on Barthele
mon's benefit night.

[3] Also on 13 June, 1774.

[4] Performers, 1774 : Fisher (violin), Dubellamy, Reinhold ;
Mons. Rodell, " musician to the King of Portugal," German flute ;
Miss Wewitzer, Miss Trelawny, Miss Wilde.

ing five shillings for an entertainment which consisted
of a few tawdry festoons and extra lamps. Some of
the visitors, we are told, "injured the stage and broke
its brittle wares." One cannot help suspecting that Dr.
Johnson was at the bottom of this outrage : at any rate
during a visit of his to the Gardens at some time between 1772–1774 a similar incident occurred.

Johnson, who had heard of the fame of Torré's fireworks, went to the Gardens one evening, accompanied
by his friend George Steevens. It was showery, and
notice was given to the few visitors present, that the
fireworks were water-soaked and could not be displayed.
"This" (said Johnson) "is a mere excuse to save their
crackers for a more profitable company. Let us both hold
up our sticks and threaten to break those coloured lamps,
. . and we shall soon have our wishes gratified. The
core of the fireworks cannot be injured : let the different
pieces be touched in their respective centres, and they
will do their offices as well as ever." Some young men
standing by indulged in the violence suggested, but
failed to ignite the fireworks. "The author of *The
Rambler*," as Mr. Steevens judiciously observes, "may
be considered, on this occasion as the ringleader of a
successful riot, though not as a skilful pyrotechnist." A
second Fête Champêtre succeeded better, and the company did not leave till six in the morning.

During this year (1774), and in 1775 and 1776 the
Gardens were open on Sunday, after five p.m., for a
promenade (without music) ; and sixpence, returned
in tea, coffee, and Ranelagh rolls, was charged for
admission. As far back as 1760 the Gardens had been
opened on Sunday, and "genteel persons were admitted
to walk gratis," and to drink tea there. But this tea-
drinking had been prohibited in 1764. The "Sunday
Rambler," who visited Marybone Gardens about this
time, speaks of them with profound contempt as a place
of tea-table recreation. Nobody was there, the table-
cloths were dirty, and the rubbish for Signor Torré's

fireworks was left lying about.   The Gardens, he adds, were " nothing more than two or three gravel roads, and a few shapeless trees."

In the same year (1774) the managers of the Gardens advertised and opened (6 June) the Marybone Spa.   In the winter of 1773 the City Surveyor, while searching for the City Wells in Marybone, had discovered in the Gardens a mineral spring.   The public were now admitted to drink this water from six o'clock in the morning.   It was suggested that the waters might be useful for nervous and scorbutic disorders, but, in any case, " they strengthen the stomach, and promote a good appetite and a good digestion."

But the end of Marybone Gardens, as an open-air resort, was rapidly approaching.   In 1775 no concerts appear to have been advertised, though there were several displays of fireworks by Caillot in June, July, and August.   Already in 1774, one of those profaners of the " cheerful uses " of the playhouse and the public garden—a lecturer and reciter—had appeared in the person of Dr. Kenrick (on Shakespeare).   The management had now (June 1775) to rely for the evening's entertainment on " The Modern Magic Lantern," consisting of whimsical sketches of character, by R. Baddeley the comedian, and on a " Lecture upon mimicry," by George Saville Carey.   In July, a conjurer was introduced.

In 1776 there was a flicker of the old gaiety.   The Forge of Vulcan was revived in May, and there were fireworks by Caillot.   A representation of the Boulevards of Paris was prettily contrived, the boxes fronting the ball-room being converted into the shops of Newfangle, the milliner ; Trinket, the toyman ; and Crotchet, the music-seller.[1]

---

[1] A large printed bill referring to this entertainment is in the possession of Mr. H. A. Rogers, and is reproduced in his *Views of Pleasure Gardens of London*, p. 30.

The Gardens closed on 23 September, 1776, and were never afterwards regularly opened. Henry Angelo (*Reminiscences*), referring to the Marybone Gardens in their later days, says they were "adapted to the gentry rather than the *haut ton*." Whatever this distinction may be worth, it is clear from the comparative paucity of the contemporary notices that the Marybone Gardens, though a well-known resort, at no period attained the vogue of Ranelagh, or the universal popularity of Vauxhall.

About 1778 the site of the Gardens was let to the builders, and the formation of streets (*see* § 1) begun. J. T. Smith[1] states that the orchestra, before which he had often stood when a boy, was erected on the space occupied by the house in Devonshire Place, numbered (in 1828) " 17." According to Malcolm, a few of the old trees of the Gardens were still standing in 1810 at the north end of Harley Street.

The old Rose of Normandy (with a skittle alley at the back) existed, little altered, till 1848–1850, when a new tavern was built on its site. The tavern (still bearing the old name) was subsequently taken by Sam Collins (Samuel Vagg), the popular Irish vocalist, who converted its concert-room into a regular music hall, The Marylebone, which he carried on till 1861, when he parted with his interest to Mr. W. Botting. The present Marylebone Music Hall (with the public bar attached to it) fronts the High Street, and standing on the site of the old Rose of Normandy, from which the Marybone Gardens were entered, may claim, in a measure, to be evolved from that once famous pleasure resort.[2]

---

[1] *Nollekens*, i. 33, chap. ii.

[2] At a bazaar held in the Portman Rooms, Baker Street, in 1887 (Nov. 22–26), for the benefit of the charities of Marylebone Church, an ingenious reproduction was attempted, under the direction of Mr. Thomas Harris, the architect, of the latticed

[Sainthill's *Memoirs*, 1659 (*Gent. Mag.* vol. 83 ; p. 524) ; advertisements, songs, &c., relating to Marybone Gardens (1763–1775), Brit. Mus. (840, m. 29); Newspaper advertisements, songs, &c., in W. Coll.   Newspaper cuttings, &c., relating to London Public Gardens in the Guildhall Library, London ; Smith's *Book for a Rainy Day*, p. 40, ff. ; Thomas Smith's *Marylebone ;* Blanchard, in *Era Almanack*, 1869, p. 32, ff. ; Grove's *Dict. of Music* (1880), art. "Marylebone Gardens," by W. H. Husk.   Angelo's *Reminiscences*, ii. p. 3 ; Timbs's *Romance of London ;* Walford, iv. 431, ff. ; Thomas Harris's *Historical and Descriptive Sketch of Marylebone Gardens*, London, 1887.]

VIEWS.

1. A view of Marybone Gardens and orchestra, J. Donnowell del. 1755 ; published by J. Tinney.   Crace, *Cat.* p. 566, No. 74.

2. Modifications of 1, published by R. Sayer, 1755, and by Bowles and Carver.   Crace, *Cat.* p. 566, Nos. 75, 76.   Also 1761, published by J. Ryall [W. Coll.].

3. Views of Rose of Normandy.   Crace, *Cat.* p. 566, Nos. 79–81; p. 567, No. 82.

---

alcoves, lamp-hung trees, &c., of the old Marybone Gardens (see *A Booke of ye olde Marybone Gardens*, 1887 (sold at the bazaar) ;. *Daily Telegraph* for 23 November, 1887).

THE QUEEN'S HEAD AND ARTICHOKE

In the neighbourhood of the Marylebone Gardens were a few much humbler places of entertainment, standing in what in the last century was a rural district ; the Queen's Head and Artichoke, the Jew's Harp house and, farther west, the Yorkshire Stingo.

The Queen's Head and Artichoke was in Marylebone Park, nearly opposite Portland Road, and about five hundred yards from the north side of the New Road (Marylebone Road). It was a small and picturesque old inn, standing in a meadow to which a footpath led, and displaying a portrait of Queen Elizabeth as its sign. Tradition attributed the building of the house to a gardener of the Queen, and the curious combination of the sign was believed to have something to do with this. The inn is marked in Rocque's map of 1745, and it probably then possessed, as it did at the beginning of the present century, a ground for skittles and "bumble-puppy," and shady bowers, in which cream, tea and cakes were served.

It was pulled down about 1811, and the Colosseum afterwards occupied part of the site. A new tavern was then built near the site of the old inn, and this is probably identical with the public-house called the Queen's Head and Artichoke, which is now No. 30 Albany Street, east side.

[*Gent. Mag.* 1819, pt. 2, p. 401 ; Larwood and Hotten, *Hist. of Signboards*, pp. 311, 312 ; Walford, v. p. 255 ; Smith, *Book for a*

Rainy Day; Wheatley, *London P. and P.,* s.v. " Jew's Harp," and " Albany Street " ; Hone's *Year Book,* p. 318 ; Clinch's *Marylebone,* pp. 40 and 45.]

VIEWS.

1. A water-colour drawing by Findlay, 1796. Crace, *Cat.* p. 569, No. 104 ; cp. an engraving of the inn in Walford, v. p. 258, and a small sketch in Clinch's *Marylebone,* p. 45 (dated 1796).

2. An engraving published in *Gent. Mag.* 1819, pt. 2, p. 401 ; reproduced in Clinch's *Marylebone,* facing p. 40.

THE JEW'S HARP HOUSE AND TEA GARDENS

The Jew's Harp House was in Marylebone Park, a little to the north-west of the Queen's Head and Artichoke, from which it was separated by fields. It is marked in Rocque's map of 1745, and while still a quiet inn, is said to have been a favourite haunt of Arthur Onslow, the famous Speaker (*b.* 1691, *d.* 1768), who used to take his pipe and glass in the chimney corner. One day when driving to the House of Commons in his coach, he was recognised by the landlord, and on his next visit to the inn was welcomed by the family as befitted Mr. Speaker. His incognito was thus betrayed, and he returned no more.

By 1772 it had become a recognised place of amusement provided with " bowery tea-gardens," skittle-grounds,[1] a trap-ball ground and a tennis court. A large upper room, reached by a staircase from the outside, was used as a dining-room for large parties and occasionally for evening dances. Facing the south of the premises was a semi-circular enclosure with boxes for ale and tea drinking, guarded by painted deal-board soldiers.

The place was in existence till about 1812, when it

[1] An account of the robbery and murder in 1808 of Mr. William Joachim in the Marylebone Fields mentions that he was on his way home to Lisson Grove, after a visit to the Jew's Harp Tavern to see the skittle-playing (F. Miller's *St. Pancras*, p. 238).

I

was removed for the formation of Regent's Park. It stood between the present Broad Walk of the Park, and the north-east corner of the Botanic Gardens.

[J. T. Smith's *Book for a Rainy Day*, pp. 17, 18 (ed. 1833); Hone's *Year Book*, p. 318 ; Larwood and Hotten, *Signboards*, pp. 340, 341, where J. T. Smith's description of the Jew's Harp,

JEW'S HARP HOUSE, 1794.

Marylebone, is wrongly referred to the Jew's Harp, Islington ; Timbs's *Club Life* (1866), ii. p. 236 ; Chambers's *Book of Days*, ii. p. 74 ; Wheatley's *London*, s.v. "Jew's Harp" ; Walford, v. p. 255 ; Clinch's *Marylebone and St. Pancras*, p. 48 ; *Picture of London*, 1802, p. 370.]

VIEWS.

The Jew's Harp public-house in Marylebone Park. A water-colour drawing by Bigot, 1794. Crace, *Cat.* p. 569, No. 106 ; cp. a sketch in Clinch's *Marylebone*, p. 48.

THE Yorkshire Stingo, a public-house on the south side of the Marylebone Road, nearly opposite Chapel Street and the entrance to Lisson Grove, is the modern representative of a rural inn of the same name that was in existence at least as early as 1733.

From 1770 (or earlier) extensive tea gardens and a bowling green were attached to the place.[1]

During the first forty years of the present century the gardens were much frequented by the middle classes, especially on Sundays, when admittance was by a six-penny ticket including refreshments. For several years, from about 1790, a fair was held on the first of May at or near the Yorkshire Stingo, and the May-dance with Jack-in-the-Green took place.[2] This fair was suppressed as a nuisance in the early part of the present century.

In 1836 and for a few years following, the Yorkshire Stingo had its Apollo, or Royal Apollo, Saloon, in

---

[1] Wheatley, *London Past and Present*, s.v. "Yorkshire Stingo," states on the authority of Cooke's *Old London Bridge*, p. 7, that a bridge designed by the celebrated Thomas Paine, being the second cast-iron bridge ever constructed, was brought to London in 1790 and set up in the bowling-green of the Yorkshire Stingo ; it was afterwards taken back to Rotherham (where it had been made in 1789) and broken up in 1791.

[2] *The Picture of London*, 1802, p. 370, mentions the Yorkshire Stingo as a house many years celebrated for rustic sports on May Day.

which concerts, vaudevilles and comic burlettas were given every evening.[1]   On gala nights, balloon ascents, fireworks and other entertainments took place in the grounds.   The admission was one shilling.

The tea-gardens and bowling green were closed about 1848, and the present County Court and the Marylebone Baths and Wash-Houses,[2] nearly adjoining the present Yorkshire Stingo on the east were built on their site.

[Thomas Smith's *Marylebone*, p. 185 ; Walford, iv. 410 ; v. 256; Larwood and Hotten, *Signboards*, p. 384; *Picture of London*, 1802 and 1829 ; Wheatley's *London P. and P.* "Yorkshire Stingo."]

VIEWS.

1. "The Yorkshire Stingo in 1770," a small sketch in Clinch's *Marylebone*, p. 46, showing the tavern and the entrance to the tea-gardens.

2. View of the new County Court and the Baths and the Wash-Houses, built upon the ground of the late tea-gardens, &c., of the Yorkshire Stingo Tavern.   A woodcut, 1849.   Crace, *Cat.* p. 567, No. 89.

---

[1] Newspaper cuttings in W. Coll. ; cp. Hollingshead's *My Lifetime*, i. 24, and *see also* Stuart and Park, *The Variety Stage*, p. 38, who mention Cave and Glindon as the comic vocalists.   The saloon, which was in the rear of the tavern, had a small but capable orchestra directed by Love, afterwards leader at the Princess's Theatre under Charles Kean.   Miss Tunstall of Vauxhall was at one time a singer there.

[2] Pulled down about 1895.

BAYSWATER TEA GARDENS

THE Bayswater Tea Gardens, situated in a region once noted for its springs and salubrious air, were originally the Physic Garden of "Sir" John Hill, botanist, playwright, and quack doctor :—

"His farces are physic, his physic a farce is,"

and in this garden he grew the plants for his wonderful Water Dock Essence and Balm of Honey.

Hill died in 1775, and his garden was (some years before 1795) turned into a place of amusement, known as the Bayswater Tea Gardens, and much frequented by the denizens of Oxford Street and neighbourhood.[1] Views of 1796 show the boxes and arbours, and a family party, more plebeian than that in George Morland's "Tea Garden," in full enjoyment of their tea. Waiters are bustling about with huge kettles crying "'Ware kettle, scaldings!"

The Bayswater Tea Gardens are mentioned in the *Picture of London*, 1823–1829, among those frequented by Londoners of the middle classes. From about 1836 they appear to have been called the Flora Tea Gardens, Bayswater.

For the 27th June, 1836, Mrs. Graham was announced to make her ascent from the gardens at five o'clock, in her silk balloon. In the evening were fire-

[1] Woodward's *Eccentric Excursions*, p. 18.

THE BAYSWATER TEA GARDENS, 1796.

works, the admission being one shilling. In August
1839, Hampton, the aëronaut, made an ascent about
seven in the evening in his Albion balloon from these
gardens, which were crowded by "a fashionable and
respectable company." The balloon moved over the
Kensington Gardens, and Hampton then descended in
his safety parachute, this descent being the feature of
the performance. The parachute struck against a tree
and fell. Hampton was extracted from the tackle in a
shaken condition, but was borne on the shoulders of
four men into the Flora Gardens amid loud applause,
and a grand display of fireworks concluded the entertainment.

At a later date the place was called the Victoria Tea
Gardens, and became well known for running matches
and other sporting meetings. The gardens continued
open till 1854, but their site, together with that of
Hopwood's Nursery Grounds, was afterwards (from
about 1860) covered by the houses of Lancaster Gate.

[Art. "Hill John, M.D." in *Dict. of Nat. Biog.*; Lysons's *Environs*, iii. p. 331 ; *Era Almanack*, 1871 ; Faulkner, *Kensington*,
p. 420 ; Wheatley, *London P. and P.* s.v. "Bayswater" and "Lancaster Gate" ; Walford, v. pp. 183, 185, 188 ; newspaper cuttings,
W. Coll.]

VIEWS.

"View of the Tea Gardens at Bayswater," two oval prints in
Woodward's *Eccentric Excursions*, plate v. Woodward del., J. C.
sculp. London, published 1796 by Allen and West.

III

NORTH LONDON GROUP

THESE Wells were situated close to old St. Pancras Church on its south side. In connection with them was a tavern originally called the Horns, and its proprietor, Edward Martin, issued in 1697 a handbill setting forth the virtues of the water, which he declares to have been found "by long experience" a powerful antidote against rising of the vapours, also against the stone and gravel. It likewise cleanses the body and sweetens the blood, and is a general and sovereign help to nature. For the summer season of this year (beginning on Whit-Monday) Martin promised to provide dancing every Tuesday and Thursday. The charge for the "watering" and such other diversions as were obtainable was threepence.

In 1722 a proprietor of the Wells laments that the credit of the place had suffered for many years "by encouraging of scandalous company" (probably some of "the pretty nymphs" mentioned [1] by Thomas Brown) and by making the Long Room a common dancing room. He promises to prevent this in the future, and to exclude undesirable characters from the garden walks.

About 1730 Pancras Wells seem to have regained their reputation; at any rate they were industriously advertised, and the London print-dealers sold views of the gardens and the rooms. The water could be

[1] Before 1702.

obtained at the pump-room, or a dozen bottles of it might be purchased for six shillings of Mr. Richard Bristow, goldsmith.[1] At this time, and for forty or fifty years later, the surroundings of the Wells were completely rural, and visitors might be seen coming across the fields by the foot-paths leading from Tottenham Court, Gray's Inn, and Islington. The gardens and premises had now (1730) reached their full extent. Facing the church was the House of Entertainment, and behind this was the Long Room (sixty feet by eighteen) with the Pump Room at its west end. The gardens lay further south, in the rear of these and other buildings. A pleasant stroll might be taken in the New Plantation or in the shaded, but formal, garden known as the Old Walk. Little is heard of the Wells during the next thirty or forty years. But in June 1769 the proprietor, John Armstrong, advertised the water as being in the greatest perfection. The place, however, was probably now chiefly frequented as a "genteel and rural" tea garden, with its hot loaves, syllabubs, and milk from the cow. Dinners were also obtainable, and the powerful refreshments of "neat wines, curious punch, Dorchester, Marlborough, and Ringwood beers."

According to Lysons, the Pancras water continued in esteem till some years before 1795, but when he wrote (1795–1811) the Well appears to have been enclosed in the garden of a private house. Part of the site of the old Wells and walks was formerly occupied by the houses in Church Row, but these have been swept away

---

[1] *The Country Journal, or the Craftsman*, 7 March, 1729–30. If an allusion in a pamphlet of 1735—*A seasonable examination of the pleas and pretensions of . . . . Playhouses erected in defiance of Royal Licence* (London, printed for T. Cooper, 1735)—may be relied on, Pancras Wells had about that time some kind of (unlicensed) theatrical or "variety" entertainments resembling those of Sadler's Wells.

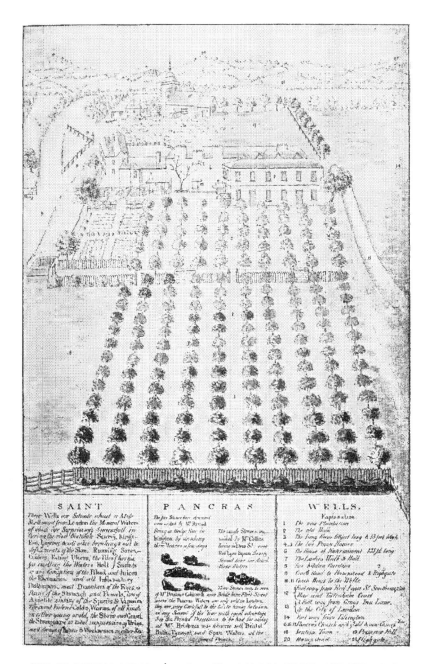

BILL OF PANCRAS WELLS, *circ.* 1730, SHOWING THE WELLS, AND THE ADAM
AND EVE TAVERN NEAR ST. PANCRAS CHURCH.

for the premises of the Midland Railway connected with the St. Pancras Terminus.[1]

[T. Brown's *Letters from the Dead to the Living*, part ii. first published 1702, "Moll Quarles to Mother Creswell"; Dodsley's *London*, 1761, s.v. "Pancras"; Lysons's *Environs*, iii. (1795), p. 381; Supplement (1811), p. 283; *Gent. Mag.* 1813, pt. 2, p. 556; *Beauties of England and Wales*, x. part iv. (1816), p. 175; Clinch's *Marylebone and St. Pancras;* Palmer's *St. Pancras;* Miller's *St. Pancras;* Roffe's *St. Pancras* (1865), p. 10; Lewis's *Islington*, p. 37, note; Walford, v. 339.]

VIEWS.

1. A bird's-eye view of St. Pancras Wells, showing the garden, house, &c., the old church, &c., with a description of the mineral waters. A tinted drawing, 1751, Crace, *Cat.* p. 580, No. 57. The original engraving is of *circ.* 1730; *see* Palmer's *St. Pancras*, p. 246, ff.; Clinch's *Marylebone*, p. 156; Walford, v. 336.

2. "The south-west view of Pancras Church and Wells." Chatelain del., J. Roberts sc., 1750. Crace, *Cat.* p. 579, No. 45; W. Coll. (Pl. 30 in Chatelain's *Fifty Views*); also the south-east view, Chatelain's *Fifty Views*, pl. 29, with "Adam and Eve."

3. Pancras Wells. A north view of the garden, house, &c. Copy of an old drawing, 1775, Crace, *Cat.* p. 580, No. 58.

4. A view of the Long Room at St. Pancras, and the Trap-Ball Ground. Copy of an old drawing, 1775. Crace, *Cat.* p. 580, No. 59.

5. Colonel Jack robbing Mrs. Smith going to Kentish Town (near the Wells). W. Jett del., J. Basire sc., 1762. Crace, *Cat.* p 580, No. 60.

---

[1] According to Roffe (*St. Pancras*), Pancras Wells occupied the south side of Church Hill from its base to its summit. Palmer in his *St. Pancras*, published in 1870, says the Well "is now enclosed in the garden of a private house, neglected and passed out of mind."

ADAM AND EVE TEA GARDENS, ST. PANCRAS

THE Adam and Eve Tavern, situated near the west end of old Saint Pancras Church, was in existence at least as early as 1730[1], and is mentioned in 1754[2] as a resort of the London " cit." In 1778 it could boast of a long room adorned with gilt-framed oval pier-glasses ;[3] and in 1786 the landlord, Charles Eaton, advertised[4] the attractions of his gardens and pleasure grounds.

About the beginning of the present century it could still be described as an agreeable retreat " with enchanting prospects," and the gardens were well laid out with arbours, flowers and shrubs. Cows were kept for making syllabubs, and on summer afternoons a regular company met to play bowls and trap-ball in an adjacent field. One proprietor fitted out a mimic squadron of frigates in the garden, and the long room was a good deal used for bean-feasts, and tea-drinking parties.[5]

[1] It is shown in the bird's-eye view of Pancras Wells of 1730. In April 1731, James Dalton, a notorious footpad, robbed a linen-pedlar at night near the Adam and Eve after drinking with him at the tavern (Pinks's *Clerkenwell*, p. 549).

[2] *The Connoisseur*, 1754, No. 26.

[3] Five of these pier-glasses were stolen from the long room in 1778 (*London Evening Post*, 11—14 July, 1778).

[4] Advertisement of 1786 quoted in Clinch's *Marylebone and St. Pancras*, p. 157.

[5] There are advertisements of the Adam and Eve issued (at the end of the eighteenth and beginning of the nineteenth century ?)

In 1803, about three and a half acres of the Adam and Eve tea-gardens were taken to form the St. Giles-in-the-Fields Cemetery (adjoining the old St. Pancras Churchyard), though the tavern still lingered on. In later years (*circ.* 1865–1874) the Adam and Eve was an ordinary public-house. It still retained (1874) a portion of its old grounds, which were used by its frequenters for bowl-playing. This ground, however, was enclosed by a high wall, and was overlooked by the mean houses that formed Eve Place. The building has since been taken down.

[F. Miller's *St. Pancras*, pp. 45 and 49 ; Palmer's *St. Pancras*, pp. 244, 245 ; Roffe's *St. Pancras*, p. 3 ; *Picture of London*, ed. 1802, p. 370 ; Wheatley's *London*, III., 20, 22, 23 ; *see also* notes.]

VIEWS.

The Adam and Eve is shown in the 1730 view of Pancras Wells, and in the views of old St. Pancras Church, *e.g.*, in the "South view of the Church of St. Pancras," printed for Bowles and Carver (W. Coll.).

---

by G. Swinnerton, Junr. and Co., and by George Lambert (quoted in Walford, vol. v. p. 338). The *Picture of London*, 1805, mentions the Adam and Eve Tea-gardens, bowling-green, &c., but the conversion of the gardens into the cemetery (authorised by Act of Parliament in 1803) appears to have been already carried out in 1804.

THE ASSEMBLY HOUSE,
KENTISH TOWN

THE Assembly House was in existence in 1725 [1] or earlier, and consisted of a large inn, partly built of wood, with a Long Room on the south, entered from outside by a covered staircase. This room for many years continued to be used for dancing by the élite of the neighbourhood.

By about 1776 the village of Kentish Town had become a somewhat populous place, and in the summertime was much resorted to by Londoners, who took lodgings there, or made brief excursions thither. In 1788 the Assembly House was taken by a Mr. Thomas Wood, who specially advertised his trap-ball and skittle-ground, pleasant summer-house, and extensive garden.

The house was pulled down in 1853, and its site and that of the garden covered by houses. The Assembly House tavern (No. 298 Kentish Town Road) and a police station have been built on the baiting ground and yard that were formerly in front of the old house.

---

[1] There is a mention of the inn in 1725 : the Assembly Rooms were certainly in existence in 1750, and perhaps at an earlier date. The original sign of the inn appears to have been the Black Bull ; see *Notes and Queries*, 1st ser. viii. p. 293 ; W. Elliot's *Some Account of Kentish Town* (1821), p. 65.

[Miller's *St. Pancras*, p. 294, ff. ; Roffe's *St. Pancras*, pp. 10, 11 ; Walford, v. p. 320 ; Palmer's *St. Pancras*, p. 62, ff.]

VIEWS.

1. "The Assembly Rooms, Kentish Town, 1750," Walford, v. p. 313.
2. "The Old Assembly House, Kentish Town," May 1853 ; drawn and etched by W. B. Rye, *Etchings*, London, 1857.

WHITE CONDUIT HOUSE was originally a small ale-house of the seventeenth century, and, according to tradition, the workmen who built it were carousing there to celebrate its completion on the day of the execution of Charles I.

It derived its name from the water-conduit, faced with white stone, which stood in a field nearly opposite. In 1731 White Conduit House was still a one-storied building, but between that date and about 1745 it was pulled down, or altered,[1] and a Long Room added.

From about 1745 the garden was well laid out, and possessed a circular fish-pond and a number of pleasant arbours. Robert Bartholomew, the proprietor in 1754, added a long walk, and, to prevent his visitors being in the "least incommoded from people in the fields," constructed a fence some seven feet in height. Hot loaves, tea, coffee and liquors 'in the greatest perfection' were the refreshments offered, and he assured those who drank his milk, procured directly from the cow, that his animals "eat no grains." Cricket was played at this time (1754) in a meadow adjoining the house ; bats and balls being provided by the proprietor.[2]

[1] The new or altered building contained the circular structure shown in so many views of the place.

[2] The White Conduit meadow long continued in use as a cricket ground. About 1784 and subsequently a club composed of gentle-

The house contained rooms for tea-drinking, and also the Long Room, from whence "is the most copious prospects and airy situation of any now in vogue," a description ungrammatical but correct, for White Conduit House at this time, and until about 1775, was picturesquely situated. Standing on rising ground, and environed by pleasant country lanes and pastures, it commanded towards the north fine views of Hampstead and Highgate.

In 1774 the gardens at the back of the house were described as being laid out with several pleasing walks, prettily disposed, with the pond in the centre, and an avenue of trees. For the accommodation of the tea-drinkers, there were "genteel boxes" let into the hedges, and decorated with Flemish paintings. A large painting was placed at the far end of the avenue, and seemed to increase its length.

Under Robert Bartholomew (who was probably proprietor until his death in 1766) White Conduit had become a popular tea-garden, and till about the end of the eighteenth century, its visitors, though never in the least people of fashion, were on the whole of a respectable class. The favourite day was Sunday in the spring and summer-time, when large numbers of holiday-folk crowded the house and gardens. The 'City prig,' in white satin waistcoat and scratch wig ; the graver man of business, clad in brown, his wife and family, were persons of consequence here ; while their dependants also spent their holiday at the same place :—

> Wish'd Sunday's come, mirth brightens ev'ry face,
> And paints the rose upon the housemaid's cheek,
> Harriot, or Mol, more ruddy. Now the heart
> Of 'prentice, resident in ample street,

men and men of rank played its matches there. Among the players were the Duke of Dorset, Lord Winchilsea, Lord Talbot, Col. Tarleton, and Thomas Lord, who afterwards established the Marylebone Cricket Club.

Or alley, kennel-wash'd, Cheapside, Cornhill,
Or Cranbourne, thee for calcuments renown'd,
With joy distends.   His meal meridian o'er
With switch in hand, he to White Conduit House
Hies merry-hearted.   Human beings here
In couples multitudinous assemble,
Forming the drollest group that ever trod
Fair Islingtonian plains.   Male after male,
Dog after dog succeeding, husbands, wives,
Fathers and mothers, brothers, sisters, friends,
And pretty little boys and girls.   Around,
Across, along the gardens' shrubby maze
They walk, they sit, they stand.   What crowds press on,
Eager to mount the stairs, eager to catch
First vacant bench, or chair in long room plac'd.
Here prig with prig holds conference polite,
And indiscriminate the gaudy beau
And sloven mix.   Here he who all the week
Took bearded mortals by the nose, or sat
Weaving dead hairs, and whistling wretched strain,
And eke the sturdy youth, whose trade it is
Stout oxen to contund, with gold-bound hat
And silken stocking strut.   The red-arm'd belle
Here shows her tasty gown, proud to be thought
The butterfly of fashion.[1]

Curtseys, bows and compliments were the order of
the day.   A White Conduit method of effecting an
introduction was for the gallant 'prentice to tread on
the lady's train, to apologise profusely, and finally to
suggest an adjournment for tea in one of the arbours.
By five o'clock on a fine Sunday afternoon a seat was
hardly procurable ; for the tea-drinking was then in
full vigour, and the famous White Conduit loaves[2] in
great request.

Among its frequenters White Conduit House could
number Oliver Goldsmith, who was wont (*circ.* 1768)
to call there at tea-time on his " shoemaker's holidays."[3]

[1] A poem by W. W[oty] printed in the *London Chronicle*, 1760,
vol. vii. p. 531.

[2] "White Conduit Loaves " was a London cry till about 1825.

[3] Forster's *Life of Goldsmith ;* cp. Goldsmith's *Citizen of the
World*, Letter 122.

(cp. Highbury Barn, *infra*).   On one occasion, meeting in the gardens the wife and daughters of a tradesman to whom he was under some obligation, he treated the ladies handsomely to refreshments ; only to find when the reckoning came, that his purse was empty.[1]   Abraham Newland, the famous cashier of the Bank of England, was also a visitor at White Conduit, and, at a later time George Cruikshank [2] made many of his character sketches there.   The visitors came to dread his sketchbook, and children who made faces were set on their good behaviour by the threat that Mr. Cruikshank would put them in his book.

In 1794, or earlier, the owner of White Conduit was Mr. Christopher Bartholomew,[3] a man of considerable means, who did much to improve the grounds.   At one time he owned the freeholds of both the Angel Inn, Islington, and White Conduit House, and was said to be worth £50,000.   Having won a lottery prize, he gave a public breakfast in the Conduit gardens " to commemorate the smiles of fortune," as the invitation tickets expressed it.   Unfortunately his taste for gambling in the Lottery increased, and soon his entire fortune was squandered, and he ultimately died in poverty at a mean lodging in March, 1809, at the age of sixty-eight.

The surroundings of White Conduit House were still agreeable, and in 1803 we find references to the fine prospect, and the mild refreshing breezes from the abundant hay crops for which the district was noted. By about 1833, however, brickfields and rows of houses had destroyed its rural aspect.

---

[1] " An Awkward Position," a painting by A. Solomon, depicts the situation.   This was exhibited in the Royal Academy, and reproduced in the *Illustrated London News*, 14 June, 1851.

[2] Ashton, *The Fleet*, p. 66.

[3] Bartholomew sold his interest in White Conduit House 25 March, 1795.

Until about the beginning of the present century,
White Conduit House appears to have had no entertainments apart from its tea-gardens, and from the
organ performances [1] in the house. But under the
proprietorship of Sharpe and Warren (from about 1811,
or earlier, till 1828) several changes took place. The
pond was filled in and planted over, and a new tea and
dancing saloon, dignified by the name of the Apollo
Room, and subsequently converted into a billiard-room,
was erected in the north-west angle of the gardens. The
tea-boxes were enlarged, and the old paintings removed
or defaced. A pretty miniature steeple, set up in the
last century, and a maze were still to be seen in the
garden. From about 1825 White Conduit House
possessed a band-stand, and a small stage erected at
the north-east end of the grounds, which were further
embellished with fountains and statuary.

Bowls and dutch-pins were played, and archery (in
1827) was a popular amusement. Balloon-ascents were
also a feature ; the most important being those made by
Graham (1823–1825) ; Mrs. Graham (1826) ; Charles
Green (1828) ; and John Hampton in 1842, and on
19 August 1844 when Hampton was accompanied by
" Mr. Wells " (Henry Coxwell). In 1824 (September)
at a Benefit and Gala Fête thirty kinds of fireworks
were displayed : fiery pigeons flew across the gardens,
and two immense snakes went in pursuit of one another.

In 1825 the place was advertised as " the New Vauxhall : White Conduit Gardens," and evening concerts,
variety entertainments and firework displays were given
in the grounds. On 21 June of this year, in
commemoration of the Battle of Waterloo, a grand
Gala and Rural Fête took place in the evening, with
a concert and fireworks. There was music in the
Quadrille Room and the Country Dance Room ; and
for dancing in the Grand Walk, the Pandean band.

---

[1] About 1772 these performances were prohibited on Sundays.

The gardens were illuminated by variegated lamps ; "vigilant officers" were in attendance, and no person was admitted "in dishabille." The admission was two shillings.

Chabert,[1] the fire-eater, was here in 1826 (June). After swallowing arsenic, oxalic acid, boiling oil and molten lead, without, it is said, feeling any inconveni-

WHITE CONDUIT HOUSE.

ence, he entered a large heated oven, supported by four pillars, and there cooked a leg of lamb and a rump steak, which he proceeded to divide among the spectators. The admission was half a crown and eighteenpence. In July of this year, Mrs. Bland here made her

[1] See a bill in the London Sections Collection, Guildhall Library, and cp. Rogers's *Views of Pleasure Gardens of London*, p. 55 ; also G. Cruikshank's Ivan Ivanitz Chabert, a print published 13 March, 1818. Hone's *Every Day Book*, ii. p. 771, ff.

last public appearance. This singer,[1] well-known for
the sweet quality of her mezzo-soprano voice and
unaffected rendering of English ballads, was long
attached to Drury Lane Theatre, and for several years
appeared at Vauxhall. About 1824 her mind became
affected, and on her recovery she was glad to accept an
engagement at an inferior place of entertainment.

In October 1826 the magistrates in granting the
license stipulated that the music should cease at 11.30
P.M., and that the gardens should close at 11.45.
Masquerades and fireworks were prohibited. These
restrictions, however, appear to have been subsequently
withdrawn or disregarded.

About this period (1826) part of the south side of
the gardens was cut off by the formation of Warren
Street ; and a few years later (before 1833) a gasometer
and a tall chimney disfigured the north-east corner of
the grounds.

The accommodation of White Conduit House having
now become insufficient, a new hotel was contemplated.
The first stone was laid on 2 February 1829, Messrs.
Bowles and Monkhouse being then the proprietors.
About the middle of June 1829 [2] the new building,
referred to in the bills as " New Minor Vauxhall :
White Conduit House, Hotel and Tavern," was opened
with a concert and ball. It was a tall, plain structure.
Its chief room, a large hall about eighty feet by sixty,
was much used for dances, dinners, and political
meetings.

From many of the laudatory press notices, from
about 1826 onwards, it might appear that White
Conduit House was a crowded and even fashionable
resort. But this was by no means the case. Surrounding buildings had spoilt the place, and at this
period " Vite Cundick Couse," as its Cockney visitors

[1] Born 1769, died 1838.
[2] Till May of 1829 the old building was still standing.

called it, was comparatively neglected : the chimes of the miniature steeple were silent, and the gardens had lost their rural charm.

Hone [1] severely describes it as a " starveling show of odd company and coloured lamps " possessing a mock orchestra with mock singing, and a dancing room, in which no respectable person would care to be seen.   In 1832 (November) the magistrates refused to grant the license, and in 1834 (15 February) the proprietor was fined £5 for the "rowdy" conduct of some of the audience.   A satirical visitor in 1838 [2] ridicules the vocal attainments of the singers, and the gaudy dresses of the female performers, whose heads were decorated with blue roses and adorned with corkscrew curls.   The audiences were now composed of the artisan class, the small shop-keeper, the apprentice and shop lad ; with a sprinkling of lawyers' clerks recognisable by their long hair, worn-out " four and ninepenny gossamers," short trousers, and blucher boots, and by their conversation, which is described as no less objectionable than their cabbage-leaf cigars.

From 1830 till the close of the place in 1849 the entertainments, beginning about 7.30, were of a very varied character ; concerts, juggling, farces and ballets. The admission, occasionally sixpence, was usually one shilling ; half of which was sometimes returned in refreshments.   Ladies and children generally came in half price.   A diorama, and moonlight view of Holyrood were exhibited in 1830 ; and about the same time Miss Clarke made one of her ascents upon an inclined rope attached to a platform above the highest trees in the garden, reaching this eminence " amidst a blaze of light."   Here, too, in 1831 (August), and also in 1836 and 1837, Blackmore of Vauxhall made some of his

---

[1] Hone's *Every Day Book*, ii. p. 1204.
[2] Cp. the White Conduit concert described in the *Sketches by Boz* (" The Mistaken Milliner," cap. viii.).

"terrific ascents." A play of T. Dibdin's entitled the 'Hog in Armour' was performed in 1831 (April), and Charles Sloman, the clever impromptu versifier, appeared in August and September 1836.

In 1839 Breach the proprietor, who exerted himself in popularising the house, placed its amusements under the management of John Dunn,[1] styled the English Jim Crow on account of his imitations of T. D. Rice in "Jump Jim Crow." In 1841 a large painting of Windsor Castle and the park-troops was placed at the end of the centre (then denominated the Chinese) walk ; and in 1842 (July and August), a Mr. Bryant being the landlord, Batty's Circus was engaged.

In 1843 R. Rouse was the proprietor, and in these later years the amusements of White Conduit House gradually deteriorated, until they were terminated on 22 January, 1849, by a Ball given for the benefit of the check-takers. Three days afterwards the demolition of the house was begun, and it was soon levelled for a new line of streets, the present White Conduit public-house being erected on part of the site.

The gardens had extended from Penton Street, in an easterly direction, to White Conduit Street, now called Cloudesley Road. Albert Street now approximately marks their southern boundary ; and Denmark Road the northern limit.

[Fillinham's collection relating to White Conduit House in Brit. Mus. ; Pinks's *Clerkenwell;* Walford's *Old and New London;* Wheatley's *London P. & P.;* Lewis's *Islington;* Tomlins's *Peramb. of Islington;* Cromwell's *Islington;* Hone's *Every Day Book*, vol. ii. p. 1201, ff.; *Mirror*, 1833, vol. xxi. p. 426 ; Nelson's *Islington;* Brayley's *Londiniana; Era Almanack*, 1871 ; newspaper cuttings in W. Coll.]

---

[1] The *Variety Stage*, by Stuart and Park, p. 8 ; 103.

VIEWS.

The Crace, Fillinham, and other collections contain numerous views, from which the following may be selected :—

1. South view of White Conduit House in Lempriere's Set of Views, 1731 ; reproduced in Lewis's *Islington* and Pinks's *Clerkenwell*.

2. White Conduit House, 1749. Engraving in Knight's *Old England*, vol. ii. fig. 2,402.

3. White Conduit House near Islington (*circa* 1771). A print, Crace, *Cat.* No. 200.

4. White Conduit House in the last century (*circa* 1780). A woodcut, Crace, *Cat.* No. 201.

5. The Old White Conduit Tea Gardens, Islington. Coloured view, 1822 (W. Coll.).

6. Old White Conduit House Tea Gardens. Sepia drawing, signed C. H. M. Fillinham Coll. p. 46.

7. White Conduit House Tavern and Tea Gardens, 1828. Engraved heading of a White Conduit bill. Fillinham Coll.

8. General View of the Gardens, White Conduit House. Fillinham Coll. p. 46.

9. White Conduit House. Engraving in Cromwell's *Clerkenwell*, p. 216.

10 White Conduit Gardens from Islington Terrace. Sepia drawing, signed C. H. M. 1829. Fillinham Coll. p. 46.

11. Old White Conduit House. P. H. D. 1831, engraved in Rogers's *Views of Pleasure Gardens of London*, p. 53 (showing balloon and old conduit).

12. The White Conduit Gardens, north view. Sepia drawing by C. H. Matthews, 1832. Crace, *Cat.* No. 204.

13. View in Gardens showing stage, &c. Water-colour drawing, signed I. F., June 2, 1832. Fillinham Coll. p. 48.

14. A view in the Gardens of White Conduit House with the rope-dancing and fireworks. Sepia drawing, 1848. Crace, *Cat.* No. 207 ; cp. Ashton's *The Fleet*.

15. White Conduit House, Hotel and Tavern. North-west view of front. A water-colour drawing by Matthews, 1849. Crace, *Cat.* No. 208.

16. Bird's-eye view of the gardens of White Conduit House, taken from the balcony. A coloured drawing by Mr. Crace, 1849. Crace, *Cat.* No. 209.

DOBNEY'S BOWLING GREEN, OR PROSPECT HOUSE

Dobney's Bowling Green, or, as it was originally called, Prospect House, stood on a portion of the site of Winchester Place (now part of Pentonville Road) near to the south-east corner of Penton Street, and opposite the New River Reservoir. It was in existence as early as the seventeenth century, a Mr. Ireland being rated in 1669 [1] for "the Prospect."

Prospect House, standing on Islington Hill, derived its name from the fine views that it commanded, and in the seventeenth and eighteenth centuries was a vantage-ground from which artists often sketched St. Paul's and the Metropolis. It possessed good bowling greens probably as early as 1633, and in the spring of 1718 these were advertised as open for the accommodation of all gentlemen bowlers.

Later on, the place was called Dobney's (or D'Aubigney's) Bowling Green House, from the name of its proprietor, whose widow, Mrs. Ann Dobney, also kept the place for many years.[2] She was succeeded by a Mr. Johnson, who called the place Johnson's Prospect and Bowling Green House. He converted the bowling green, which was near the corner of Penton Street,

---

[1] The place appears to be referred to as early as 1633 as "the bowling place in Islington Fields" (Pinks, p. 710).

[2] Mrs. Dobney died at about the age of ninety on 15 March, 1760.

into an *al fresco* amphitheatre, and in 1767 engaged
the equestrian Price[1] who drew large audiences by his
performances, which lasted during the spring and
summer season, beginning at six o'clock. Price is

"A REPRESENTATION OF THE SURPRISING PERFORMANCES OF MR. PRICE"
AT DOBNEY'S. *Circ.* 1767.

said to have made, by his exhibitions at Dobney's and
elsewhere, a fortune of £14,000.

[1] Pinks states that Price had been starring at the Three Hats,
Islington, prior to his performance at Dobney's in 1767 (cp.
Memoirs of J. de Castro (1824), p. 29, who says that Price, Thomas
Johnson, and old Sampson exhibited at the Three Hats). This
may have been the case, though from 1758 to the spring of 1767,
Thomas Johnson was certainly the chief equestrian performer at
the "Three Hats."

In 1769 Philip Jonas performed there feats of manual dexterity, and the exhibition of the skeleton of a whale, three score feet long, was reckoned an attraction. In 1770, the house was occupied as a boarding-school by the Rev. John Davis, but the place was soon again re-opened as the Jubilee Gardens, in allusion to the Stratford Jubilee of Shakespeare.

In 1772, Daniel Wildman, an expert in bee-keeping, gave on summer evenings a curious performance called " Bees on horse-back," described as follows :—

"Daniel Wildman rides standing upright, one foot on the saddle, and the other on the horse's neck, with a curious mask of bees on his face. He also rides standing upright on the saddle with the bridle in his mouth, and by firing a pistol makes one part of the bees march over a table, and the other part swarm in the air, and return to their places again." This performance, together with other entertainments, began at a quarter before seven, and the admission was one shilling, or two shillings to the boxes and gallery.

In 1774, the gardens were still open, but in a much neglected condition, as the walks were not kept in order nor the hedges properly cut. There were, however, at this time several good apartments in the house and two tea-rooms on the north side of the bowling green, built one above the other, and Dobney's (as it was still popularly called) was a favourite Sunday resort of the London apprentice :—

> On Sabbath day who has not seen
> In colours of the rainbow dizened,
> The 'prentice beaux and belles, I ween,
> Fatigued with heat, with dust half-poisoned,
> To Dobney's strolling, or Pantheon,
> Their tea to sip or else regale,
> As on their way they shall agree on,
> With syllabubs or bottled ale.[1]

[1] *London Evening Post*, August 1776. The Pantheon is the tea-house in Exmouth Street.

In 1780, we hear of lectures and debates taking place in the house ; but in 1781 " the lease and trade of the Shakespeare Tavern and Jubilee Gardens, formerly called Dobney's Bowling Green," were offered for sale by auction. At that time, according to the auctioneer's advertisement, Dobney's consisted of a dwelling house, a building containing a bake-house, kitchens, &c., with an adjoining erection comprising two spacious rooms, capable of dining near two hundred people each, a trap-ball ground, bowling green and "extensive gardens properly laid out."

The place, however, ceasing to be frequented, the ground was, about 1790, partly built over with the houses forming Winchester Place. The gardens, or a part of them, remained until 1810, when they disappeared.[1] Dobney's Court, an alley on the east side of Penton Street, now occupies a small part of the original site.

[Pinks's *Clerkenwell ;* Nelson's *Islington ;* Lewis's *Islington ; Sunday Ramble ;* Tomlins's *Perambulation of Islington,* pp. 160, 187 ; *Memoirs of De Castro,* p. 29.]

VIEWS.

1. A drawing of Prospect House taken about 1780 was at one time in the possession of Mr. Upcott (*Notes and Queries,* 1st series, ix. 1854, p. 572).

2. " A representation of the surprising performances of Mr. Price," engraved for the *Universal Museum and Comp. Mag. (circ.* 1767), W. Coll.

---

[1] Tomlins in his *Perambulation of Islington,* published in 1858, but written in part about 1849, describes Prospect House as still existing behind Winchester Place, though the bowling green (he says) had been already covered by Winchester Place.

BELVIDERE TEA GARDENS,
PENTONVILLE ROAD

The Belvidere tavern and tea gardens in the Penton-ville Road, at the south-west corner of Penton Street, occupied the site of Busby's Folly, itself a house of entertainment with a bowling green attached to it. Busby's Folly, which was in existence at least as early as 1664,[1] afterwards (between 1731 and 1745) acquired the name of Penny's Folly.

In August 1769, Penny's Folly was taken by a German named Zucker, who exhibited there his Learned Little Horse, while Mrs. Zucker played favourite airs on the musical glasses, and " the so-much admired and unparalleled Mr. Jonas " displayed his "matchless and curious deceptions." The entertain-ment began at 6.30, and took place in a large room commanding a "delightful prospect" from its fourteen windows. The admission was one shilling, and it was announced that " The Little Horse will be looking out of the windows up two pair of stairs every evening before the performances begin."

The performances of Zucker had already been for some years in repute with holiday folk, and in 1762 he had received honourable mention in a prologue spoken at the Haymarket Theatre :—

[1] Busby's Folly is first mentioned in 1664 as a meeting-place of the Society of Bull Feathers Hall, a fraternity of Odd Fellows. It is supposed to have derived its name from Christopher Busby, landlord of the White Lion Inn, Islington, in 1668.

L

How dull, methinks, look Robin, Sue and Nancy
At Greenwich Park did nothing strike your fancy ;
Had you no cheese-cakes, cyder, shrimps or bun,
Saw no wild beastis, or no jack-ass run ?
Blest Conduit House ! what raptures does it yield ;
And hail, thou wonder of a Chelsea field !
Yet Zucker still amazingly surpasses
Your Conduit-house, your pigmy, and your asses.[1]

Penny's Folly was afterwards pulled down and the Belvidere tavern came into existence about 1780.

In the early part of the present century, and probably twenty years earlier, the Belvidere possessed a bowling green, and a large garden, with many trees and plenty of accommodation for tea-drinking parties. The chief attraction was a large racket-court. The garden and racket-court continued to be frequented till 1860 or later. In 1876, the Belvidere was rebuilt and is now used as a public-house, the garden, or part of it, being occupied by the pianoforte works of Messrs. Yates.

[Pinks's *Clerkenwell*, 531–533 ; Tomlins's *Perambulation of Islington*, 40, 41, 163, 164 ; *Picture of London*, 1802, p. 370.]

VIEWS.

1. South front of Busby's Folly, one of C. Lempriere's Set of Views, 1731 (woodcut in Pinks, p. 530) ; cp. woodcut in Tomlins's *Perambulation of Islington*, p. 164, and a water-colour drawing by C. H. Matthews in Crace, *Cat.* p. 606, No. 212.

2. The Belvidere Gardens, early in the present century, woodcut in Cromwell's *Clerkenwell* (1828), p. 414, J. and H. S. Storer del. et sculp. (copied in Pinks, p. 531).

3. The "Belvidere Gardens at the present time" (*circ.* 1860 ?), Pinks, p. 532.

---

[1] Prologue written and spoken by Mr. Gibson before the Orphan at the New Theatre in the Haymarket on 31 May, 1762 (*Owen's Weekly Chronicle or Universal Journal*, June 5 to 12, 1762). The "wonder of a Chelsea field" mentioned in this prologue is evidently Coan, the dwarf (called "the jovial pigmy"), who attracted visitors to the Dwarf's Tavern in Chelsea Fields (see *infra*, Star and Garter, Chelsea).

THE Castle Inn is mentioned in 1754 a
resort of the London " cit.," who frequented it in
evening to smoke his pipe and obtain the light refreshment of cyder and heart-cakes. The house must have
stood nearly alone till 1768, when the oldest portion
of the street called Colebrooke Row was built. The
Castle Inn, with its tea gardens, was then the last house
but one at the northern end of the Row.[1] A pleasant
nursery garden occupied, till about 1822, six acres of
the ground in the rear of Colebrooke Row.

The inn and tea gardens were still in existence about
1772, but the house had ceased to be a place of public
entertainment at the time when Nelson published his
Islington, *i.e.* 1811.

[*The Connoisseur*, No. 26 (1754) ; Nelson's *Islington* (1811), p. 385 ;
Lewis's *Islington* (1842), pp. 351, 352.]

---

[1] According to Nelson and Lewis, the house facing to the south
at the northern termination of Colebrooke Row, was occupied
about 1772 by the Rev. John Rule, who there kept a school, of
some repute, for gentlemen's sons. The Castle Inn was the adjoining house and a house next to the Castle was supposed by a
doubtful tradition (cp. J. Knight, art. "Cibber" in *Dict. Nat. Biog.*)
to be that in which Colley Cibber died 12 December, 1757 (*see*
Nelson and Lewis). The old house with a red-tiled roof, still
existing, though divided into the dwelling houses Nos. 56 and 57
Colebrooke Row, was apparently the Castle Inn. The southern
end of Colebrooke Row was built in the present century. The
Row also now extends a little farther to the north than when
Nelson wrote, so that Rule's house is not now at the extreme
northern end of the Row.

THREE HATS, ISLINGTON

THE Three Hats was a picturesque old inn standing in the Upper Street, Islington, a few doors from the corner of the Liverpool Road and on the site of the present Islington branch of the London and County Bank.

It first became known as a place of amusement in 1758, when, in the field adjoining, Thomas Johnson, "the Irish Tartar," one of the earliest equestrian performers in England, made his *début*. He galloped round the field standing first on one horse, then on a pair, then on three horses. At one time he rode the single horse standing on his head, but as this posture "gave pain to the spectators" he discontinued it. His feats seem to have been of a simpler kind than those afterwards performed by the rider Price at Dobney's in 1767. One of Johnson's performances at the Three Hats (17 July, 1766) took place in the presence of the Duke of York and of about five hundred spectators.

In the spring of 1767 Johnson was succeeded by the equestrian Sampson, who announced his appearance at five o'clock at a commodious place built in a field adjoining the Three Hats. "A proper band of music" was engaged for this entertainment. In the summer of this year Sampson introduced his wife into his entertainment, and inserted the following advertisement in the *Public Advertiser* for 23 July : "Horsemanship at Dingley's, Three Hats, Islington. Mr. Sampson begs to inform the public that besides the usual feats which he exhibits, Mrs. Sampson, to diversify the entertainment and prove that the fair sex are by no means inferior to the male, either in courage or agility, will this and every evening during the summer season perform various exercises in the same art, in which she hopes to acquit herself to the universal approbation of those ladies and gentlemen whose curiosity may induce them to honour her attempt with their company."

JOHNSON AT THE THREE HATS, 1758.

The Three Hats had other attractions besides the horsemanship and at least as early as 1768 had become a favourite Sunday resort. In Bickerstaffe's comedy the "Hypocrite," published in 1768, Mawworm says : "Till I went after him (Dr. Cantwell) I was little better than the devil. My conscience was tanned with sin like a piece of neat's leather, and had no more feeling than the sole of my shoe, always aroving after fantastical delights. I used to go every Sunday evening to the Three Hats at Islington—mayhap your ladyship

may know it. I was a great lover of skittles, but now
I can't bear them."

Sampson's performances still continued in 1770 and
additional diversions were occasionally provided : " At
the Three Hats, Islington, this day, the 1st of May
(1770) will be played a grand match at that ancient
and much renowned manly diversion called Double
Stick by a sett of chosen young men at that exercise
from different parts of the West country, for two
guineas given free ; those who brake the most heads to
bear away the prize." " To begin precisely at four."
" Before the above mentioned diversion begins, Mr.
Sampson and his young German will display alternately on one, two, and three horses, various surprising
and curious feats of famous horsemanship in like
manner as at the Grand Jubilee at Stratford-upon-Avon.
Admittance one shilling each person."

In 1771 Sampson was under a cloud—he is said to
have been ensnared " into gay company " by Price, his
rival at Dobney's—and sold his horses to Coningham,
who performed in the evening at the Three Hats
(1771 and 1772), and was announced as follows :—
" First : He rides a gallop, standing upright on a single
horse, three times round the room without holding.
Second : He rides a single horse on full speed, dis-
mounts, fires a pistol, and performs the boasted feat of
Hughes's leaping over him backwards and forwards for
forty times without ceasing ; also flies over three horses
on full speed, leaps over one and two horses on full
speed as they leap the bar, plays a march on the
flute, without holding, upon two horses, standing upright." It was also announced that " Mr. and Mrs.
Sampson, Mr. Brown, &c., will perform to make these
nights the completest in the kingdom. The Tailor and
Sailor upon the drollest horses in the kingdom. The
doors to be opened exactly at five, and to mount at a
quarter to five. Admittance in the front seats two

shillings, and the back seats one.   Mr. Coningham will engage to fly through a hogshead of fire upon two horses' backs, without touching them, and, for a single person, will perform activity with any man in the world."

In 1772 Sampson resumed his performances at the Riding School of the Three Hats and gave lessons there.   On Whit Monday some other curious attractions were advertised in the *Gazetteer* (June 6, 1772) : " A young gentleman will undertake to walk and pick up one hundred eggs (each egg to be the distance of one yard apart) and put them in a basket within an hour and fifteen minutes ; if any egg breaks he puts down one in its place, for a wager of ten guineas.   And on Whitsun Tuesday will be run for an holland shift by a number of smart girls, six times round the School."

About this period the riding seems to have come to an end,[1] though the Three Hats continued for many years to be a favourite tea-garden until the ground at the back of the house was built over.   The *Morning Chronicle* gives us a glimpse of the place in 1779 (21 July) : " Yesterday morning upwards of twenty fellows who were dancing with their ladies at the Three Hats, Islington, were taken by the constables as fit persons to serve his Majesty, and lodged in Clerkenwell Bridewell, in order to be carried before the commissioners."

On 6 January, 1839, a fire (which destroyed two neighbouring houses) so damaged the roof of the Three Hats, then a mere public-house, that in April of the same year the whole place was demolished, and the present branch office of the London and County Bank was erected on the site.

---

[1] Sampson's Riding School at Islington is mentioned in the *Macaroni and Theatrical Magazine* for January 1773, p. 162, together with Astley's and Hughes's.

[Lewis's *Islington ;* Pinks's *Clerkenwell.*]

VIEWS.

1. Engraving of Three Hats and other old houses adjacent, in *Gent. Mag.* 1823, pt. 2, frontispiece ; cp. p. 113.

2. A sepia drawing by C. H. Matthews, 1839.   Crace, *Cat.* p. 596, No. 110.

3. Engraving in the *Grand Magazine*, showing Johnson's eques-trian feats, 1758, W. Coll. ; cp. Crace, *Cat.* p. 596, No. 108.

BARLEY MOW TEA HOUSE AND GARDENS, ISLINGTON

THE Barley Mow Tea House and Gardens were on the west side of Frog Lane, now Popham Road, Islington. They are first mentioned in 1786.[1] About 1799, the Barley Mow was kept as a public-house by a man named Tate, and George Morland lived there for several months, indulging in drinking and low company, but finding time to paint some good pictures which he generally sold for small sums. He often borrowed for sketching purposes old harness and saddles from a farm-house opposite, and was wont " to send after any rustic-looking character " to obtain a sitting. The Barley Mow has been used as a public-house to the present time, and is now No. 31, Popham Road, but it has been modernised, or rebuilt, and the garden has disappeared.

[Nelson's *Islington*, 128, 197 ; Cromwell's *Islington*, p. 194, ff. ; Lewis's *Islington*, 154, ff. ; Walford, ii. 262 ; *Morning Herald*, 22 April, 1786.]

[1] They were probably in existence before this date, but are not marked in the survey of Islington of 1735. An advertisement in *The Morning Herald* of 22 April, 1786, announces the sale of the ground-rents of an Islington copyhold estate. This estate, situated " in the Lower Street, opposite Cross Street, Islington, and extending down to Frog Lane," comprised a brick mansion and garden, four dwelling-houses and gardens, and the Barley Mow Tea House and Gardens. A plan of the estate was to be seen at Mr. Spurrier's, the auctioneer's, Copthall Court, Throgmorton Street. The estate was therefore between the present Essex Road, where it is touched by Cross Street, and Popham Road.

CANONBURY HOUSE TEA GARDENS

THE Canonbury House tea-gardens, a quiet and un-pretending resort of Londoners, derive a certain anti-quarian interest from their situation within the ancient park attached to Canonbury House, the mansion built by the Priors of St. Bartholomew's, Smithfield, for their summer residence. Houses in Canonbury Place, first erected about 1770, occupy the site of the old mansion, though a substantial relic still exists in Canonbury Tower, built in the sixteenth century, and during the last century let out for summer lodgings to various tenants, the best known of whom was Oliver Gold-smith.

About 1754 a small ale-house was built by a Mr. Benjamin Collins on the eastern side of the mansion. This afterwards came into the possession of James Lane, who made additions to the premises, utilising, it would seem, a range of tiled outhouses on the east of the house which were supposed to have originally been its stables.

The place had a good reputation and became much frequented as a tea-garden under the name of Canonbury House. Lane died in 1783, and about 1785 the tavern was taken by a Mr. Sutton, who died soon after, leaving the premises to his wife.

The "Widow Sutton" enlarged the tavern, which was then known as Canonbury House Tavern (or Canonbury Tavern), laid out a bowling green and improved the tea-gardens.   The house was much used for the dinners of Societies.

The gardens, which at this time occupied about four acres, were almost entirely situated within the old park wall of the Priors of St. Bartholomew's, and the wall on the east divided them from the open fields.   The old fish-pond of the Priors was also connected.

The *Sunday Ramble* describes Canonbury House in 1797 as "a place of decent retreat for tea and sober treatment."   In 1810 an Assembly was established at the tavern, and about 1811 the grounds consisted of a shrubbery and bowling green with Dutch-pin and trap-ball grounds and butts for ball-firing used by the Volunteers.   The old tiled outhouses were used as a bake-house for the pastry and rolls till 1840, when they were pulled down.

About 1823 the builders had invaded the rural neighbourhood of Canonbury, but the tea-gardens continued to be frequented as a pleasant resort till 1843, or later.

At some time between 1843 and 1866 the Canonbury Tavern was rebuilt.   It now stands on the north side of Canonbury Place, a little to the east of Canonbury Tower and on the opposite side of the road.

A garden, though not of the old dimensions, is still attached to the tavern and open to the public during the summer.

[Nichols's *Canonbury*, 1788, 33 ; *The Ambulator*, 1st ed. 1774, s.v. "Canonbury House" ; Kearsley's *Strangers' Guide* (1793 ?), s.v. "Canonbury or Cambray House" ; *A Modern Sabbath*, 1797, chap. vii.; Nelson's *Islington*, 252 ; Brayley's *Londiniana*, iii. 269, ff.; *Picture of London*, eds. 1802 and 1829 ; Lewis's *Islington*, p. 310 ; Timbs's *Club Life*, 1866, ii. 228.]

VIEWS.

Exterior of Canonbury Tavern (north view), a small engraving published in 1819 by R. Ackermann (W. Coll.) ; Crace, *Cat.* p. 602, No. 174.

COPENHAGEN HOUSE stood alone on an eminence in the fields, on the right-hand side of Maiden Lane, the old way leading from Battle Bridge to Highgate, being about midway between those places.[1]

It is known to have been a house of public entertainment in 1725 [2] and was probably one much earlier, seeing that the oldest part of the building was in the style of the seventeenth century. " Coopen-hagen " is marked in a map of 1695.[3]

There are various accounts of the origin of the the name. A Danish Prince or a Danish Ambassador is said to have resided in the house during the Great Plague. Or, again, an enterprising Dane is said to have built the inn for the accommodation of his countrymen who had come to London in the train of the King of Denmark on his visit to James I. in 1606.[4] In the

[1] See the survey of roads in Islington parish in 1735 (Nelson's *Islington*, p. 20).

[2] Hone, *Every Day Book*, i. p. 860. Tomlins (*Islington*, 204, 205) discovered that in 1753 it was occupied by a currier, and supposes, therefore, that it was not a place of entertainment till after that date. The meeting of the Highbury Society there before 1740 seems however to bear out Hone's assertion that Copenhagen House was already an inn in the first half of the eighteenth century.

[3] Map in Gibson's edition of Camden's *Britannia*, 1695.

[4] Hone, however, shows (*op. cit.* 860) that there is some reason for supposing that Copenhagen House was not in existence until after 1624.

early part of the eighteenth century Copenhagen House is not often mentioned, though the curious Highbury Society [1] used to assemble here previous to the year 1740, when it began to meet at Highbury.

In 1780 a brutal robbery [2] of which the landlady, Mrs. Harrington, was the victim, attracted attention to the place. A subscription was opened for her benefit, and visitors came in such numbers that Mr. Leader, the owner of the House, pulled down the old wooden building attached to its western end, and built in its stead a long room for tea-drinking parties, with a large parlour below for drinking and smoking. There were gardens attached, with the usual accommodation for skittles and Dutch-pin playing.

Under Mrs. Harrington's management, Copenhagen House first became celebrated for its Fives Courts. A young Shropshire woman (afterwards Mrs. Tomes) who assisted Mrs. Harrington, gave Hone an interesting little account of the introduction of the game :—" I made the first fives ball (she said) that was ever thrown up against Copenhagen House. One Hickman, a butcher at Highgate, a countryman of mine, used the house, and seeing me ' country,' we talked about our country sports, and amongst the rest, *fives :* I told him we'd have a game some day. I laid down the stone in the ground myself, and against he came again, made a ball. I struck the ball the first blow, and he gave it the second, and so we played ; and as there was company they liked the sport, and it got talked of. This was the beginning of the *fives-play*, which has since become so famous at Copenhagen House."

John Cavanagh (*d.* 1819), the famous Irish fives player, had many matches at Copenhagen House for wagers and dinners. The wall against which the combatants played was (says Hone) the same that supported the kitchen chimney, and when the wall resounded louder than usual, the cook exclaimed, "Those are the *Irishman's* balls," and the joints trembled on the spit. Hazlitt, in a pleasant memoir of Cavanagh,[1] says that he had no equal in the game or second. He had no affectation in his playing. He was the best up-hill player in the world, and never gave away a game through laziness or conceit. His "service" was tremendous, but a peculiarity of his play was that he never volleyed, though if the ball rose but an inch from the ground he never missed it. "His eye," adds Hazlitt, "was certain, his hand fatal, his presence of mind complete."

In 1795 the house was kept by Robert Orchard, notorious for his connexion with the London Corresponding Society, which at that time held tumultuous meetings in the adjoining Copenhagen Fields. Orchard was succeeded by a man named Tooth, who gained custom by encouraging brutal sports. At this time, " on a Sunday morning, the fives ground was filled by bull-dogs and ruffians, who lounged and drank to intoxication : so many as fifty or sixty bull-dogs have been seen tied up to the benches at once, while their masters boozed and made match after match, and went out and fought their dogs before the house, amid the uproar of idlers attracted to the 'bad eminence' by its infamy."

There was also a common field, east of the house, wherein bulls were baited, and this was called the bull-field. At last the magistrates interfered, and in 1816 Tooth lost his license. The next landlord, a Mr. Bath, conducted the house respectably, and refused admittance

---

[1] Hazlitt's memoir is published in the *Examiner* for February 17, 1819 ; most of it is reprinted in Hone's *Every Day Book,* i. 865, ff.

to the bull-dogs. The bull-field was afterwards used for the harmless purpose of cow-keeping.

From about this period (1816–1830) Copenhagen House was a favourite Sunday tea-garden with the middle-classes [1] who flocked there, especially in the summer-time during the hay harvest in the fields around.[2] Although the builders were making their way up to Copenhagen House from London on the south, it still commanded an extensive view of the metropolis and western suburbs, with the heights of Hampstead and Highgate, "and the rich intervening meadows." In 1841 [3] the tavern and tea-gardens were still in existence, and the space between them and Highgate was still open fields. Attached to the house at that time was a well known cricket ground.[4]

About 1852 the Corporation of London purchased Copenhagen House with its grounds and adjacent fields to the extent of about seventy-five acres, and began to build there the present Metropolitan Cattle Market, between the York and Caledonian Roads, which was opened in 1855. The old tavern (pulled down in 1853 [5]) and tea-gardens were thus swept away, and their site is approximately marked by the Great Clock Tower in the market.[6]

[Hone's *Every Day Book*, i. 858, ff. ; Nelson's *Islington* ; Lewis's *Islington* ; Larwood and Hotten, *Signboards*, 435, 436 ; Walford, ii. 275, 276, 283 ; v. 374 ; Tomlins's *Perambulation of Islington*, 204, 205.]

[1] *Picture of London*, 1823 and 1829 ; Hone's *Every Day Book*, i. 859, 870.

[2] The hay-harvest is referred to in Nelson's *Islington*, 1811, 74. A view of 1809, published by Cundee in the *Juvenile Tourist*, 1810, shows cockney visitors playing in the hay.

[3] Plan in Lewis's *Islington*.

[4] J. Hollingshead's *My Lifetime*, i. 13. The cricket ground was between Copenhagen House and Maiden Lane.

[5] Tomlins, *Perambulation of Islington*, p. 205.

[6] F. Miller, *St. Pancras*, 269.

VIEWS.

1. Copenhagen House, Islington, as it appeared in 1737, sepia drawing by Bernard Lens. Crace, *Cat.* p. 604, No. 191.

2. South-east view of Copenhagen House, printed for R. Sayer and J. Bennett, 20 March, 1783 (W. Coll.); the woodcut in Lewis's *Islington*, p. 283, is derived from this.

3. Copenhagen House, Islington. J. Swaine del. 1793 ; J. Swaine, sculp. 1854. Woodcut (W. Coll.).

4. There are several views of Copenhagen House in the nineteenth century, see *e.g.* Hone's *Every Day Book*, i. 858 ; Cromwell's *Islington*, p. 204 ; Crace, *Cat.* p. 605, Nos. 194, 196 (views of 1853).

5. "The Grand Meeting of the Metropolitan Trades' Unions in the Copenhagen Fields on Monday, April 21, 1834." Coloured engraving by Geo. Dorrington (W. Coll.). This shows Copenhagen House and an enormous concourse in the fields.

HIGHBURY BARN

HIGHBURY Barn Tavern with its gardens is, like the Canonbury House Tavern and gardens, rooted in a respectable antiquity, for it stood on the site of Highbury Barn[1] which formed part of the farm attached to the old country seat[2] of the Prior of the Knights of St. John of Jerusalem.

Highbury Barn (the tavern) was originally a small cake and ale house which was in existence at least as early as 1740[3]. It was occasionally (about 1768) honoured by a visit from Oliver Goldsmith on one of his Shoemaker's holidays. Goldsmith and three or four of his friends would leave his Temple chambers

---

[1] Highbury Barn, *i.e.*, the grange or farm of Highbury Manor, is mentioned by that name at an early period, and there are extant various leases of it of the fifteenth century, granted by the Prior and Convent of St. John of Jerusalem (*e.g.* " our certain grange, situate upon the site of our manor of Highbury called Highbury Barn " · see Tomlins's *Perambulation of Islington*). The name Highbury Barn is, therefore, much older than the date of the incorporation of the large barn of Highbury Farm with the Highbury Tavern premises.

[2] The site of the Prior's house was occupied by a private residence called Highbury House built in 1781 and immediately opposite the Highbury Barn Tavern.

[3] The Highbury Society, formed by Protestant Dissenters to commemorate the abandonment of the Schism Bill at the end of the reign of Anne, met at first at Copenhagen House, but about 1740 assembled at Highbury Barn. The members beguiled their pilgrimage from Moorfields to Highbury by bowling a ball of ivory at objects in their path. This society was dissolved about 1833.

M

in the morning and proceed by the City Road and
through the fields to Highbury Barn, where at one
o'clock they enjoyed a dinner of two courses and pastry,
at the cost of tenpence a head including the waiter's
penny.   The company then to be met with at the inn
consisted of Templars and literary men, and a citizen
or two retired from business.   At about six, Goldsmith
and his party adjourned to the White Conduit House
for tea, and ended the day with supper at the Globe or
Grecian.

The trade of the place greatly increased under the
management of Mr. Willoughby, who, dying in December 1785, was succeeded by his son. The younger
Willoughby (landlord 1785–1818 ?)[1] laid out the gardens, bowling green and trap-ball ground.[2] A large
barn belonging to the neighbouring Highbury Farm
(or Grange) was incorporated with the premises and
fitted up suitably for a Great Room.   Here a monthly
assembly subscribed to in the neighbourhood was held
in the spring and winter and monster dinner-parties
of clubs and societies were accommodated.   In 1800
a company of eight hundred persons sat down to dinner,
and seventy geese were to be seen roasting on the fire.
Three thousand people were accommodated at the
Licensed Victuallers' Dinner in 1841.

[1] The younger Willoughby was certainly proprietor in 1792 and
later, and Lewis says he succeeded his father on the death of the
latter in December 1785.   In May 1789 Highbury House (Nichols,
Canonbury, p. 31, note) opposite the Tavern was sold by auction,
as were also Highbury Tea House with gardens and bowling-green
and two good messuages adjoining, together with many fields in
the neighbourhood.   This sale does not, however, necessarily imply
any change in the management of Highbury Barn, which may at
that time have been only rented by Willoughby from the owner of
Highbury House and the adjoining property.

[2] A few years previous to 1811 Willoughby cultivated at one
end of the gardens a small plantation of hops, and afterwards
erected a brewery on the premises.   Highbury Barn was sometimes
called " Willoughby's Tea Gardens " (*Picture of London*, 1802).

Highbury Assembly House, near Islington, kept by M.ʳ Willoughby.

Published Jan.ʸ 1.ˢᵗ 1792 by Rob.ᵗ Sayer & C.ᵒ Fleet Street London.

HIGHBURY BARN IN 1792.

M 2

About 1793 the garden commanded an extensive prospect, and as late as 1842 Highbury could be described as " a beautifully situated hamlet."

In 1818 the property was purchased by the former proprietor of the Grove House, Camberwell, and High-bury Barn was much resorted to as a Sunday tea-garden (*circ.* 1823–1830). The place then passed (before 1835) into the hands of John Hinton (previously landlord of the Eyre Arms, St. John's Wood) who with his son Archibald Hinton, ultimately the sole proprietor, gave new life to the place and made High-bury Barn a kind of North London Cremorne. By about 1854 the number of monster dinner-parties and bean-feasts had much fallen off, and on Whit-Monday of that year Hinton opened his establishment for musical entertainments with a performance by the band of the Grenadier Guards.

A license for dancing was granted in October 1856, and in July 1858 Leviathan dancing platform, with an orchestra at one end, was erected in the grounds. It was open to the sky with the exception of one side, which consisted of ⌐oofed structure of ornamental ironwork. The w ɔle platform occupied four thousand feet. A standard of gas lamps in the centre of the platform and lamps placed round its railing lit up the place in the evening, when the gardens were frequented by large masses of people. In a more secluded part of the gardens was an avenue of trees, flanked by female statues, each holding a globular gas lamp. About 1858 the admission was sixpence, and at this time Highbury Barn was much frequented on Sunday evenings, when little parties might be seen on the lawn before the Barn or in the bowers and alcoves by its side. The gardens occupied five acres.

Archibald Hinton gave up possession in 1860 ; and in 1861 Edward Giovanelli opened Highbury Barn, after having improved the grounds and erected a spacious hall for a ball and supper room. In 1862 Miss Rebecca Isaacs and Vernon Rigby were the principal singers, and Leotard the gymnast was engaged for the summer season. On 20 May 1865 the Alexandra Theatre was opened in the grounds, but the entertainments in the gardens were also continued. "The splendid Illuminations" were boldly advertised, and Blondin (1868), Natator the man-frog, and the Siamese Twins were engaged (1869). The riotous behaviour, late at night, of many frequenters of the gardens caused annoyance to the neighbours, who regularly opposed the renewal of the license. In October 1870 the dancing license was refused, and next season Mr. E. T. Smith took the place of Giovanelli as manager, but the license being again refused in October 1871, Highbury Barn was finally closed. The flowerbeds became choked with grass and weeds, and nightshade luxuriated around the dism. itled orchestra. By the spring of 1883 the place had been covered with buildings, and a large public-house, the Highbury Tavern (No. 26, Highbury P ' N.), on part of the old site, alone commemorates this ̭nce popular resort.

[Nelson's *Islington*; Cromwell's *Islington*; Lewis's *Islington*; Tomlins's *Perambulation of Islington*; Kearsley's *Strangers' Guide*; Walford, ii. 273. ff.; Forster's *Life of Goldsmith*, bk. iv. chap. 2; *Picture of London*, 1802, 1823 and 1829; Ritchie's *Night-side of London* (1858); *Era Almanack*, 1871, pp. 3, 4; M. Williams's *Some London Theatres*, 1883, p. 33, ff.; newspaper cuttings and bills, W. Coll.]

VIEWS.

1. Highbury Barn (gabled buildings), an etching from a drawing by B. Green, 1775 (W. Coll.).

2. Highbury Assembly House, near Islington, kept by Mr. Willoughby, 1792, print published in 1792 by Sayer (W. Coll.; also Crace. *Cat.* p. 603, No. 182).

3. "Highbury Barn, Islington," engraving published May 1, 1819, for R. Ackermann.

4. Highbury Barn (exterior) (*circ.* 1835), engraving in Cromwell's *Islington*, p. 247, J. and H. S. Storer, del. et. sc.

5. "The Leviathan Platform, Highbury Barn," woodcut in *Illustrated London News*, July 1858.

6. Two views of "The Gardens, Highbury Barn Tavern" (*circ.* 1851), in Tallis's *Illustrated London*, ed. Gaspey.

THE DEVIL'S HOUSE, HOLLOWAY.

THIS place, in spite of its unpromising name, deserves a brief notice as a quiet summer resort of Londoners.

The Devil's House was a moated timber building which originally formed the manor-house of Tolentone (afterwards Highbury) Manor. It stood on the east of Devil's Lane, previously (before 1735) called Tallington or Tollington Lane, and now known as the Hornsey Road. It was within two fields of Holloway Turnpike.[1]

There was a tradition that the house was a retreat of Claude Duval's, and the house and Lane were sometimes known as " Duval's." There is, however, no direct evidence to connect the famous highwayman with the house, and Duval's House may be considered as a popular corruption of Devil's House. In a survey of Highbury Manor made in 1611, this house already bears the name of " Devil's House in Devil's Lane " and is described as being at that date an old building " with a mote, and a little orchard within." In the Islington Survey of 1735, it appears as " Devol's House," an apparent compromise between the fiend and the highwayman.

[1] Lysons, Nelson and Lewis all identify the moated house called in the Survey of 1611 "The Devil's House " or the " Lower House " with the old Tallington or Tollington Manor House. In the survey of the roads of Islington (Nelson's *Islington*, p. 20), however, both Tallington House and Devil's House are separately marked, the two being divided by Heame Lane, a lane running at right angles to Tallington (Devil's) Lane. This Tallington House must therefore have been an eighteenth-century residence and not the old Manor House.

It is not known to have been a place of entertainment till 1767 when the landlord,[1] who attempted to change the name to the Summer House, offered to London anglers and pedestrians the attraction of "tea and hot loaves, ready at a moment's notice, and new milk from the cows grazing in the pleasant meadows adjoining." The house was still encompassed with a wide moat crossed by a bridge, and there was an orchard with a canal. The garden which surrounded the house was well laid out, and the water was stocked with abundance of tench and carp. The place was still occupied and used as an inn in 1811,[2] though about that time the landlord nearly filled up the moat with earth.

The house was in existence in 1849 (or later),[3] being on the east of the Hornsey Road near the junction with the Seven Sisters' Road.

[Lysons's *Environs* (1795), "Islington," p. 127, note ; Nelson's *Islington*, 133, 173 ; Lewis's *Islington*, pp. 67, 279, 280 ; Larwood and Hotten, *Signboards*, 294, 295, quoting a letter signed H. G., 25 May, 1767, in the *Public Advertiser*, which describes the place at that period ; Walford, ii. 275 ; Tomlins's *Perambulation of Islington*, pp. 31, 32.]

VIEWS.

1. A view of the house, gardens and bridge appears in Walford, v. 378, "Claude Duval's House in 1825."

2. Devil's or Du Val's House, Holloway, a sepia drawing by C. H. Matthews (1840) ; Crace, *Cat.* p. 604, No. 190.

---

[1] Nelson (*Islington*), writing about 1811, says that about thirty or forty years before his time (1776 ?) the landlord's name was Fawcett.

[2] This seems to be implied by Nelson (*Islington*, 1811), who says that in his time the old "house had been fitted up in the modern taste."

[3] Lewis's *Islington*, 1841, mentions the house as still existing, and it is described as still standing in Tomlins's *Perambulation of Islington*, a work published in 1858, but in part written nine years before the date of publication.

HORNSEY WOOD HOUSE.

HORNSEY Wood House was situated on the summit of rising ground on the east of Hornsey and at the entrance to Hornsey Wood. It began to be frequented about the middle of the last century,[1] and in the earlier years of its existence aspired to be "a genteel tea-house," though unpretending in appearance. On popular holidays, such as Whit-Sunday, its long room might be seen crowded as early as nine or ten in the morning with a motley assemblage of "men, women and children eating rolls and butter and drinking of tea at an extravagant price."[2]

The pleasures of Hornsey Wood House were of an unsophisticated kind—unlimited tea-drinking, a ramble in the wood, and a delightful view of the surrounding country. An excursion to Little Hornsey to drink tea was a favourite with London citizens' wives and daughters.[3] Hone remembered the old Hornsey Wood

---

[1] Tea-drinking on Sunday at Little Hornsey is mentioned in the *Connoisseur*, No. 68, May 15, 1755, and Hornsey Wood is referred to in *The Idler*, No. 15, July 1758, in a way which implies that its reputation as a place of Sunday recreation was already well established. It appears from a passage in *Low Life*, referred to in the next note, that in or before 1764 the sign of the tavern was The Horns. The place was, however, usually known as Hornsey Wood House, and in its latest days as Hornsey Wood Tavern.

[2] *Low Life* (1764), p. 46.

[3] Mr. Rose, the "citizen at Vauxhall," described in the *Connoisseur*, May 1755, No. 68, used to grumble when his wife and daughters went " to Little Hornsey to drink tea."

House, as it stood (apparently before 1800), "embowered and seeming a part of the Wood." It was at that time kept by two sisters, Mrs. Lloyd and Mrs. Collier, and these aged dames were usually to be found before their door on a seat between two venerable oaks, wherein swarms of bees hived themselves.

Soon after their death (before 1800?) the house was pulled down and the proprietor expended £10,000 in improvements and in erecting the roomy brick building known as Hornsey Wood Tavern. The tea-gardens were enlarged and a lake formed, for the benefit of those who wished for a little angling or boating. To effect these improvements, a romantic part of the wood was destroyed, but the remaining portion still continued an attraction. About 1835 the "lower order of citizens" as T. Cromwell (*Islington*, p. 138) calls them, used to go "palming" to the wood on Palm Sunday. All through the present century Hornsey Wood House (or Tavern) was a favourite Sunday resort of Londoners.

In 1866 at the time of the formation of Finsbury Park, the house was pulled down and its site and that of the gardens and the Wood must be looked for in the Park, which was opened as a public recreation ground in 1869.

[*The Idler*, No. 15, July 1758 ; Dodsley's *London*, 1761 ; *Low Life* (1764), p. 46 ; *Sunday Ramble*, 1776 and 1797 ; Kearsley's *Strangers' Guide ;* Lambert's *London*, iv. 274 ; *Picture of London*, eds. 1802, 1823 and 1829 ; Hone's *Every Day Book*, i. 759, ff. ; Lewis's *Islington*, pp. 190, 282 ; J. F. Murray's *World of London*, 1845, ii. p. 82, ff. ; Walford, v. 430, ff. ; *Illustrated London News*, 14 August, 1869 ; J. H. Lloyd's *Highgate*, 1888.]

VIEWS.

1. An engraving of old Hornsey Wood House &c., in Lewis's *Islington*, p. 282.

2. There are many views of the later Hornsey Wood House (or Tavern), *e.g.* one engraved in Walford, v. 426, and there assigned to the year 1800. This is substantially the same as one (undated) in Hone's *Every Day Book*, i. 759. Hone, *ib.* 761, also gives a woodcut of the Lake. There is an engraving of the house of 1809, published by J. Cundee (W. Coll.), and there are views of it of a later date ; *e.g.* an engraving in Cromwell's *Islington*, p. 138.

THE SPRING GARDEN, STOKE NEWINGTON.

THIS Spring Garden is marked in Warner's *Survey of Islington*, 1735, rather to the south of Newington Green. About 1753 the tavern connected with the garden was taken by W. Bristow, who advertised the place as an afternoon tea-garden, appending to his advertisement the note " beans in perfection for any companies." [1]

It is mentioned in *Low Life*, 1764 as resorted to on Whit-Sunday evening by Londoners of the lower classes. Cromwell in his *Islington* (p. 199) published in 1835, speaks of the tavern and tea-gardens as existing " within memory."

[1] Newspaper cutting, 1753 (W. Coll.).

THE BLACK QUEEN COFFEE-HOUSE AND TEA GARDENS, SHACKLEWELL.

THE Black Queen Coffee-house situated on Shackle-well Green had attached to it a bowling green and tea-gardens planted with fruit trees, yews, limes, and poplars. It is said to have been resorted to by " genteel company," but little is known of it, except that in 1793 (when in possession of a Mr. Moore) the lease was advertised to be sold by auction (13th September, 1793).

[*The Daily Advertiser* for 3 September, 1793.]

IV

HAMPSTEAD GROUP

THE outlet of the once famous spring of Hampstead is at the present time to be found on the north side of Well Walk, and the water now trickles out slowly into a basin, which forms part of a modern fountain. The earliest mention of the spring occurs in the time of Charles II. when one Dorothy Rippin appears to have made some profit by the sale of the water, as she issued a halfpenny token which has on its obverse the words, DOROTHY RIPPIN AT THE WELL IN HAMSTED, and a representation of a well and bucket.[1] The well was in 1698 on the estate of Susanna Noel and her son Baptist, third Earl of Gainsborough, and was given by them conjointly on 20th December of that year, together with six acres of land, for the benefit of the Hampstead poor. A tablet on the present fountain records this gift.

The first to draw attention to the medicinal value of the water, was a well-known physician, Dr. Gibbons,[2] who in the early part of the eighteenth century described it as being as fully efficacious as any chalybeate water in England.

In April 1700 the water was advertised as being of the same nature and virtue as that at Tunbridge Wells,

[1] See Boyne's *Trade Tokens*, ed. Williamson, ii. p. 818. This token is undated. The only dated token of Hampstead is one of 1670.

[2] The " Mirmillo " of Garth's *Dispensary*.

and was sold by Phelps, an apothecary, at the Eagle and Child in Fleet Street, for threepence a flask. It was also obtainable from the lessee of the Wells at the Black Posts, King Street, near the Guildhall ; at Sam's Coffee House, Ludgate Hill, and at several other places in the City.

From this time there grew up around the spring various places of entertainment—a tavern [1] and coffee room, a bowling green and raffling shops, and, as will be presently seen, a chapel.

The chief building was the Great Room situated on the south side of Well Walk, about one hundred yards from the East Heath. It was a large house lit with long windows, and within its walls took place concerts and dances for the amusement of the Wells visitors up to 1733. The first recorded entertainment was given there in 1701 (18 August), when there was a " consort " of both vocal and instrumental music by the " best masters." The performance began at ten o'clock in the morning, and dancing took place in the afternoon. The tickets for the dancing cost sixpence, and one shilling was charged for the concert. In September of the same year, another concert was given at eleven o'clock, at which one Jemmy Bowen sang and two men performed on the violin. There was dancing in the afternoon as usual. These performances were continued every Monday during the season. " Very good music for dancing all day long " was announced for 12 May, 1707, and on 22 July, 1710, a girl of nine, a pupil of Mr. Tenoe, sang several operatic songs, and this performance began at five for the " conveniency of gentlemen's returning." The admission was two shillings and sixpence.

In the vicinity of the Great Room, stood Sion

---

[1] The modern public-house in Well Walk called the Wells Tavern, though at one period. (before 1840) bearing the sign of the Green Man, is probably on the site of the original tavern.

Buttaura Delin. et Sculp.

Published according to Act of Parliament 1752.

A View of y^e Long Room at Hampstead from the Heath. | Vüe de la Chambre longue a Hampstead du Côté de la Colline.

London Printed for & Sold by C. Dicey & Co in Aldermary Church Yard.

Chapel,[1] where couples on presenting a license and the sum of five shillings could be married at any time. A clergyman was always in attendance, and if the newly married would take their wedding dinner in the garden of the tavern nothing beyond the license was required. In 1716 the chapel was referred to as a "private and pleasure place" where many persons of the best fashion were married. It may be suspected, however, that the marriages were often, like those at the Fleet and Mayfair, irregular, and that the license was occasionally dispensed with.

During the first ten or twenty years of the eighteenth century, Hampstead Wells presented a gay and varied scene. When tired of the music and dancing in the Great Room, the visitor could adjourn to the bowling green, or to the raffling shops, where the cards were flying and the dice rattling, while fine gentlemen lost their money with "ease and negligence." There was the promenade in Well Walk beneath the avenue of limes, or a stroll might be taken on the breezy Heath. Court ladies were there "all air and no dress"; city ladies all dress and no air, and country dames with "broad brown faces like a Stepney bun." Citizens like Mr. Deputy Driver in the comedy[2] came down from town, perhaps to find their ladies coquetting with a beau, or retired to picquet with some brisk young Templar. "This Hampstead's a charming place," exclaims Arabella the citizen's wife: "To dance all night at the Wells; be treated at Mother Huff's,[3] have presents

---

[1] Sion Chapel (the exact site of which is unknown) is of course distinct from the Episcopal Chapel into which the Great Room was converted in 1733.

[2] Baker's comedy, *Hampstead Heath*, London, 1706.

[3] *The Country Journal, or the Craftsman* for 16 October, 1736, has the notice :—"On Sunday between seven and eight in the evening one Mr. Thomas Lane, a farrier of Hampstead, going home from the Spaniards upon the Heath near the house called Mother Huff's," was attacked and robbed and stripped naked by three men who jumped out of the bushes

made one at the raffling shops, and then take a walk in Cane Wood with a man of wit that's not over rude."

With this gay and fashionable throng there mingled company of a lower class, such as the Fleet Street sempstresses who danced minuets " in their furbeloe scarfs " and ill-fitting clothes. By about 1724 the more rakish and disreputable element had become predominant.[1] Bad characters came from London in " vampt up old cloaths to catch the apprentices." Lord Lovemore might still court his " mimic charmer "[2] there, but modest people did not care to join the company on the walks. The playing and dicing were kept up as formerly, but gentlemen no longer lost with ease and negligence, and one sharper tried to cheat another. In 1733 the Great Room was converted into an Episcopal Chapel and was used for church services until 1849. In 1869 the West Middlesex Volunteers occupied the building. About 1880 it was demolished, and to-day a modern red brick house in Well Walk (erected in 1892), and the entrance to Gainsborough Gardens occupy the site. A tablet on the house testifies that the "Old pump room " (*i.e.* Great Room) once stood on the spot.

In 1734 Dr. John Soame published a pamphlet in which he extolled with somewhat suspicious optimism the virtues of the neglected spring, recommending the water for cutaneous affections and nervous disorders. According to Soame, the spring [3] then threw off water at the rate of five gallons in four minutes, and could be made to throw a stream upwards to a height of at least

---

[1] Lysons's *Magna Britannia*, vol. iii. 1724, p. 44.

[2] This lady had made an earlier appearance at Cuper's Gardens ; *see* Welsted's *Epistle on False Fame*.

[3] The spring at this time was adjacent to the Great Room, and was in this position, *i.e.* on the opposite side to the existing fountain, at any rate as late as 1806.

twelve feet. "The Beautys of Hampstead," a song of this period, extols the "Chrystal bub'ling Well," [1] but the water-drinking does not appear again to have become the vogue, though as a place of amusement the Wells still enjoyed some degree of popularity. Another assembly-house, known as the Long Room, took the place of the old Great Room. This was a substantial red brick building of one storey. The ground floor consisted of an entire room with two small ante-rooms, one on either side of the entrance, used for tea-parties and card-playing. The floor above was divided up into rooms, where a cosy supper or a game of cards might be enjoyed. The house (probably built, in part, in the seventeenth century) still exists, and is to be found on the opposite side to the old Great Room, about a hundred yards further down Well Walk, going from the Heath. It is now a private residence called Weatherall House. It was in the Long Room that the Hampstead Balls took place of the kind described by Frances Burney. Here Evelina [2] was worried by Beau Smith, and refused the offers of "inelegant and low-bred" partners, who "begged the favour of hopping a dance" with her. Samuel Rogers (*Table Talk*) says that in his youth (*circ.* 1783) the Hampstead Assemblies were frequented by "a great deal of good . company," and that he himself danced four or five minuets there in one evening.

In 1802 a surgeon named John Bliss published a treatise, in which, without success, he endeavoured once more to awaken an interest in the medicinal properties of the Well. Mr. Keates, consulting chemist to the Metropolitan Board of Works, in recent times stated that it was a distinctly chalybeate water containing sufficient iron to render it capable of producing marked therapeutic effects. It was extremely pure, and in

---

[1] In Bickham's *Musical Entertainer* (1733, &c.).
[2] *Evelina* (1778), letter li.

general character, though with a larger proportion of iron, resembled that of Tunbridge Wells.[1]

[Dodsley's *London* (1761) ; *Ambulator*, 1774 ; Kearsley's *Strangers' Guide* (1793 ?) ; Walford, v. 467, ff. ; Thorne's *Environs of London* (1876), 281 ; Sir Gilbert Scott's *Proposed Destruction of the Well Walk* (Hampstead, 1879), with plan of Well Walk ; Park's *Hampstead ;* Baines's *Hampstead.*]

VIEWS.

1. The Pump-room, Well Walk (*i.e.* Great Room), since, the Episcopal Chapel, in Baines's *Hampstead*, from a drawing by Blanche Cowper Baines, after E. H. Dixon.

2. The old Well Walk, Hampstead, about 1750 (Walford, v. 463).

3. A view of " Ye Long Room at Hampstead from the Heath." Chatelain del. et sculp. 1752 (W. Coll.).

4. Well Walk, engraving in Howitt's *Northern Heights*, from a photograph.

5. Well Walk in 1870 in Baines's *Hampstead*, from a sketch by Walter Field.

---

[1] The house, No. 17 in Well Walk, which is just behind the existing fountain, has a shallow well supposed to contain the source of the original spring.

THE old Spaniards inn, still standing on the north side of the road between the upper and lower Heath of Hampstead, deserves a brief mention, seeing that about the middle of the eighteenth century or earlier, it had attached to it a curious garden laid out by one William Staples, who was probably the keeper of the inn.[1]

A contemporary account describes how " out of a wild and thorny wood full of hills, valleys, and sand-pits," the ingenious Mr. Staples " hath now made pleasant grass and gravel walks, with a mount, from the elevation whereof the beholder hath a prospect of Hanslope steeple in Northamptonshire, within eight miles of Northampton ; of Langdon hill, in Essex, full sixty miles east," and of other eminences, the visibility of which was perhaps less mythical.

The walks and plats were ornamented with a number of curious devices picked out with pebble stones of variegated colours. There were over forty of these quaint designs, such as the sun in its glory, the twelve signs of the Zodiac, the Tower of London, the grand colossus of Rhodes, the pathway of all the planets, the spire of Salisbury, Adam and Eve, the shield of David, the Egyptian pyramids, and an Egyptian sphinx : an odd association of things earthly and celestial.

Towards the end of the eighteenth century the

[1] MS. *History of Middlesex*, 1752, quoted by Park.

Spaniards was much resorted to, especially on Sundays.[1]
During the Gordon Riots of 1780, its landlord, Giles
Thomas, is said to have arrested the progress of the
mob bent on the destruction of Caen Wood House,
Lord Mansfield's residence, hard by, through rolling
out his beer barrels into the road, and setting them
abroach, thus gaining time to summon the military for
the defence of the house.

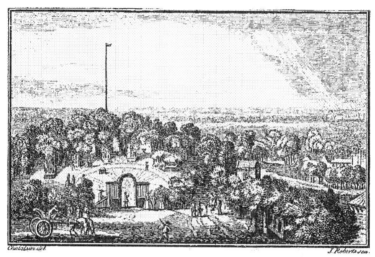

SOUTH VIEW OF THE SPANIARDS, 1750.

In the present century, though the mount and the
pebbled plots had disappeared, the Spaniards gardens
were rendered attractive by a bowling-green, and by
pleasant arbours and parterres : it was resorted to by
many a party of tea-drinkers like that of Mr. Raddle,
Mrs. Bardell and her friends.[2]

---

[1] *A Modern Sabbath*, 1797, p. 53 ; see also Woodward's *Eccentric
Excursions*, 13.
[2] Dickens, *Pickwick Papers*, cap. xlvi.

[Park's *Hampstead*; Baines's *Hampstead*; Walford, v. 445, ff.; Thorne's *Environs of London*, 1876.]

VIEWS.

1. The south view of the Spaniards (showing the garden as laid out by Staples) near Hampstead (Chatelain del., J. Roberts sculp. 1750, W. Coll., reproduced in Chambers's *Book of Days*, ii. 71).

2. The Spaniards Tavern, Hampstead, Middlesex, drawn and engraved for Dugdale's *England and Wales*.

3. View of the inn as at present, Walford, v. 445.

4. " View of a skittle ground at Hampstead " (either the Spaniards or Jack Straw's Castle), Woodward's *Eccentric Excursions*, coloured print, pl. iv. p. 14 (1796).

NEW GEORGIA

New Georgia was situated in Turner's Wood to the north-east of the Spaniards tavern, Hampstead, and at the northern extremity of the road opposite the western lodge of Caen Wood. It was a wooden cottage, two storeys high, irregularly constructed, and standing in a wilderness and garden laid out "in a delightful romantic taste." The proprietor, Robert Caston, built the cottage in 1737, and opened New Georgia to the public.

He was his own architect, builder, and gardener, and probably compared his labours to those of the founders of the American colony of Georgia established in 1733. An inscription on the cottage explained the origin of New Georgia as follows :—" I Robert Caston, begun this place in a wild wood, stubbed up the wood, digged all the ponds, cut all the walks, made all the gardens, built all the rooms, with my own hands ; nobody drove a nail here, laid a brick or a tile, but myself, and thank God for giving me such strength, being sixty-four years of age when I begun it."

Tea was supplied in the cottage or the gardens, but the chief attractions were a number of mechanical oddities set in motion in the garden and in the various little rooms into which the house was divided. London shopkeepers, like Zachary Treacle,[1] often made their way to the place on Sunday afternoons, and were

---

[1] Cp. *The Idler*, No. 15, July 1758.

diverted by reptiles that darted forth when a board or spring was trodden upon, by a chair that collapsed when sat upon, and by various contrivances of waterworks.

The more boisterous, who on other Sundays delighted in a roll down the hill in Greenwich Park, found amusement in thrusting their heads into the New Georgia pillory to receive in that position the kisses of the ladies. A thickly-planted maze was another source of diversion.

The place does not appear to have been frequented after about 1758, and was subsequently (before 1795)[1] enclosed in the estate of Lord Mansfield.

[*Gent. Mag.* 1748, vol. 18, 109 ; *The Connoisseur*, No. 26, 25 July, 1754 ; *The Idler*, No. 15, 22 July, 1758 ; Lysons's *Environs*, ii. 527 ; Lambert's *London* (1806), iv. 255 ; Park's *Hampstead ;* Prickett's *Highgate*, 72, ff. ; Walford, v. 446.]

VIEWS.

New Georgia is clearly marked in Rocque's Survey, 1745, but there appear to be no views.

[1] Lysons, *Environs*, ii. 527.

BELSIZE HOUSE

Belsize House was a large Elizabethan mansion, modified in the time of Charles II. Pepys, who visited it in 1668 (17 August) when it was the residence of Lord Wotton, describes its gardens as " wonderful fine : too good for the house the gardens are, being, indeed, the most noble that ever I saw, and brave orange and lemon trees." [1]

The house was a private residence until 1720, when it was converted into a place of public amusement, under the management of a Welshman named Howell. At this time it was a somewhat imposing structure, with wings, and a tower in the centre. The entrance was by a door placed between the wings, and also by an external staircase at one wing.

The inaugural entertainment took place about April, 1720, and consisted of an "uncommon solemnity of music and dancing." The place was usually open from 6 a.m. till 8 p.m., without charge for admission. The Park, Wilderness and Garden, about a mile in circumference, were advertised (about 1721 ?), as being wonderfully improved and filled with a variety of birds, " which compose a most melodious and delightful harmony." Those who wished for an early stroll in the park could " breakfast on tea or coffee as cheap as at their own chambers." As the journey from London was

[1] Evelyn (*Diary*, 2 June, 1676) describes the gardens as very large and woody, but ill kept.

not unattended with risks, twelve stout fellows (afterwards increased to thirty), completely armed, were announced as "always at hand to patrol timid females or
other."

Belsize became a fashionable rendezvous. In July
1721 the Prince and Princess of Wales, attended by
several persons of rank, dined at the house, and were
entertained with hunting and other diversions. In June,
1722, on the occasion of a wild deer hunt, three or four

BELSIZE HOUSE AND PARK.

hundred coaches brought down the "Nobility and
Gentry" from town. Athletic sports were introduced,
and the proprietor gave a plate of several guineas to be
run for by eleven footmen (1721). Gambling and intrigue were the less wholesome results of this influx of
the nobility and gentry. In May 1722 the Justices took
steps to prevent the unlawful gaming, while in the
same year "A serious Person of Quality" published a
satire called *Belsize House*, in which he undertook to

expose " the Fops and Beaux who daily frequent that Academy," and also the " characters of the women who make this an exchange for assignations."

> This house, which is a nuisance to the land
> Doth near a park and handsome garden stand
> Fronting the road, betwixt a range of trees
> Which is perfumed with a Hampstead breeze.
> The Welsh Ambassador has many ways
> Fool's pence, while summer season holds, to raise.
> For 'tis not only chocolate and tea,
> With ratafia, bring him company.
> Nor is it claret, Rhenish wine or sack
> The fond and rampant Lords and Ladies lack
> Or ven'son pasty for a certain dish
> With several varieties of fish ;
> But hither they and other chubs resort
> To see the Welsh Ambassador make sport,
> Who in the art of hunting has the luck
> To kill in fatal corner tired buck,
> The which he roasts and stews and sometimes bakes,
> Whereby His Excellency profit makes.
> He also on another element
> Does give his choused customers content
> With net or angling rod, to catch a dish
> Of trouts or carp or other sorts of fish.

The Welsh Ambassador was the nickname of the proprietor, James Howell, an enterprising though not very reputable person, who had once been imprisoned for some offence in Newgate.

Races [1] and similar amusements continued for several years to be provided, and music was performed every day during the season. In the spring of 1733 (31 May) a race was advertised for ponies twelve hands six inches high. The length of the race was six times round the course ; " Mr. Treacle's black pony," which distinguished itself by winning the plate at Hampstead Heath in the previous year, being excluded.

In 1736 a fat doe was advertised to be hunted to

[1] *E.g.* "Galloway Races" in 1725 and 1729.

death by small beagles, beginning at nine in the morning, and sportsmen were invited to bring their own dogs, if " not too large." In the same year (16 September) a boys' race was run, beginning at three o'clock, six times round the course : a prize of one guinea was given to the winner, and half a guinea to the second runner. " Each person to pay sixpence coming in, and all persons sitting on the wall or getting over will be prosecuted."

For an afternoon in August 1737, there was announced a running match six times round the park, between " the Cobler's Boy and John Wise the Mile-End Drover," for twenty guineas. In 1745 there were foot-races in the park, and this is the last notice we have of Belsize as a place of amusement.

The mansion falling into a ruinous state [1] was pulled down at the close of the eighteenth century (before 1798), and a large, plainly-built house was erected in its stead. From 1798–1807 this new Belsize House was tenanted by the Right Hon. Spencer Perceval and others. In the autumn of 1853 the house was pulled down (cp. *The Illustrated London News* for 9th September, 1854, p. 239), and the buildings of the Belsize Estate were subsequently erected on the site of the Park.

The present Belsize Avenue (on the west side of Haverstock Hill) is the representative of a beautiful avenue of elms, which originally led up to the old Belsize House, the site of which was near the present St. Peter's Church.

[Palmer's *St. Pancras*, 227, ff. ; Baines's *Hampstead;* Walford v. 494, ff. ; Howitt's *Northern Heights;* Lambert's *London*, 1806, iv. 256 ; Thorne's *Environs of London*, s.v. " Hampstead " ; Park's *Hampstead;* newspaper advertisements, W. Coll.]

---

[1] *Ambulator*, 1774 ; Dodsley's *London*, 1761.

VIEWS.

1. Old Belsize House. A view on a Belsize House advertisement, *circ.* 1721 ? and a view by Maurer, 1750; cp. Howitt's *Northern Heights* and C. Knight's *Old England*, ii. fig. 2404.

2. Belsize House in 1800 (Walford, v. 492).

KILBURN WELLS

THE spring known as Kilburn Wells was situated in the Abbey Field near the site of the old Kilburn Priory, and in the rear of the Bell Tavern. It attracted public notice about the middle of the last century ;[1] and some endeavours were made, probably by the proprietor of the Bell, to bring Kilburn Wells into vogue : at any rate, in 1752 it is referred to as a place in some respects akin to Sadler's Wells :—

> Shall you prolong the midnight ball
> With costly supper at Vaux Hall,
> And yet prohibit earlier suppers
> At Kilburn, Sadler's Wells or Kupers ?[2]

About 1773 Kilburn Wells began to be more widely known, and the proprietor's advertisement of 17 July in that year announced that the water was then in the utmost perfection, the gardens enlarged and greatly im-

---

[1] From the manuscript history of Middlesex quoted by Park (*Hampstead*), the spring would appear to have been discovered about 1742 ; the date on the reservoir containing the water was, however, 1714, and Walford (v. 245) states that the spring was known before 1600. But there is no evidence that Kilburn Wells was a place of entertainment earlier than about 1742, though the Bell tavern dated from about 1600.

[2] Richard Owen Cambridge, *Dialogue between a master and his servant* (1752). "Kupers" = Cuper's Gardens, Lambeth.

proved, and the house and offices "repainted and beautified in the most elegant manner." The Great Room was described as specially adapted for "the use and amusement of the politest companies" who might require it for music, dancing, or entertainments. "This happy spot is equally celebrated for its rural situation, extensive prospects, and the acknowledged efficacy of its waters ; is most delightfully situated on the site of the once famous Abbey of Kilburn on the Edgware Road, at an easy distance, being but a morning's walk from the metropolis, two miles from Oxford Street ; the footway from Mary-bone across the fields still nearer. A plentiful larder is always provided, together with the best of wines and other liquors. Breakfasting and hot loaves."

An account of the medicinal water drawn up by the usual "eminent physician" was given away to visitors, and in one of the rooms was a long list of the diseases said to have been cured. In 1792 Godfrey Schmeisser made a careful analysis of the water. It was a mild purgative, milky in appearance, and had a bitterish saline taste. The use of the water for curative purposes appears to have ceased in the early part of the present century (before 1814), but the Old Bell, or Kilburn Wells as the place was generally denominated, enjoyed popularity as a tea-garden as late as 1829.[1]

About 1863 the Old Bell was pulled down, and the present Bell public-house erected on the spot. A brick reservoir long enclosed the spring, but some years ago it was demolished and built over. It stood immediately behind the Bank at the corner of Belsize Road.

[Thorne's *Environs of London ;* Lambert's *London,* iv. 288 ; Howitt's *Northern Heights ;* Baines's *Hampstead ;* Park's *Hampstead ;* Walford, v. 245, ff.]

---

[1] *Picture of London,* 1802 and 1829.

VIEWS.

1. The Bell Inn, Kilburn, 1750 (Walford, v. 246).

2. The Bell Inn, Kilburn, from a mezzotint, 1789, reproduced in Baines's *Hampstead*.

3. View of the Old Bell Inn at Kilburn on the Edgware Road. Rathbone del. Prestal sculp. 1789.   Crace, *Cat.* p. 670, No. 76.

4. An engraved handbill, describing the waters, at the top of which is a print of the Long Room, by F. Vivares ; mentioned in Park's *Hampstead*, p. xxxi*, additions.

V

CHELSEA GROUP

RANELAGH HOUSE AND GARDENS

§ 1. *Origin of Ranelagh*

ABOUT the year 1690 Richard, Viscount (afterwards Earl of) Ranelagh, Paymaster-General of the Forces, built for himself on the east side of Chelsea Hospital a private residence known as Ranelagh House, and laid out a garden.   In 1691 [1] the house is described as " very fine within, all the rooms being wainscotted with Norway oak," and the garden plats and walks were " curiously kept and elegantly designed."   Bowack in 1705 says that the gardens were " esteemed to be the best in England, the size considered."   Here Lord Ranelagh lived till his death in 1712.

In 1733 the property was sold, and at that time Lacy, patentee of Drury Lane Theatre, made arrangements for forming Ranelagh into a place of public amusement.   Nothing decisive was done till 1741, when a large circular building, the famous Rotunda (at first generally called the Amphitheatre), was erected in the Ranelagh grounds by William Jones, architect to the East India Company.[2]

The capital for the undertaking was furnished by a few shareholders, and was divided into thirty-six shares of £1,000 each.   The principal shareholder and

[1] Gibson, *View of the Gardens near London*, Dec. 1691.
[2] Lord Ranelagh's house remained standing till 1805, and was used in connexion with the Ranelagh entertainments.

manager was Sir Thomas Robinson, Bart., M.P.,
whose gigantic form was for many years familiar to
all frequenters of the Rotunda : a writer of 1774 calls
him its Maypole and Garland of Delights.[1]

The Rotunda and Gardens were first opened on
5 April, 1742, with a public breakfast, and a visit to
Ranelagh became the vogue. Of the early fortunes of
the place the best chronicler is Horace Walpole. On
April 22, 1742, he writes to Mann :—" I have been
breakfasting this morning at Ranelagh Garden : they
have built an immense amphitheatre, with balconies
full of little ale-houses : it is in rivalry to Vauxhall and
costs above twelve thousand pounds."[2]

On May 26[3] he again describes the "vast amphitheatre, finely gilt, painted and illuminated ; into
which everybody that loves eating, drinking, staring,
or crowding, is admitted for twelvepence." In 1744,[4]
Mr. Walpole goes "every night constantly" to Ranelagh, "which has totally beat Vauxhall." "Nobody
goes anywhere else ; everybody goes there. My Lord
Chesterfield is so fond of it, that he says he has ordered
all his letters to be directed thither." "The floor is
all of beaten princes" ; "you can't set your foot without treading on a Prince or Duke of Cumberland."
In 1748,[5] "Ranelagh is so crowded, that going there
t'other night in a string of coaches, we had a stop of
six and thirty minutes."

In 1745 Mr. Thomas Gray had written to a friend [6]

---

[1] Robinson lived at Prospect Place adjoining the gardens. He
died on 3 March, 1777.

[2] Cp. Walpole's letter to Mann of 26 May, 1742 : "The
building and disposition of the gardens cost sixteen thousand
pounds."

[3] Walpole to Mann, 26 May, 1742.

[4] Walpole to Conway, 29 June, 1744.

[5] Walpole to Montagu, 26 May, 1748.

[6] Gray to Chute, July 1745 (Gray's *Works*, ed. Gosse, ii.
125, ff.).

that he had no intention of following the stream to Ranelagh, and he touched a weak spot in the delights of the London Pleasure Gardens—the uncertainty of the London weather. " I have never been at Ranelagh Gardens since they were opened. . . . They do not succeed : people see it once, or twice, and so they go to Vauxhall. Well, but is it not a very great design, very new, finely lighted ? Well, yes, aye, very fine truly, so they yawn and go to Vauxhall, and then it's too hot, and then it's too cold, and here's a wind and there's a damp." But in August 1746 we find Gray declaring [1] that his evenings lately have been chiefly spent at Ranelagh ' and Vauxhall.

Other literary people, at least as interesting as Walpole's Dukes and Princes, frequented Ranelagh. The learned Mrs. Carter was there in 1748, and found the gardens very pleasant on a June evening, though she did not relish such " tumultary torchlight entertainments." Goldsmith and Reynolds used to go there together about 1771, and Dr. Johnson " often went to Ranelagh," which he deemed, as the Rev. Dr. Maxwell apologetically observes, " a place of innocent recreation."

§ 2.   The Rotunda

The guide-books abound with architectural details of the Ranelagh Rotunda.[2] A sufficient idea of its general appearance may be gained by glancing at some of the contemporary prints and by noticing a few salient features. Writers of the time compare it to " the Pantheon at Rome " : the Londoner of to-day will think rather of the British Museum Reading Room which it resembled in size and, to some extent, in general appearance. The circumference was 555 feet and the internal diameter 150 feet. It was entered by four Doric

[1] *Works*, ed. Gosse, ii. 139.
[2] See especially Kearsley's *Strangers' Guide* (1793 ?).

porticoes opposite one another, and the interior architecture corresponded with the exterior.

On the exterior was an arcade encircling the building,
and above this arcade was a gallery reached by steps
placed at the porticoes.

In the interior was a circle of fifty-two [1] boxes,
separated by wainscotting. Each box had its "droll
painting" and its bell-lamp with candles ; and in each
seven or eight people could be accommodated with
refreshments. Benches covered with red baize were
dispersed about the area, and the plaster floor was
covered with matting.

Above the circle of boxes was a gallery containing
a similar range of boxes which were entered by folding-
doors from the gallery outside the building. The
Rotunda was lighted by sixty windows, and the chief
material used in its construction was wood.

The ceiling was painted an olive colour, with a rainbow round the extremity, and there hung from it
numerous chandeliers, each ornamented with a gilt
crown and containing crystal bell-lamps of candles.
When all the candles were lighted, the sight, we are
told, was "very glorious."

In the centre of the building was a remarkable square
erection supporting the roof, and made up of pillars
and arches elaborately decorated. This "grand and
elegant structure" was nothing more or less than a fireplace containing a chimney and an open fire. On cold
days in February and March the best place was "one
of the hot blazing red-cloth benches" by the fire. This
fireplace structure had originally contained the orchestra,
but after a few years the orchestra was, for acoustic
reasons, moved to the side of the Rotunda. Behind the
orchestra was an organ by Byfield, set up in 1746.[2]

---

[1] This was the number about 1793.
[2] Burney says that the first organist was Keeble, who was succeeded by Butler. Burney himself was organist in 1770.

Johnson declared that "the *coup d'œil*" of Ranelagh was "the finest thing he had ever seen."[1]   When Johnson first entered Ranelagh and its brilliant circle, it gave, as he told Boswell,[2] "an expansion and gay sensation" to his mind, such as he had never experienced anywhere else.   Miss Lydia Melford, in *Humphry Clinker*, wrote about Ranelagh to her 'dear Willis' with an enthusiasm less restrained, and without Dr. Johnson's moralising comment :—"Alas, Sir, these are only *struggles* for happiness."   "Ranelagh (she writes) looks like the enchanted palace of a genio, adorned with the most exquisite performances of painting, carving, and gilding, enlightened with a thousand golden lamps that emulate the noonday sun ; crowded with the great, the rich, the gay, the happy and the fair ; glittering with cloth of gold and silver, lace, embroidery, and precious stones.   While these exulting sons and daughters of felicity tread this round of pleasure, or regale in different parties, and separate lodges, with fine imperial tea and other delicious refreshments, their ears are entertained with the most ravishing delights of music, both instrumental and vocal."

§ 3.   *The entertainments and the company.*

The usual charge for admission was half a crown,[3] which always included the 'regale' of tea, coffee and bread and butter.   Foote called Ranelagh the Bread and Butter Manufactory, and, except on ball nights, no other refreshments seem to have been procurable.

[1] Boswell, *Life*, chap. xxvi. p. 236, ed. Croker.
[2] *Life*, 1777–1778, chap. lxi. p. 561, ed. Croker.
[3] In the early days, sometimes one shilling and two shillings, including the breakfast and the morning concert.   On special nights when fireworks were displayed, the price was raised to three shillings or more.   Tickets costing from half a guinea to two guineas were issued for the masquerades.

The place was usually open on three days in the week, Mondays, Wednesdays and Fridays.[1] The regular season for the evening concerts and garden-promenade began at Easter, but the Rotunda was often open in February, or earlier, for the dances. In the early days of Ranelagh the public breakfastings and the morning concerts at twelve were a constant feature. About 1754 the proprietors of Ranelagh were refused a license for music, and the breakfasting took place that year without concerts : these breakfasts and morning concerts do not appear to have been subsequently renewed.

The evening concerts (from May 1742, onwards) generally began at 6.30 or 7. Between the Acts the company walked in the gardens to the music of horns and clarinets, and a garden-orchestra was erected about 1764. The gardens were illuminated, but fireworks did not become a prominent feature till about 1767.

The gardens themselves were somewhat formally laid out. There were several gravel walks, shaded by elms and yews ; a flower-garden, and "a beautiful octagon grass plat." The principal walk led from the south end of Ranelagh House to the bottom of the gardens, where there was a circular Temple of Pan. At night the walks were prettily lit with lamps attached to the trees. There was also a canal with a Temple indifferently described as the Chinese House and the Venetian Temple.

In its earliest as well as in its latest days masquerades attracted many to the Rotunda and the gardens, but the chief diversion was the promenade in the Rotunda. A guide-book of 1793 states that " walking round the Rotundo " was " one of the pleasures of the place." We hear much at all periods of " the circular labour "

---

[1] Sometimes it was advertised as open "every evening." People were allowed to walk in the gardens and view the Rotunda during the daytime for one shilling.

of the company and "the ring of folly."[1]   Matthew
Bramble found one half of the company "following
one another's tails in an eternal circle like asses in an
olive mill while the other half are drinking hot water
under the denomination of tea."   Mr. Bramble exacted
much from places of amusement, but it is to be suspected from other testimonies that there was an
atmosphere of dulness, a note of ennui, about the
ordinary diversions of this fashionable rendezvous.
"There's your famous Ranelagh (says 'Evelina') that
you make such a fuss about ; why what a dull place is
that ! "   A Frenchman describing Ranelagh about 1800
—foreigners were always expected to visit it—calls it
"le plus insipide lieu d'amusement que l'on ait pu
imaginer," and even hints at Dante's Purgatory.   Another Frenchman writing much earlier, *circ.* 1749,
briefly comments "on s'ennuie avec de la mauvaise
musique, du thé et du beurre."

Samuel Rogers (*Table Talk*), who must have known
Ranelagh from about 1786 till its close, was struck by
the solemnity of the whole thing : "all was so orderly
and still that you could hear the whishing sound of the
ladies' trains as the immense assembly walked round
and round the room."   An "affray" of the kind
familiar at Vauxhall and not infrequent at Marylebone
was practically unknown at Ranelagh.   On May 6th,
1752, Dr. John Hill was caned in the Rotunda by an
angry gentleman, and the newspapers and caricaturists
were momentarily excited, chiefly because Hill's injuries
were supposed to be a sham.   One almost welcomes a
scene at Ranelagh.   On the 12th of May, 1764, four
footmen were charged before Sir John Fielding with
riotous behaviour at Ranelagh House, "hissing several
of the nobility, relative to their not giving or suffering
vails to be taken, pelting several gentlemen with brick-
bats and breaking the windows."[2]

[1] "Harlequin in Ranelagh," *London Magazine*, May 1774.
[2] Cp. *Gent. Mag.* 1764, p. 247.

Throughout its career of more than a hundred and sixty years, Ranelagh fairly maintained its position as a fashionable resort, but at all periods the company was a good deal mixed. Philomides, "a gentleman of sprightly wit, and very solid judgment," has described [1] the frequenters of the place four or five years after it was first opened. My Lord (he says) was sure to meet his tailor there, and Statira would see her toyman "cursing himself for letting this Statira have a service of very fine Dresden china, which she assured him her Lord would pay for immediately." The ubiquitous Templar was easily recognised—a pert young fellow in a fustian frock, and a broad-brimmed hat "in an affected impudent cock." There was an Oxford scholar, a political pamphleteer and a spruce military spark smelling of lavender water. A coxcomb just returned from his travels was more absurd. He had set up as virtuoso, and brought home a headless Helen and a genuine 'Otho' coined at Rome two years ago. He might now be heard talking Italian in a loud voice and "pronouncing the word Gothic fifty times an hour."

In 1760 a fashionable lady complains that there were too many tradesmen's wives at Ranelagh. But compared with Vauxhall it was fashionable, at least according to a lady's maid in "High Life Below Stairs" (*circ.* 1759, Act I. sc. 2) :—

Lady Charlotte's Maid : Well, I say it again, I love Vauxhall.

Lady Bab's Maid : Oh, my stars ! Why, there is nobody there but filthy citizens—*Runelow* for *my* money.

From about 1774 it was considered fashionable to arrive at the Rotunda about 11 P.M., one hour after the concert was over. In 1777, according to Walpole, the company did not arrive till twelve. "The people of the true ton," says the satirical "Harlequin in Ranelagh," [2]

---

[1] *Ranelagh House : a satire*, 1747.
[2] *London Magazine*, 1774.

A NIGHT SCENE at RANELAGH on Wednesday 6ᵗʰ of May 1752.
Thus I bore my point, six rogues in buckram let drive at me.

Extract from the Covent Garden Journal.

THE ATTACK ON DR. JOHN HILL AT RANELAGH, 6 MAY, 1752.

(1774), " come in about eleven, stare about them for half an hour, laugh at the other fools who are drenching and scalding themselves with coffee and tea . . . . despise all they have seen, and then they trail home again to sup." The citizens, on the other hand, came to stare at the great, at the Duke of Gloucester or Lady Almeria Carpenter, or whoever it might be. They came to see how the great folks were dressed, how they walked and how they talked. Some worthy men were compelled by their wives to wear swords, and in the circling promenade found it hard " to adjust the spit to the humour of those behind and before" them. The 'Harlequin' enlarges on some unpleasant characters who haunted Ranelagh, Baron H——g (for instance), who trails about like a wounded worm, and Lord C——y who " runs his nose under every bonnet." It is not to be denied that Ranelagh, though on the whole decorous, had a tolerable reputation as a place of assignation.

§4. *Annals of Ranelagh* 1742–1769.

From this general sketch of Ranelagh and its frequenters, we may pass on to some details of its amusements year by year.

The principal performer at the concerts in the earliest days (1742—*circ.* 1760) was the well-known actor and vocalist Beard, who was considered by Dibdin to be, " taken altogether, the best English singer." Giulia Frasi, young and interesting, with her " sweet clear voice," was heard in 1751 and 1752. Michael Festing at first led the band, and was succeeded (about 1752) by Abram Brown, a performer who (according to Burney) had " a clear, sprightly and loud tone, with a strong hand," but who was deficient in musical knowledge and feeling. Parry, the Welsh harper (1746), and Caporale, the violoncello player, were also among the earlier performers.[1]

At first, choruses from oratorios (this was still the case in 1763) were a feature of the concerts, but the performances soon came to differ little from those of Vauxhall and Marylebone. In 1754 an entertainment of recitation, with a procession, was given under the name of Comus's Court. In 1757 " Acis and Galatea " was performed for the benefit of the Marine Society. On 10 June, 1763 [2] Bonnell Thornton's ' Burlesque Ode on St. Cecilia's Day ' was performed, " adapted (by Burney) to the antient British music, viz. : the salt-box, the Jew's-harp, the marrow-bones and cleavers, the hum-strum or hurdy-gurdy, etc., etc." The performers sang the recitative, airs and choruses in masquerade dresses, and the salt-box song was especially successful. The fun must have been rather forced, though Johnson, who read the Ode when printed, " praised its humour," seemed much diverted with it, and repeated the lines :—

> In strains more exalted the salt-box shall join,
> And clattering and battering and clapping combine ;
> With a rap and a tap while the hollow side sounds,
> Up and down leaps the flap, and with rattling rebounds.

---

[1] Other early vocalists were :—Mrs. Storer (1751) ; Miss Young (1755) ; Miss Formantel (*Ten favourite songs sung by Miss Formantel at Ranelagh*, music by Mr. Oswald, published July 1758).

[2] According to a statement of Burney's (note in Croker's ed. of Boswell's *Johnson*, p. 143, anno " 1763 "), the salt-box song was sung by Beard accompanied on that instrument by Brent, the fencing master, while Skeggs played on the broomstick as bassoon. Croker assigns the composition, and apparently the first performance, of the Ode to 1769, and states that the first edition (which he himself had seen) of it bears the date 1749, a date which he considered to be a misprint for 1769. But the date 1769 is, as some later writers have seen, clearly erroneous, and the composition—and possibly the *first* performance at Ranelagh—must be assigned to 1759. The published edition of the Ode, in the British Museum, is dated (May) 1763, and the Ode was undoubtedly performed at Ranelagh on 10 June of that year (1763). (See *Annual Register ; Lloyd's Evening Post*, 8–16 June, 1763.)

In 1762–1764 the principal singer was the Italian Tenducci,[1] whose voice, according to Miss Lydia Melford, was "neither man's nor woman's; but it is more melodious than either, and it warbled so divinely, that while I listened I really thought myself in Paradise."

On 29 June, 1764, Mozart, then eight years old, performed on the harpsichord and organ several of his own compositions. On 12 May, 1767,[2] Catches and Glees were rendered with instrumental parts by Arne, an addition considered necessary on account of the size of the Rotunda. This was stated to be the first public performance of the kind in England.

In 1769 Dibdin was a singer of ballads, and on 12 May of this year there was a Jubilee Ridotto, an event at which we may pause to recall some of the earlier masquerades and balls which, from time to time, enlivened the routine of Ranelagh.

The most famous of these entertainments was the "Grand Jubilee Masquerade, in the Venetian taste," that took place on Wednesday, 26 April, 1749, to celebrate the proclamation of the peace of Aix-la-Chapelle. The Masquerade (says Horace Walpole[3]) "had nothing Venetian in it, but was by far the best understood and prettiest spectacle I ever saw; nothing in a fairy tale ever surpassed it. . . . It began at three o'clock; at about five, people of fashion began to go; when you entered, you found the whole garden filled with masks and spread with tents, which remained all

---

[1] Cp. *Six new English songs composed by Ferdinando Tenducci, and to be sung by him at Ranelagh*. Sold by the author at his lodging in the Great Piazza, Covent Garden, 1763 (W. Coll.).

Other performers at this period were :—1762 : Champness, Hudson, Miss Thomas, Miss Brent. 1763 : Dearle, Miss Wright, Miss Brent. 1765 (?) : the elder Fawcett.

[2] *Gent. Mag.* 1767, p. 277.

[3] Walpole's *Letters*, ed. Cunningham, ii. 150, ff. (Walpole to Mann, 3 May, 1749).

night very commodely. In one quarter was a May-pole dressed with garlands, and people dancing round it to a tabor and pipe, and rustic music, all masked, as were all the various bands of music that were disposed in different parts of the garden ; some like huntsmen with French-horns, some like peasants, and a troop of harlequins and scaramouches in the little open temple on the mount. On the canal was a sort of gondola, adorned with flags and streamers, and filled with music, rowing about. All round the outside of the amphi-theatre were shops, filled with Dresden china, Japan, &c., and all the shopkeepers in mask. The amphitheatre was illuminated, and in the middle was a circular bower, composed of all kinds of firs in tubs, from twenty to thirty feet high ; under them, orange trees, with small lamps in each orange, and below them all sorts of the finest auriculas in pots ; and festoons of natural flowers hanging from tree to tree. Between the arches, too, were firs, and smaller ones in the balconies above. There were booths for tea and wine, gaming-tables, and dancing, and about two thousand persons. In short, it pleased me more than the finest thing I ever saw."

Later masquerades, though attended by fashionable people, were less select, as appears, for example, from an advertisement which a gentleman inserted in the *Public Advertiser* of 8 March, 1753 [1] :—" This is to inform the Lady that was in a wite mask, red Beard and Ey's at the last Masquereade but one, in a brown and silver flora Pethecoat and head-dress, remarkable gentle, very finely maid, who lost her company and walked with several masks, perticuler with one, who in raptorous heared her declare a dislike to gameing and the intention of Maskquerdes. . . . . on which he asked, wathere single

---

[1] It is to be feared that this advertisement was an invention of the editor's, but it would have had little point for his readers had it not been actually based on familiar incidents of the Ranelagh masquerades.

or ingaged, and under whos care that Night? the lady
pointing to a tall gentleman in black and a bag wigg,
said his, my Brother." His intentions were honourable,
and he begged to see her face. In reply, "she repetted
Part out of the Orphin 'Trust not a man'; said he had
taken notice enough of her to know her again; bid him
look sharp at the next Makquered, at wich and all
other Places he as been dispionted of seeing her; he
therefore hops (if not ingaged) will get her Brother or
some Friend to call on him" as he feels assured he could
be happy for life with her.

On the occasion of the Jubilee Ridotto on 12 May,
1769, the gardens and the Chinese House were illuminated. "A large sea-horse stuck full of small lamps
floated on the Canal, and had a very agreeable aspect."
A favourite Ranelagh 'serenata,' Dibdin's 'Ephesian
Matron,' was performed at ten, and the Rotunda and
gardens were gradually filled by a brilliant company.
The Dukes of York and Cumberland were there, and
one of the prettiest characters was "a rural nymph in
rose-coloured sattin, trimmed with silver." The tickets,
which cost a guinea, included the supper. Unfortunately, the wine and sweetmeats were not immediately
forthcoming, and some gentlemen broke open the wine
cellar and helped themselves. Sir Thomas Robinson,
to make things pleasant, thereupon sent a general invitation to the company to sup with him. The dancing
began at twelve, and was continued till four, a comparatively early hour at Ranelagh masquerades.

§ 5.   *Later history of Ranelagh*, 1770–1805.

A "Gentleman in Town," writing in *The Town and
Country Magazine* for April 1770 (p. 195) to his friend
in the country, enlarges on the fashionable assemblages
to be then seen at Ranelagh three times a week. And we
may note that about this time the tradesmen advertised

their silver Ranelagh silks and Ranelagh waistcoats in
gold, silver and colours. The sweet voice of "the
lovely Mrs. Baddeley" was then to be heard in the
Rotunda, and she sang (in the autumn, 1770) in "The
Recruiting Sergeant," together with Mrs. Thompson,
Dibdin, and Bannister.[1]

The garden concerts, and the fireworks, and transparent pictures in a building in the grounds had by this
time become prominent features of the place.[2]

The event of 1775 was the Ranelagh Regatta and
Ball,[3] which took place on June 23rd. Early in the
afternoon of that day the whole river from London
Bridge to Millbank was covered with pleasure boats,
and scaffold erections were to be seen on the banks, and
even on the top of Westminster Hall. Gambling tables
lined the approaches to Westminster Bridge : men went
about selling indifferent liquor, Regatta songs and Regatta cards. The river banks now resembled a great
fair, and the Thames itself a floating town. Wild cal-
culations fixed the number of the spectators at 200,000,
or "at least" three millions. At 7.30 a cannon sig-
nalled the start of the racing-boats, and about 8.30, when
the prizes had been awarded, the whole procession began
to move "in a picturesque irregularity towards Ranelagh." The Directors' barge, with its band playing and
gold REGATTA ensign flying, led the way, and the
fortunate persons who had ball-tickets landed at Ranelagh Stairs at nine o'clock.

Dancing took place in the Temple of Neptune, a
temporary octagon erection in the grounds. Mrs.
Cornelys had been given seven hundred guineas (it is

---

[1] Mrs. Baddeley also sang there in 1772.

[2] An impetus to the fireworks seems to have been first given by
Angelo, father of Henry Angelo, who directed the displays in 1766.
In 1771 the fireworkers were Clitherow and Caillot.

[3] The admission ticket for the Regatta Ball (Lake scene) was
prepared by Cipriani and Bartolozzi.

said) to supply the supper, and it is lamentable to re-
flect that the supper was "indifferent, and the wine
very scarce." However, there was a great company : the
Duke of Gloucester, the Duke of Northumberland,
Lord North, the Duchess of Devonshire, Sir Joshua
Reynolds, Garrick, Colman, Samuel Foote.   A band

REGATTA BALL AT RANELAGH
XXIII JUNE MDCCLXXV

ADMISSION TICKET, BY CIPRIANI AND BARTOLOZZI.

of two hundred and forty instrumentalists, under Giardini, performed in the Rotunda, and there was singing
by Vernon and Reinhold, including the cheering
ballad :—

> Ye lords and ye ladies who form this gay throng,
> Be silent a moment, attend to our song,
> And while you suspend your fantastical round,
> Come, bless your sweet stars that you're none of you drowned.

From this time (1775) till about 1790 the concerts continued as usual, but Ranelagh seems during the period to have suffered a certain eclipse. In May 1788 the shares are said to have fallen from their par value (£1,000) to £900. Ranelagh was "voted a bore with the fashionable circles," and its distance from town began to be considered an obstacle.

About 1791, however, its fortunes revived, and numerous masquerades, sometimes lasting till six or eight in the morning, and firework displays (chiefly by Caillot and by Rossi and Tessier) remained a feature of Ranelagh till its close.

Henry Angelo (*Reminiscences*, ii. *p.* 3 *f.*), speaking of its later days, declares that it was frequented by "the élite of fashion." The gentlemen wore powder, frills and ruffles, and had gold-headed canes. "Cropped heads, trousers or shoe-strings" were not to be seen there. The men used to buy in the ante-room myrtles, hyacinths and roses, not to wear themselves, but for presentation to the ladies.

A masquerade of 1792 (14 February) was attended by Mrs. Jordan, "supported" (as the newspapers said) "between the friendly arms of the Prince of Wales and the Duke of Clarence." Mr. Petit was good as a man walking in his sleep with a candle, and amid the usual crowd of harlequins, sailors and flower-girls, "a monkey of the largest size was offensively dexterous."[1] At another masquerade this year (16 May) a Guy Faux, a 'Bath Maccarony,' an African Princess, and three or four Romps attracted attention.

On May 7th, 1792, the exhibition called Mount Etna was introduced and remained popular at Ranelagh for several years. A special building with a scene designed by G. Marinari, 'painter to the Opera,' was prepared for it in the gardens. The idea was evidently borrowed from Torré's Forge of Vulcan, the great

[1] *Evening Mail*, Feb. 15–17, 1792.

attraction at the Marylebone Gardens some twenty years earlier. The scene represented Mount Etna and the Cavern of Vulcan with the ' Cyclops ' forging the armour of Mars, " as described (the advertisements add) in the Aeneid of Virgil." To an accompaniment of music " compiled from Gluck, Haydn, Giardini, and Handel," we see the ' Cyclops ' going to work. " The smoke thickens, the crater on the top of Etna vomits forth flames, and the lava rolls dreadful along the side of the mountain. This continues with increasing violence till there is a prodigious eruption, which finishes with a tremendous explosion."

On June 27th, 1793, the Chevalier D'Eon fenced in the Rotunda with M. Sainville, and received the congratulations of the Prince of Wales and Mrs. Fitzherbert.[1]

In 1797 (April) there was an enjoyable masquerade, at which there reigned (we are told) "good nature and pleasant hilarity, without riot " : all this, in spite of a crowd of imaginary Dutch skippers, lunatics, coachmen, quack doctors and watercress girls.

At a concert in 1798 (June) Incledon and Madame Mara sang. In 1799 a January masquerade was diversified by a drawing for fifty twelfth cakes as prizes for the masks.

The Directors now began to offer prizes for regattas and volunteer shooting-matches, and a few splendid entertainments mark the closing years of Ranelagh.

On 2 June, 1802, Boodle's Club gave an elegant dance at which the ladies " wore white and silver, ornamented with laurel "—and diamonds, and amused themselves by drawing prizes of trinkets in a Lottery

[1] Newspaper cutting [W. Coll.] assigned to 28 June (referring to 27 June), 1793. Mr. Vizetelly (*Chevalier D'Eon*, p. 322) states that D'Eon fenced at Ranelagh in 1794. The managers of Ranelagh had given the Chevalier, who was then in money difficulties, a benefit night in 1791 (24 June).

Booth. On the 28 June (1802) the Picnic Society gave an "afternoon breakfast," and at five o'clock Garnerin, the French aeronaut, and Captain Sowden ascended in a balloon from the gardens.[1]

On 23 September (1802) Mr. Thomas Todd descended into a reservoir of water twenty-five feet deep, prepared for him in the gardens. His awkward diving-tub, and his dress of leather and metal excited the laughter of spectators born too early to know the diver of the Polytechnic. Nor is this praiseworthy experiment to be counted among the splendid entertainments of Ranelagh, for Mr. Todd was "misfitted by his coppersmith," forgot to take down his lamp, and did not remain under water more than five minutes.[2]

On 1 June, 1803, a ball in commemoration of the Installation of the Knights of the Bath took place and proved one of the finest of the entertainments. Yet these were only 'struggles for happiness,' and attempts to galvanise a nearly lifeless Ranelagh. The unending promenade, with its sentimental songs and elegant regale of tea and coffee, had ceased to attract, and the lamp-hung trees, the Chinese House and the music on the Canal had lost their ancient charm. On 8 July, 1803, the Rotunda of Ranelagh was opened for the last time as a place of amusement.

On 30 September, 1805, the proprietors gave directions for the demolition of Ranelagh House and the Rotunda ; the furniture was sold by auction shortly afterwards, and the buildings were removed. The organ was bought for Tetbury Church, Gloucestershire, where it remained till 1863, when it was purchased by a builder.

The Ranelagh grounds had extended from the old Burial Ground (east of Chelsea Hospital) to the river-

[1] Another great fête of this period (June 1802 or 1803 ?) was the Ball given by the Spanish Ambassador.

[2] *The European Magazine*, October 1802, and several newspapers of the time.

marshes on the south, and the Chelsea Bridge Road
now crosses their eastern boundary.   When the buildings were removed the grounds were, by degrees, purchased of the shareholders by General Richard R.
Wilford to add to his property adjoining.   A poet of
the *Gentleman's Magazine* in June 1807 laments the
Fall of Ranelagh, and the site already overgrown with
weeds.   The foundation walls of the Rotunda and
the arches of some of the cellars could, however,
be traced as late as 1813, and part of the site was a
favourite playground for Chelsea children.   By 1826, the
Ranelagh grounds had become by purchase the property
of Chelsea Hospital and were parcelled out into allot-
ments.   The ground is, at the present time, once more a
' Ranelagh Garden,' in which the public are admitted,
as the old advertisements would say, " to walk gratis."

All traces of Ranelagh have been thus obliterated,
and a London historian (Jesse, *London*, iii, 420) on
visiting the site in 1871, could find as its memorial
only a single avenue of trees with one or two of the old
lamp-irons—the ' firetrees ' of the early advertisements
—still attached.

[From the numerous authorities, the following may be selected :—
Gent. Mag. 1742, 418, ff. ; *Ranelagh House : a Satire in prose*,
London, 1747 (W. Coll.) ; Dodsley's *London*, 1761 ; Sir John
Fielding's *Brief Description of London*, 1776 ; Burney's *Hist. of
Music*, iv. 668, ff. ; Kearsley's *Strangers' Guide* (1793 ?) ; Lysons's
Environs, Supplement, p. 120 ; Faulkner's *Chelsea*, ii. 299, ff. ;
Blanchard in *The Era Almanack*, 1870 ; Grove's *Dict. of Music*, art.
" Ranelagh House," by W. H. Husk ; L'Estrange's *Village of
Palaces*, ii. 296 ; Walford, v. 76, ff. ; Austin Dobson's *Eighteenth
Century Vignettes*, 2nd ser. p. 263, ff. ; collections relating to
Ranelagh in British Museum and Guildhall libraries, and a large
series of cuttings from newspapers, magazines, &c., W. Coll.]

VIEWS.

A good representative series of the principal early views of
Ranelagh is in the Crace Collection (*Catal.* p. 164 ; pp. 312–314).
The site is well marked in Horwood's Plan A, 1794.

STROMBOLO HOUSE AND GARDENS, CHELSEA

STROMBOLO House [1] was a minor place of entertainment, dating from 1762, or earlier, with tea-gardens and "a fine fountain" [2] attached to it. The gardens [3] are said to have been most frequented about 1788. They were open chiefly in the afternoons of week-days and Sundays for tea-drinking during the summer season. The house, opposite the famous Royal Bun House, Chelsea, in Jew's Row (now Pimlico Road), was still standing in 1829, when Faulkner's *Chelsea* (second edition) was published, but it appears to have been disused as a place of amusement long before that date.

The ground was afterwards occupied by the Orange Tavern and tea-gardens to which was attached the Orange Theatre, a small private playhouse, where local geniuses performed (1831–32). St. Barnabas Church, Pimlico, built 1848–1850, standing off the south side of Pimlico Road (entrance in Church Street) is now nearly on the site.

[O'Keefe's *Recollections*, i. p. 88 ; Faulkner's *Chelsea*, ii. p. 357 ; Davis's *Knightsbridge* (1859), p. 263 ; Wheatley's *London P. and P.* s.v. "Strombello" ; Timbs's *Club Life* (1866), ii. p. 260.]

[1] The name was spelt Strumbels, Strombels and Strumbello. Davis (*Knightsbridge*) calls it Stromboli House.

[2] O'Keefe's *Recollections*.

[3] Davis's *Knightsbridge*. Strumbelo is marked in the map of 1789 in Fores's *New Guide*.

STAR AND GARTER TAVERN AND GARDENS, CHELSEA

In the grounds attached to the Star and Garter Tavern in the Five Fields between Chelsea and Pimlico,[1] displays of fireworks and horsemanship took place in 1762 (July–September) to celebrate the birth of the Prince of Wales, and the visit of the chiefs of the Cherokee Indians[2] who were duly exploited by the proprietor. Carlo Genovini, an Italian artificer, exhibited stars and moving suns, a guilloche of a varied coloured rose, reprises of water cascades and many pyrotechnic devices, together with the Temple of Liberty, a machine thirty-two feet long and forty high " painted in a theatrical manner " with Britannia triumphant over the portico. The fireworks began at eight or nine and the tickets were usually half-a-crown.

On other evenings at seven o'clock Thomas Johnson, the well-known equestrian, performed feats with two and three horses similar to those undertaken by him at the Three Hats, Islington. The admission was one shilling. The proprietor of the Star and Garter also kept the neighbouring Dwarf's Tavern, with Coan, " the

---

[1] The Star and Garter was at the end of Five Fields Row. In Faulkner's time (*Chelsea*, ii. p. 354), about 1829, the house, no longer used as a tavern, was Mr. Homden's Academy.

[2] On the Cherokee Chiefs, see Forster's *Goldsmith* bk. iii. chap. vi. (ann. 1762).

jovial Pigmy," as Major Domo,[1] and to this place visitors were invited to adjourn after the fireworks, there to sup on "a most excellent ham, some collared eels, potted beef, etc., with plenty of sound old bright wine and punch like nectar."[2]

[Faulkner's *Chelsea*, ii. 354–356, where further details of the fireworks and horsemanship may be found; Davis's *Knightsbridge*, p. 264.]

---

[1] John Coan, "the unparalleled Norfolk Dwarf," died there 16 March 1764 (*Daily Advertiser*, 17 March, 1764).

[2] The Dwarf's Tavern according to Faulkner (*Chelsea*, ii. 354), was situated in Chelsea Fields "on the spot which was afterwards called Spring Gardens, between Ebury Street and Belgrave Terrace," and which was subsequently (a few years before 1829) occupied by Ackerman's Waterproof Cloth Manufactory. This Spring Garden is the place usually marked in the maps (*e.g.*, Horwood's Plan, B. 1795) as the *New Spring Gardens, Chelsea*, and was a place of public entertainment, as may be inferred from a newspaper advertisement of January 1792 : " J. Louis, of New Spring Gardens, Chelsea, having fitted up *likewise* the above house (*i.e.* York Coffee House) in Norris Street, Haymarket, for the winter, serves dinners and suppers there."
This Spring Garden was distinct from the *Spring Gardens, Knightsbridge*, a place frequented by Pepys, and perhaps identical with the World's End, Knightsbridge (see Davis's *Knightsbridge*, p. 149, ff.). The Knightsbridge Spring Gardens (which stood about where William Street joins Lowndes Square) ceased to be a place of entertainment before 1773, in which year the house belonging to them was occupied by Dr. C. Kelly, who had his anatomical museum there. Walford (v. 18) engraves from a drawing in the Crace Collection a view of the "Spring Gardens," which he assigns to the Knightsbridge Spring Gardens, but it is possibly a representation of the *Chelsea* Spring Gardens.

JENNY'S WHIM, PIMLICO

ST. GEORGE's Row, near Ebury Bridge, formerly called The Wooden Bridge or Jenny's Whim Bridge, marks the site of Jenny's Whim, a tavern and pleasure-garden popular in the last century.

Jenny's Whim is said to have been established as a place of amusement by a firework artificer and theatrical machinist, in the reign of George II. About 1750 it appears to have been a good deal frequented during the day-time, and people of rank and fashion occasionally visited it. Walpole once encountered Lord Granby "arrived very drunk from Jenny's Whim," where he "had dined with Lady Fanny [Seymour] and left her and eight other women and four other men playing at Brag."

A writer in *The Connoisseur* comparing it in 1755 with Ranelagh and Vauxhall, describes it, however, as a resort of "the lower sort of people," rather than of the quality.

The gardens possessed, in addition to the usual bowers, alcoves and prim flower-beds, a bowling-green, a grotto, a cock-pit and a ducking pond. In the centre was a large fish pond. Mechanical devices, similar to those at New Georgia, Hampstead, attracted many visitors. A Harlequin, a Mother Shipton, or some terrific monster, started up in the recesses of the garden when an unsuspected spring was trodden upon, and

A West VIEW of Chelsea BRIDGE ...... Un VUE du Pont de Chelsea du COTE du West.

SHOWING JENNY'S WHIM, 1761.

huge fish and mermaids rose at intervals from the water of the pond.

The admission about 1755 appears to have been sixpence.

Before the close of the eighteenth century, the popularity of the place had declined, though it was still frequented as a summer tea-garden, and by 1804 Jenny's Whim had become a mere public-house. The house, a red brick building with lattice work, containing a large room originally used for breakfasting parties, continued in existence for many years, and was not pulled down till 1865.

[Walford, v. 45, ff. ; Walpole's *Letters*, ii. 212, 23 June, 1750 ; *The Connoisseur*, No. 68, 15 May, 1755 ; *Low Life*, 1764 ; Davis's *Knightsbridge*, 253, ff. ; *Notes and Queries*, 3rd ser. viii. 166 ; Angelo's *Picnic* (1834), s.v.]

VIEWS.

1. The north front of Jenny's Whim Bridge and the Old Public House at the foot of the Bridge, water colour drawing, 1761. Crace, *Cat.* p. 311, No. 58.

2. "A west view of Chelsea Bridge" (showing Jenny's Whim). Boreman pinx. Lodge sculp. (1761), W. Coll. ; Crace, *Cat.* p. 311, No. 59 (cp. Walford, v. 43).

CROMWELL'S GARDENS,

Afterwards FLORIDA GARDENS, BROMPTON

CROMWELL'S GARDENS consisted of grounds immediately adjoining (and perhaps at one time belonging to)
Hale House, Brompton, a mansion popularly known as
Cromwell House from a tradition, seemingly unfounded,
that the Protector or his family had once resided there.
Some of the entrance tickets of Cromwell's Gardens
consisted of rude imitations of Oliver's pattern-shillings,
and had his effigy on the obverse.

The Gardens were in existence at least as early as
1762,[1] and in 1776 they are described as frequented by
fashionable gentlemen of Kensington and the West End,
and by various ladies who were apparently not always
of irreproachable character. Brompton was then and
long afterwards in the midst of gardens and nurseries,
and was noted for its salubrious air. Cromwell's
Gardens were within a pleasant rural walk from the
Park, Chelsea and Knightsbridge. The grounds were
neatly kept: there were " agreeable " arbours for drinking tea and coffee, and in one part of the garden trees,
curiously cut, surrounded an elevated grass plat. Their
retired situation rendered them (in the opinion of the

---

[1] O'Keefe's *Recollections*, vol. i. p. 88 : " 1762. At Cromwell
House, Brompton, once the seat of Oliver, was also a tea-garden
concert."

Q

" Sunday Rambler ") " well adapted for gallantry and intrigue."

Music of some kind seems to have been provided, and at one time equestrian performances in the open air were exhibited by Charles Hughes, the well-known rider, who in 1782 founded with Dibdin the Royal Circus, afterwards the Surrey Theatre. The admission was sixpence,[1] and the gardens were open at least as late as nine at night.[2]

In 1781 (or 1780) the gardens were in the hands of Mr. R. Hiem, a German florist, who grew his cherries, strawberries, and flowers there. About that time he changed the name to Florida Gardens,[3] erected a great

[1] The price appears on the (undated) pewter and brass admission tickets to Cromwell's Gardens. The British Museum has four specimens in pewter, with Cromwell's head ; and one of the brass tickets.

[2] The Sunday Rambler visits the gardens between 7.30 and 9 p.m.

[3] I follow the *Modern Sabbath*, ed. 1797, in stating that Cromwell's Gardens were identical with the Florida Gardens. In the second edition of the *Sunday Ramble* (1776) Cromwell's Gardens at Brompton are described under that name, and in the 1797 ed. (*A Modern Sabbath*) almost the same description is repeated, and it is expressly stated that the name of the place had been changed from Cromwell's to Florida Gardens. On the other hand, Faulkner describes the Florida Gardens as having been originally a nursery garden kept by "Hyam" (he is called Hiem in the advertisements) and converted by him (for the first time, it is implied) into a place of public amusement. Faulkner after describing Hale House, mentions Cromwell's Gardens as a separate place of amusement earlier than the Florida Gardens. The contemporary authority of the *Modern Sabbath* seems, however, preferable ; especially as Faulkner does not appear to be able to state the precise site of Cromwell's Gardens. A further complication may perhaps be thought to be introduced by the passage in O'Keefe (cited in Note 1) where Cromwell's Gardens are described as "at Cromwell House " (*i.e.* Hale House). But the inhabitants of Cromwell House from 1754 to 1794, or later, are well known to have been people of substance, and the gardens proper of Hale House could hardly have been employed as a tea-garden. The Florida Gardens (afterwards occupied by Canning's Gloucester Lodge) were (as stated above)

room for dining in the centre of the gardens, and
opened the place to the public at a charge of sixpence.
A bowling-green was formed and a band (said to be
subscribed for by the nobility and gentry) played twice
a week during the summer. An air-balloon and fireworks were announced for 10 September, 1784. It
was a pleasant place where visitors could gather flowers,
and fruit "fresh every hour in the day," and take the
light refreshment of tea, coffee, and ice creams, or wine
and cyder if they preferred it. Hiem specially recommended his Bern Veckley as "an elegant succedaneum
for bread and butter, and eat by the Noblesse of
Switzerland." However, like many proprietors of
pleasure-gardens, he subsequently became bankrupt,
between 1787 and 1797 (?).

Maria, Duchess of Gloucester, having procured a
lease (before September 1797) [1] of the place, built there
a villa, at first called Maria Lodge, then Orford Lodge,

adjacent to Hale House, and may possibly at one time have be-
longed to its owners, and have been let out partly as a tea-
garden and partly as a nursery. The writer of the *Modern Sabbath*
in fact remarks that Cromwell's Gardens is supposed to have taken
its name from the ground being formerly the patrimonial estate of
the Protector who once had a palace here upon the site of which
is a handsome seat (*i.e.* Hale House). The change of name from
Cromwell to Florida took place (as appears from the various editions
of a *Sunday Ramble*) at some time between 1776 and 1797. I
suggest that the change took place about 1780, because Lysons (who,
however, does not mention Cromwell's Gardens) says that the place
was "much puffed in the daily papers between the years 1780 and
1790 by the name of Florida Gardens." In any case they certainly
were advertised by Hiem as the Florida Gardens as early as 1781.

[1] The Florida Gardens are described as a place of entertainment
in the *Modern Sabbath*, published in 1797, but they were already
in the possession of the Duchess of Gloucester in September 1797.
Cp. a newspaper paragraph of 25 September, 1797, in "Public
Gardens" Collection in Guildhall Library : "Florida Gardens, at
present in the possession of the Duchess of Gloucester, were fitted
up in an elegant manner as a place of resort by the late Mr. Wilder
[a successor of Hiem ?] but did not answer the purpose for which
they were intended."

at which she died in 1807. Shortly after 1807 the premises consisting of about six acres were purchased by the Rt. Hon. George Canning, who changed the name of the house to Gloucester Lodge, and lived there for many years.

The house was pulled down about 1850 and the ground let on building leases. Part of Courtfield Road, Ashburn Place, and perhaps other streets, occupy the site of Gloucester Lodge which stood immediately south of the present Cromwell Road, and west of Gloucester Road near the point where the Gloucester Road intersects Cromwell Road.

[*Sunday Ramble* (1776); *A Modern Sabbath* (1797), chap. vii.; Faulkner's *Kensington* (1820), pp. 438, 441; Lysons's *Environs*, supplement to first ed. (1811), p. 215; Wheatley, *London P. and P.* s.v. "Cromwell House" and "Gloucester Lodge"; Fores's *New Guide* (1789), preface, p. vi.; *The Public Advertiser*, 10 July, 1789; *The Morning Herald*, 7 July, 1786; and newspaper cuttings in W. Coll.]

VIEWS.

There seem to be no views of the Cromwell and Florida Gardens. There is a view of the garden front of Gloucester Lodge in Jerdan's *Autobiography* (1852), vol. ii. frontispiece.

VI

SOUTH LONDON GROUP

BERMONDSEY SPA GARDENS

THE Bermondsey Spa Gardens owe such celebrity as they attained to the enterprise of their founder and proprietor, Thomas Keyse, a self-taught artist, born in 1722, who painted skilful imitations of still life and exhibited pictures at the Royal Academy. About 1765 he purchased the Waterman's Arms, a tavern in Bermondsey, together with some waste ground adjoining, and opened the place as a tea-garden, exhibiting there a collection of his own pictures. At that time, and for several years in the present century, Bermondsey was surrounded by open country.

About 1770 a chalybeate spring was discovered in the grounds, and Keyse's establishment thereupon acquired the name of the Bermondsey Spa Gardens. Keyse was a cheery, ingenious landlord, remarkable among other things for his preparation of cherry-brandy. In 1784 he obtained a license for music from the Surrey magistrates, and spent £4,000 in improvements. The gardens (covering not less than four acres) were opened during the summer months on week-day evenings and Sundays, and the price of admission on week-days was a shilling. Each visitor was, however, given on entering a metal check,[1] which was exchanged for refreshments

---

[1] These checks in copper and lead resemble the tradesmen's halfpenny tokens of the end of the eighteenth century, and are usually described as tokens : see descriptions in Sharpe's *Catalogue*,

to the extent of sixpence. On special occasions the
admission was half-a-crown or three shillings.

In the gardens were the usual arbours and benches
for tea-drinking. The space before the orchestra was
about a quarter of the size of that at Vauxhall, and on
the north-east of the garden was a lawn of about three
acres. A row of trees leading from the entrance to the
picture gallery was hung at night with lamps of red,
blue, green, and white, in humble imitation of the
Grand Walk at Vauxhall.[1]

Jonas Blewitt, one of the most distinguished organists
of the latter half of the eighteenth century, composed
the music of many songs for the entertainments at the
Spa.[2] The Spa poets were Mr. J. Oakman and Mr.
Harriss. Songs of hunting, drinking, and seafaring took
their turn with ditties full of what may be described as
sprightly sentiment. The other music [3] consisted of burlettas, duets, and interludes, performed by vocalists of only
local fame. In a burletta called the ' Friars,' certain
nuns who had been forced by wicked guardians to take
the veil, make their escape with the assistance of two
friars. These reverend men, after singing an anacreontic
song, divide the gold which the ladies have given them
as their reward, and the whole concludes with a chorus.
The words of the burlettas and songs were printed in
little books, sold for sixpence at the bar and in the
exhibition room.[4]

p. 89 ; Atkins, p. 193. Miss Banks, in the MS. catalogue of her
tokens (p. 210) now in the Department of Coins, British Museum,
says respecting the leaden check : "One shilling was paid on going
in, and this ticket given in exchange which would count for sixpence if the person chose liquor."

[1] Smith's *Book for a Rainy Day* : the description strictly applies
to the year 1795 ; *A Modern Sabbath*, chap. ix. (1797), implies that
the place was more refined than Smith's description would suggest.

[2] Blewitt lived in Bermondsey Square, where he died in 1805.

[3] Cp. "X" in *The Musical Times* for October 1, 1893, p. 588.

[4] It is possibly worth while to record the names of some of the
forgotten performers at Bermondsey Spa. *Circ.* 1785–1788 the

An occasional display of fireworks took place, and the gardens and a cascade (introduced about 1792) were illuminated.[1] From time to time there was a representation of the Siege of Gibraltar by means of fireworks, transparencies and bomb shells.[2] The apparatus for the Siege, which was designed by Keyse himself, was set up in a field divided from the lawn by a sunk fence, the rock being fifty feet high and two hundred feet long. The blowing up of the floating batteries and the sinking of boats in 'fictitious water' were (we are assured) ' so truly represented as to give a very strong idea of the real Siege.'

A permanent attraction was the Gallery of Paintings, an oblong room described as being about the same size as W. M. Turner's studio in Queen Anne's Street. Here were exhibited Keyse's pictorial reproductions of

vocalists were Mr. Birkett, Mr. C. Blewitt, Mr. Burling (or Birling), Mr. Harriss ; Mrs. Thompson, Mrs. Byrn, Mrs. Piercy ; Miss Stephenson, Miss Pay, Miss Cemmitt ; Mme. Floranze. In 1792 the leader of the band was Mr. Peile, and the vocalists were Mr. Burton, Mr. Milward, Mrs. Freeman, and Mrs. Peile.

Among the burlettas (1785–1788) were "The Quack Doctor," "The Fop," and "The Auctioneer."

[1] The fireworks in 1792 were by Rossi and Tessier, of Ranelagh. On 25 September, 1792, "by particular desire, the Battle of the Fiery Dragons, and the line comet to come from the Rock of Gibraltar and cause the Dragons to engage."

[2] This entertainment was probably first introduced in 1786, in which year (2 September) the *Public Advertiser* announces "the representation of the storming of a fort which with the fortifications cover (*sic*) 3 acres of ground, the rock being fifty feet high and 200 feet long." From about 1789 to 1792 it was advertised as a representation of the Siege of Gibraltar. The writer of *A Modern Sabbath* (1797) gives further details. "On the north-east side of the gardens is a very fine lawn consisting of about three acres, and in a field parted from this lawn by a sunk fence is a building with turrets, resembling a fortress or castle." At each side of this fortress at unequal distances were two buildings, from which on public nights bombshells, &c., were thrown. The fire was returned and the whole exhibited the "picturesque prospect of a siege."

a Butcher's Shop and a Greengrocer's Stall and many
other paintings, including a Vesuvius, and a candle that
looked as if it were really lighted.

On the whole, the Bermondsey Spa appears to have
been a respectable, though hardly fashionable, resort,
which brought its proprietor a moderate income and
supplied harmless, if not very exalted, means of
recreation.

It being not unnecessary to provide for the safe
convoy of the visitors after nightfall, Keyse inserted
the following advertisement in the newspapers :—" The
Spa Gardens, in Grange Road, Bermondsey, one mile
[the distance is rather understated] from London
Bridge ; for the security of the public the road is
lighted and watched by patroles every night, at the sole
expense of the proprietor." The lighting and patrol-
ling were probably somewhat mythical, but no doubt
the announcement served to reassure the timid.

J. T. Smith, the author of *A Book for a Rainy Day*,
has left a graphic description of a visit that he paid on
a bright July evening of 1795. The popularity of the
gardens was then waning, and on entering he found no
one there but three idle waiters. A board with a
ruffled hand within a sky-blue painted sleeve directed
him to the staircase which led " To the Gallery of
Paintings," and he made a solitary tour of the room.

The rest of the visit may be described in Smith's own
words. " Stepping back to study the picture of the
the ' Greenstall,' I ask your pardon,' said I, for I had
trodden upon some one's toes. ' Sir, it is granted,'
replied a little, thick-set man, with a round face, arch
look, and closely-curled wig, surmounted by a small
three-cornered hat put very knowingly on one side, not
unlike Hogarth's head in his print of the ' Gates of
Calais.' ' You are an artist, I presume ; I noticed you
from the end of the gallery, when you first stepped back
to look at my best picture. I painted all the objects

in this room from nature and still life.' 'Your Green-grocer's Shop,' said I, 'is inimitable; the drops of water on that savoy appear as if they had just fallen from the element. Van Huysum could not have pencilled them with greater delicacy.' 'What do you think,' said he, 'of my Butcher's Shop?' 'Your pluck is bleeding fresh, and your sweetbread is in a clean plate.' 'How do you like my bull's eye?' 'Why, it would be a most excellent one for Adams or Dollond to lecture upon. Your knuckle of veal is the finest I ever saw.' 'It's young meat,' replied he; 'anyone who is a judge of meat can tell that from the blueness of its bone.' 'What a beautiful white you have used on the fat of that Southdown leg! or is it Bagshot?' 'Yes,' said he, 'my solitary visitor, it is Bagshot: and as for my white, that is the best Nottingham, which you or any artist can procure at Stone & Puncheon's, in Bishopsgate Street Within.' 'Sir Joshua Reynolds,' continued Mr. Keyse, 'paid me two visits. On the second, he asked me what white I had used; and when I told him, he observed, 'It's very extraordinary, sir, how it keeps so bright. I use the same.' 'Not at all, sir, I rejoined: 'the doors of this gallery are open day and night; and the admission of fresh air, together with the great expansion of light from the sashes above, will never suffer the white to turn yellow. Have you not observed, Sir Joshua, how white the posts and rails on the public roads are, though they have not been re-painted for years; that arises from constant air and bleaching.' 'Come,' said Mr. Keyse, putting his hand upon my shoulder, 'the bell rings, not for prayers, nor for dinner, but for the song.'

"As soon as we had reached the orchestra, the singer curtsied to us, for we were the only persons in the gardens. 'This is sad work,' said he, 'but the woman must sing, according to our contract.' I recollect that the singer was handsome, most dashingly

dressed, immensely plumed, and villainously rouged ;
she smiled as she sang, but it was not the bewitching smile of Mrs. Wrighten, then applauded by
thousands at Vauxhall Gardens. As soon as the Spa
lady had ended her song, Keyse, after joining me in
applause, apologised for doing so, by observing that
as he never suffered his servants to applaud, and as
the people in the road (whose ears were close to the
cracks in the paling to hear the song) would make a
bad report if they had not heard more than the clapping
of one pair of hands, he had in this instance expressed
his reluctant feelings. As the lady retired from the
front of the orchestra, she, to keep herself in practice,
curtsied to me with as much respect as she would had
Colonel Topham been the patron of a gala-night.
' This is too bad,' again observed Mr. Keyse, ' and I am
sure you cannot expect fireworks ! ' However, he
politely asked me to partake of a bottle of Lisbon,
which upon my refusing, he pressed me to accept of a
catalogue of his pictures."

Keyse died in his house at the Gardens on 8 February,
1800[1] and his pictures were subsequently sold by
auction. His successors in the management of the
Bermondsey Spa failed to make it pay,[2] and it was
closed about 1804.[3] The Site, now in Spa Road, was
afterwards built upon.

[1] *Gent. Mag.* 1800, pt. i. p. 284. Keyse's house was a large
wooden-fronted building, consisting of square divisions in imitation
of scantlings of stone (J. T. Smith). The entrance to the
Gardens was next to the house, beneath a semi-circular awning.

[2] Hughson's *London*, vol. v. (1808), p. 60. *The Picture of
London* for 1802 mentions in the "Almanack of Pleasures" under
July 17, "A silver cup run for at Spa Gardens, Bermondsey, by
gentlemen's ponies."

[3] Blanchard in *Era Almanack*, 1870, p. 18 (followed by Walford).
Brayley and Mantell (*Surrey*, iii. 200, 201) say the Gardens were
closed about 1805. Lambert in his *London* (iv. 140) published in
1806, speaks of the Spa as still open, but the passage may have
been written a year or more before the date of publication.

[Lysons's *Environs*, vol. i. (1792), p. 558 ; Smith's *Book for a Rainy Day*, p. 135, ff. under "1795" ; G. W. Phillips's *History and Antiquities of Bermondsey*, 1841, pp. 84, 85 ; *Dict. Nat. Biog.* art. "Keyse" ; Walford, vi. 128, 129 ; *Histories of Surrey* ; E. L. Blanchard in the *Era Almanack* for 1870, p. 18 ; Rendle and Norman's *Inns of Old Southwark*, pp. 394–396 ; *A Modern Sabbath* (1797), chap. ix. ; Kearsley's *Strangers' Guide to London* (1793 ?) ; Fores's *New Guide* (1789), preface, p. vi. ; *Picture of London*, 1802, p. 370, where "the pictures of the late Mr. Keys" are mentioned ; "Public Gardens" Coll. in Guildhall Library, London ; *Description of some of the Paintings in the Perpetual Exhibition at Bermondsey Spa*, Horselydown (*circ.* 1785 ?) 8vo. (W. Coll.). Song-books (words only) of Bermondsey Spa, W. Coll.]

VIEWS.

A pen and ink sketch of Bermondsey Spa and a portrait of Keyse were in J. H. Burn's Collection, and at his sale at Puttick's were bought by Mr. Gardner (*Notes and Queries*, 6th ser. i. 506).

THESE gardens were opened in 1770, and in May 1776 music and dancing were advertised to take place there in the evenings. Towards the close of the century the Prince of Wales (George IV.) and various fashionable people are said to have occasionally visited the place. St. Helena's was a good deal frequented as a tea-garden during the first thirty years of the nineteenth century,[1] chiefly by the dockyard population of the neighbourhood. In 1831 fireworks and other entertainments were introduced on the week-day evenings and the place was for some years styled the Eastern Vauxhall. In 1832 the gardens occupied about five acres and a half, and in this year the performers advertised included Mr. G. R. Chapman "from the Adelphi and Astley's" as organist and musical director, Mrs. Venning, "from the Nobility's Concerts," Miss Wood, "the Infant Prodigy, only six years of age," and Miss Taylor who performed "many difficult airs on that delightful instrument, the Musical Glasses." Concerts, dancing and other amusements continued till about 1869 when the gardens appear to have been closed.

In 1874, the gardens passed into the hands of Messrs. W. H. and J. R. Carter who erected an

---

[1] *Picture of London*, eds. 1802, 1829; Tallis's *Illustrated London*, ed. Gaspey.

orchestra and a dancing platform, and provided music and fireworks for an admission of sixpence.   The gardens had fallen into a neglected state, but the walks were once more well laid out, and the old chestnut trees, the elms and planes were still standing.

The gardens ceased to exist in 1881 and were eventually built over.[1]   The site was to the west of

ℱORCHESTRA AND DANCING-PLATFORM, ST. HELENA GARDENS, *circ.* 1875.

Deptford Lower Road, and just south of Corbett's Lane and the present St. Helena Road.   St. Katharine's Church (consecrated 18 October, 1884) in Eugenia Road (south of St. Helena Road) stands on part of the site.

[Newspaper cuttings, W. Coll. ; and see notes.]

---

[1] In the *Era Almanack*, 1871, p. 6, it is stated that the gardens "disappeared in 1869."   Walford, vi. 133, says they ceased to exist in 1881.

VIEWS.

1. The entrance to the St. Helena Tavern and tea-garden, water-colour drawing, signed R. B. 7 June, 1839 (W. Coll.).

2. Admission ticket in white metal. Size 1·5 inch. Nineteenth century, *circ.* 1839? (British Museum). *Obverse:* View of the entrance to the tavern and gardens (similar to No. 1); in foreground, two posts supporting semicircular board inscribed "St. Helena Tavern and Tea Gardens. Dinners dress'd": in exergue, "Rotherhithe." *Reverse:* "Refreshment to the value of sixpence" within floral wreath.

3. Lithographed poster of the St. Helena Gardens, *circ.* 1875, showing the orchestra, dancing-platform, and gardens illuminated at night (W. Coll.).

FINCH'S GROTTO GARDENS

Finch's Grotto Gardens situated on the western side of St. George's Street, Southwark, near St. George's Fields,[1] derived their name from Thomas Finch, a Herald Painter, who, having inherited from a relation a house and garden, opened both for the entertainment of the public in the spring of 1760. The garden possessed some lofty trees, and was planted with evergreens and shrubs. In the centre was a medicinal spring over which Finch constructed a grotto, wherein a fountain played over artificial embankments and formed " a natural and beautiful cascade." The spring enjoyed some local celebrity, and was recommended to his patients by a doctor named Townshend, who resided in the Haymarket and afterwards in St. George's Fields. In our own time Dr. Rendle has described the water as " merely the filtered soakage of a supersaturated soil," which could be obtained almost anywhere in Southwark.

---

[1] " The principal site of Finch's Grotto Gardens appears to have been a triangular piece of ground forming the western side of St. George's Street, Southwark, and bounded on the south by the road called Dirty Lane and on the north by a vinegar yard in Lombard Street, and the extremity of St. Saviour's Parish." Wilkinson, *Londina*. A way from Falcon Stairs through Bandy Leg Walk (now Guildford Street) led directly to the place, and Williams, Finch's successor, made an entrance from St. George's Fields. Those who came by water landed at Mason's Stairs.

R

A subscription ticket of a guinea entitled the holder to such benefits, as Finch's spring conferred and gave admission to the evening entertainments that were introduced from about 1764. The ordinary admission was a shilling, raised on special nights to two shillings. The gardens were open on Sunday when sixpence was charged, though the visitor was entitled for his money to tea, half a pint of wine, cakes, jelly or cyder.

ADMISSION TICKET,
FINCH'S GROTTO.

An orchestra containing an organ by Pike, of Bloomsbury, stood in the garden, and there was another orchestra attached to a large octagonal music-room decorated with paintings and festoons of flowers. This Octagon Room was used for occasional balls and for the promenade and concert on wet evenings.

The place appears to have been respectably conducted, but there is little evidence that it was ever a modish resort, in spite of the assertion of the country-bred Mrs. Hardcastle[1] that no one could " have a manner that has never seen the Pantheon, the Grotto Gardens, the Borough and such places where the nobility chiefly resort." [2]

The vocal and instrumental concerts which took place every evening in the season (May-September) were of a creditable though not very ambitious character. About fifteen hundred persons are said to have been present on some of the Freemasons' nights and on the benefit nights of the performers.

Numerous singers and instrumentalists were engaged,[3]

[1] Goldsmith's *She Stoops to Conquer*, act. ii.
[2] The Dukes of York and Gloucester, brothers of George III., are, however, said to have visited the gardens many times.
[3] List of performers under Finch and Williams :—Messrs. Oldfield (or Offield ?, 1765), Lauder, Dearle, Baker, Barnshaw of Covent Garden Theatre, Moore, Tom Lowe, Kear (sang at Mary-

(M.ʳˢ Baddely)

of whom the best known are Robert Hudson the organist, Miss Snow and Thomas Lowe. Sophia Snow, the daughter of Valentine Snow, sergeant trumpeter to the King, married Robert Baddeley the comedian, who introduced her to the stage at Drury Lane in 1765. As Mrs. Baddeley, she became notorious for her beauty and intrigues. She had some powers as an actress in genteel comedy and her melodious voice made her popular at Ranelagh (from 1770) and Vauxhall.

Lowe was the well-known tenor singer of Vauxhall and lessee of Marylebone Gardens from 1763 to 1768. Becoming bankrupt in 1768, he was glad to accept engagements at the humbler Finch's Grotto. He was announced to sing in August 1769, and appeared under the designation of Brother Lowe at one of the Freemasons' Concerts at the Grotto.

Finch died on October 23, 1770, and his successor, a Mr. Williams, advertised the place as Williams's Grotto Gardens. The concerts were continued and among the musical entertainments were Bates's " The Gamester " (1771) and Barnshaw's " Linco's Travels." [1]

The programmes of entertainments under Finch and Williams included concertos on the organ, pieces for horns and clarionets, Handel's Coronation Anthem, an Ode to Summer with music by Brewster, and songs,

---

lebone 1754, and at Sadler's Wells in 1771 and later), Nepecker, Clarke, Thomas and A. Smith from the Richmond Theatre, Weston from Drury Lane (1772), Aitken and Murphin, Master Adams, Master Suett (in 1771, from Ranelagh, supposed to be Dick Suett the actor), Master Green, and Master Lyon. The female singers were Mrs. Forbes, Reed, Smith, Taylor, Clark, and Dorman, and Misses Garvey, Thomas (in August 1765), Carli, Moyse, Snow, Dowson (sang at Sadler's Wells 1775), Cantrell, Marshall, and Oakes. The instrumentalists included Cocklin and Smart, *violins ;* Hudson, *organ ;* Palmer, *flute.*

[1] " Linco's Travels " was also performed at the Patagonian Theatre, Exeter Change. Humphreys's *Memoirs of Decastro,* 237.

such as "Thro' the Wood, Laddie"; "Water parted
from the Sea"; "Oh what a charming thing is a
Battle"; "British Wives"; "O'er Mountains and
Moorlands"; "Cupid's Recruiting Sergeant" (with
drum and fife accompaniment); "Swift Wing'd Vengeance," from Bates's Pharnaces; "Shepherds cease
your soft complainings;" a satirical song on Garrick's
Stratford Jubilee; "Hark, hark, the joy inspiring
horn"; "The Season of Love," sung by Mr. Dearle,
(1765):—

> Bright Sol is return'd and the Winter is o'er,
> O come then, Philander, with Sylvia away.[1]

Fireworks were occasionally displayed, and when a
ball was given, the place was illuminated at a cost of
about five pounds, and horns and clarionets played
till twelve in the garden. In 1771 and 1772 a grand

---

[1] A programme of a benefit night for 12 September, 1771 (under
Williams), may be inserted as a specimen :—
"Act i.—An Overture. A favourite song from the opera of
Pharnaces : 'Swift wing'd vengeance nerves my arm,' by Mr. A.
Smith, set by Mr. Bates. A favourite Scotch air by Miss Dowson,
words and music by Mr. A. Smith. An overture by Abel. The
Act to conclude with a celebrated song from Anacreon, set by Mr.
Starling [Sterling ?] Goodwin, by Mr. A. Smith. Act ii.—'The
soldier tired of war's alarm,' by Miss Dowson. A new song, 'O
what a charming thing is a battle,' by Mr. Barnshaw. An overture
in Otho, Handel. 'Sweet Echo,' by a young gentleman from Italy.
Trumpet Concerto by Master Green, pupil of Mr. Jones. The
celebrated song of the 'British Wives,' by Mr. A. Smith. A new
song by Miss Dowson. Concerto on the violin by Mr. Smart.
The Act to conclude with 'Russel's triumph,' by Mr. A. Smith,
by particular desire. To which will be added an entertainment
called 'The Gamester,' to be sung by Mr. A. Smith, Mr. Barnshaw, Miss Dowson, and Mrs. Dorman, with a hornpipe in the
character of a sailor, by Mr. Rawlins from the Opera House in
the Haymarket. At the end of the hornpipe Mr. A. Smith will
sing the celebrated song of 'The storm or the danger of the sea,'
in character. After which will be displayed a Grand Transparent
Painting."

transparent painting forty feet wide and thirty high, with illuminations, was displayed. Over the centre arch of this masterpiece was a medallion of Neptune supported by Tritons : on each side were two fountains "with serpents jetting water, representing different coloured crystal." On one wing was Neptune drawn by sea-horses ; on the other, Venus rising from the sea ; and the back arches showed a distant prospect of the sea. In June 1771 a representation was given " of the famous Fall of Water call'd Pystill Rhiader near the seat of Sir Watkin Williams Wynne, Bart., in Denbighshire."

Apparently these entertainments failed to pay the proprietor and in 1773 (?) he pulled down the grotto over the spring and rooted up the shrubs to form a skittle ground in connection with the tavern, which still continued to be carried on.

About 1777 the "messuages and lands known as the Grotto Gardens" were purchased for the parish of St. Saviour's, Southwark, part of the ground being used for the erection of a workhouse and part for a Burial Ground (consecrated in 1780). In 1799 the Workhouse was sold to Mr. John Harris, hat manufacturer, and M.P. for Southwark in 1830, who used it as his manufactory and residence. Some relics of the old Grotto were to be found many years after the closing of the Gardens, notably the Octagon Room, which was converted into a mill and at one time used as the armoury of the Southwark Volunteers.

In 1824 "a very large and old mulberry tree" was standing at the end of a long range of wooden tea-rooms formerly belonging to the gardens and converted into inferior cottages. Behind the cottages was a water-course derived from Loman's Pond dividing them from a field, once part of the gardens, though only occupied at that time by dust and rubbish.

The tavern attached to the Gardens continued to be

carried on under the sign of the Grotto till 28 May,
1795, when it was destroyed by fire. The new tavern
erected in its place bore the sign of The Goldsmith's
Arms, and afterwards of the "Old Grotto new
reviv'd."

In the front of this house was inserted a stone bearing the inscription :—

> Here Herbs did grow
> And Flowers sweet,
> But now 'tis call'd
> Saint George's Street.[1]

This building was removed for the formation of the
present Southwark Bridge Road in 1825 and a public
house named The Goldsmith's Arms—still standing—
was built on the western side of the new road, more
upon the site of the old Grotto Gardens. The main
site of the gardens is now occupied by the large red-
brick building, which forms the headquarters of the
Metropolitan Fire Brigade.

[Wilkinson's *Londina Illustrata*, vol. ii., "Finch's Grotto Gardens" ; Manning and Bray's *Surrey*, iii. 591; Brayley and Mantell's
Surrey, v. 371 ; Rendle and Norman's *Inns of Old Southwark*, 360–
364 ; Walford, vi. 64 ; newspaper cuttings, W. Coll.]

VIEWS.

The only view is one of the second tavern published in Wilkinson's *Londina Illustrata*, 1825 :—

"South-east view of the Grotto, now the Goldsmith's Arms in
the Parish of St. George's, Southwark." This shows the inscription : "Here Herbs did grow."

---

[1] In 1827 this stone was used as a step in the yard of the house
of a Mrs. Stevens near the site of the Gardens, the verses being
then almost illegible (Wilkinson).

CUPER'S GARDENS

CUPER'S GARDENS, a notable resort during the first half of the last century, owe their name and origin to Boyder Cuper, who rented, in the parish of Lambeth on the south side of the Thames opposite Somerset House, a narrow strip of meadow land surrounded by water-courses.

About 1691 or earlier he opened the place as a pleasure garden with agreeable walks and arbours and some good bowling-greens. As an old servant of the Howard family he obtained the gift of some of the statues that had been removed when Arundel House in the Strand was pulled down. These, though mutilated and headless, appeared to the proprietor to give classic distinction to his garden, and they remained there till 1717, when his successor, a John Cuper, sold these 'Arundel Marbles' for £75.[1]

During the first twenty or thirty years of the last century, Cuper's was a good deal frequented in the summer-time. A tavern by the water-side, called The Feathers, was connected with the grounds.

It is not certain that music and dancing were provided at this period, and the company appears to have consisted chiefly of young attorneys' clerks and Fleet Street sempstresses, with a few City dames, escorted by

---

[1] Nichols's *Lambeth*, 1786 (in vol. ii. of *Bibl. Topog. Brit.* p. 77, ff.) ; Michaelis's *Ancient Marbles in Great Britain*, 35–37.

their husbands' 'prentices, who (perhaps after paying a visit to the floating ' Folly ') sat in the arbours singing, laughing, and regaling themselves with bottle-ale.[1]

The place was popularly known as Cupid's Gardens, and is even thus denominated in maps of the last century. This name is preserved in the traditional song, once very popular, " 'Twas down in Cupid's Garden " :—

> 'Twas down in Cupid's Garden
> For pleasure I did go,
> To see the fairest flowers
> That in that garden grow :
> The first it was the jessamine,
> The lily, pink and rose,
> And surely they're the fairest flowers
> That in that garden grows.[2]

In 1738 the tavern and gardens were taken by Ephraim Evans, a publican who had kept the Hercules Pillars opposite St. Dunstan's Church, Fleet Street. During his tenancy (1738-1740) he improved the gardens and erected an orchestra in which was set up an organ by Bridge. A band played from six till ten and Jones, the blind Welsh harper, was engaged to perform selections from Handel and Corelli. The admission was then and thenceforward one shilling, and the gardens were opened on Sunday free of charge.[3] It was announced that care would be taken to keep out bad company and that no servant in livery would be admitted to walk in the garden.

There was a back way to the gardens leading from St. George's Fields, and watchmen were appointed " to guard those who go over the fields late at night." The favourite approach, however, was by water, and the

---

[1] Prologue to Mrs. Centlivre's *Busybody*.

[2] Chappell (*Popular Music in the Olden Time*, ii. 727, 728) gives words and music.

[3] The gardens were closed on the Sundays of 1752.

visitors landed at Cuper's Stairs, a few yards east of the present Waterloo Bridge. The season lasted from April or May till the beginning of September.

Evans died on 14 October, 1740,[1] but the tavern and gardens were carried on by his widow. It was under the spirited management of the widow Evans that Cuper's Gardens especially flourished, and her advertisements figure frequently in the newspapers (1741-1759). 'The Widow,' as she was called, presided at the bar during the evening and complimentary visitors described her as "a woman of discretion" and "a well-looking comely person." By providing good music and elaborate fireworks, she attracted a good deal of fashionable patronage. The Prince and Princess of Wales visited the place and some of Horace Walpole's friends,[2] Lord Bath and Lord Sandys, for instance, both of whom had their pockets picked there. The well-dressed sharper was, in fact, by no means unknown at Cuper's. One night in 1743 a man was caught stealing from a young lady a purse containing four guineas, and while being taken by a constable to Lambeth was rescued by a gang of thieves in St. George's Fields. On the whole, Cuper's was looked upon as a decidedly rakish place at which a prudent young lady was not to be seen alone with a gentleman.[3]

For the evening concert of 16 June, 1741, Mrs. Evans announced "a new grand concerto for the organ by the author, Mr. Henry Burgess, junior, of whom it may be said without ostentation that he is of

---

[1] *Gent. Mag.* 1740, 525.

[2] Walpole's *Letters*, ed. Cunningham, ii. 32, 24 June, 1746. Bad company was not unknown in the earlier days of the gardens : see Welsted's *Epistle on False Fame*, 1732 :—

"For Cupid's Bowers she hires the willing scull . . . .
While here a 'prentice, there a captain bites."

[3] *The Complete Letter-writer*, Edinburgh, 1773, quoted in *Notes and Queries*, 7th ser. ii. 469.

as promising a genius and as neat a performer as any of the age." Composers better known to fame than Mr. Henry Burgess, junior, were also represented. The programme, for instance, of one July evening in 1741 consisted of " The Overture in Saul, with several grand choruses composed by Mr. Handel " ; the eighth concerto of Corelli ; a hautboy concerto by Sig. Hasse ; " Blow, blow thou wintry wind," and other favourite songs composed by the ingenious Mr. Arne, and the whole concluded with a new grand piece of music, an original composition by Handel, called ' Portobello,' in honour of the popular hero, Admiral Vernon, " who took Portobello with six ships only." On other occasions there were vocal performances (1748–1750) by Signora Sibilla and by Master Mattocks. The Signora was Sibilla Gronamann, daughter of a German pastor and the first wife of Thomas Pinto, the violinist. She died in or before 1766. Mattocks, who had " a sweet and soft voice," was afterwards an operatic actor at Covent Garden. Mrs. Mattocks sang at the gardens in 1750.

After the concert, at half-past nine or ten, a gun gave the signal for the fireworks for which the place was renowned.

On 18 July, 1741, the Fire Music from Handel's opera, " Atalanta," was given, the fireworks consisting of wheels, fountains, large sky-rockets, " with an addition of the fire-pump, &c., made by the ingenious Mr. Worman, who originally projected it for the opera " when performed in 1736. The *Daily Advertiser* for 28 June, 1743, announced that " this night will be burnt the Gorgon's head . . . . in history said to have snakes on her hair and to kill men by her looks, such a thing as was never known to be done in England before." For another night (4 September, 1749) the entertainment was announced to conclude with " a curious and magnificent firework, which has given great satisfaction to the nobility, wherein Neptune will be drawn on the canal by sea-horses and set fire to an Archimedan (*sic*) worm and return to the Grotto."

In 1746 (August 14) there was a special display to celebrate "the glorious victory obtained over the rebels" by the Duke of Cumberland, consisting of emblematic figures and magnificent fireworks, with "triumphant arches burning in various colours." In 1749 (May) there was a miniature reproduction with transparencies and fireworks of the Allegorical Temple that had been displayed in the Green Park on 27 April, 1749, to commemorate the peace of Aix-la-Chapelle. At the opening of the gardens on April 30 for the season of 1750, the edifice from which the fireworks were displayed was altered "into an exact model of that at the Hague, made on account of the General Peace."

The season of 1752, practically the last at Cuper's, lasted from May till near the end of September. The principal vocalist was Miss Maria Bennett.[1] The fireworks and scenic effects were novel and elaborate. A song commemorating the Prince of Wales's birthday was "shown curiously in fireworks in the front of the machine." The fireworks building, when the curtain was withdrawn, disclosed a perspective view of the city of Rhodes—sea, buildings, and landscape, with a model of the Colossus, from under which Neptune issued forth and set fire to a grand pyramid in the middle of the canal. Dolphins spouted water ; water-wheels and rockets threw up air-balloons and suns blazed on the summit of the building.

On one occasion the crowd near the fireworks was so great that a gentleman took up his position in a tree, and when St. George and the Dragon came to a close engagement and the clockwork began to move the arms of St. George to pierce the Dragon, he let go his

[1] Twelve songs by Lewis Granom, as sung at Cuper's Gardens by Miss Maria Bennett, published London, 24 November, 1752.

hands to clap like the rest and fell headlong upon the bystanders.[1]

The 'Inspector' of the *London Daily Advertiser* took his friend the old Major, to Cupid's Gardens (as they were still called) on a pleasant August evening in this year. The Major was delighted with all he saw. "Now I like this. I am always pleased when I see other people happy : the folks that are rambling about among the trees there ; the jovial countenances of them delight me . . . . here's all the festivity and all the harmless indulgence of a country wake."[2]

The country wake element was in evidence late in the evening, and constables stationed at the gate had occasionally to interfere. One night, for instance, a pretty young woman, accompanied by a friend, promenaded the gardens dressed as a man wearing a long sword. No small sensation was caused in the miscellaneous company, which included a physician, a templar, a berouged old lady and her granddaughter, and the sedate wife of a Cheapside fur-seller. "A spirited young thing with a lively air and smart cock of her hat" passed by. "Gad," said she, as she tripped along, "I don't see there's anything in it ; give us their cloathes and we shall look as sharp and as rakish as they do." "What an air ! what a gate ! what a tread the baggage has !" exclaimed another.

But the days of Cuper's were numbered. In the early part of 1752 the statute-book had been dignified by the addition of 25 George II., cap. 36, entitled, "An Act for the better preventing thefts and robberies

---

[1] The fireworks at Cuper's in 1751 are described in the *London Daily Advertiser* for 10 September, 1751.

[2] 'The Inspector,' No. 448, in the *London Daily Advertiser* for 6 August, 1752. The details that follow are derived from the same journal for 4 August, 1752, where they are related of "one of the public gardens on the other side of the water." Possibly Vauxhall is intended, but if not literally true of Cuper's Gardens, they seem sufficiently applicable to them.

and for regulating places of public entertainment and punishing persons keeping disorderly houses." By section 2 of this enactment it was required that every house, room, garden, or other place kept for public dancing or music, &c., within the cities of London and Westminster, or twenty miles thereof, should be under a licence. The Act took effect from December 1, 1752, and the necessary licence for the season of 1753 was refused to the management of Cuper's Gardens. The widow Evans complained bitterly that she was denied the liberty of opening her gardens, a misfortune attributed by her to the malicious representations of ill-meaning persons, but which was really owing, no doubt, to the circumstance that Cuper's was degenerating into the place which Pennant says he remembered as the scene of low dissipation. Meanwhile Mrs. Evans threw open the grounds (June 1753) as a tea-garden in connection with the Feathers, and the walks were " kept in pleasant order."

In the summer of 1755 entertainments of the old character were revived, but they were advertised as fifteen private evening concerts and fireworks, open only to subscribers, a one guinea ticket admitting two persons. It is to be suspected that the subscription was mythical, and was a mere device to evade the Act. However, a band was engaged, and on June 23 loyal visitors to Cuper's commemorated the accession of King George to the throne by a concert and fireworks. Clitherow, who had been the engineer of Cuper's fireworks from 1750 (or earlier), was again employed, but had to publish in the newspapers a lame apology for the failure of the Engagement on the Water on the night of August 2 (1755), a failure which he explained was not due to his want of skill but " owing to part of the machinery for moving the shipping being clogg'd by some unaccountable accident, and the powder in the ships having unfortunately got a little damp."

From 1756–1759 Cuper's Gardens were again used as the tea-garden of the Feathers. There was no longer a Band of Musick but (as the advertisements express it) "there still remains some harmony from the sweet enchanting sounds of rural warblers."

The last recorded entertainment at the place was a special concert given on August 30, 1759 by "a select number of gentlemen for their own private diversion," who had "composed an ode alluding to the late decisive action of Prince Ferdinand." Any lady or gentleman inspired by Prussian glory was admitted to this entertainment on payment of a shilling.

For several years the gardens remained unoccupied, but from about 1768 three acres of them were leased to the firm of Beaufoy, the producers of British wines and vinegar. The orchestra, or rather the edifice used from 1750 for the fireworks, was utilised for the distillery. Dr. Johnson once passed by the gardens : "Beauclerk, I, and Langton, and Lady Sydney Beauclerk, mother to our friend, were one day driving in a coach by Cuper's Gardens which were then unoccupied. I, in sport, proposed that Beauclerk, and Langton, and myself, should take them, and we amused ourselves with scheming how we should all do our parts. Lady Sydney grew angry and said, ' An old man should not put such things in young people's heads.' She had no notion of a joke, sir ; had come late into life, and had a mighty unpliable understanding." [1]

J. T. Smith [2] tells us that he walked over the place when occupied by the Beaufoys, and saw many of the old lamp-irons along the paling of the gardens, humble reminders of the days when the walks of Cuper's Gardens were "beautifully illuminated with lamp-trees in a grand taste, disposed in proper order." In

[1] Boswell, *Life of Johnson*, ed. Croker, chap. xli. p. 366.
[2] *Nollekens*, ii. 201.

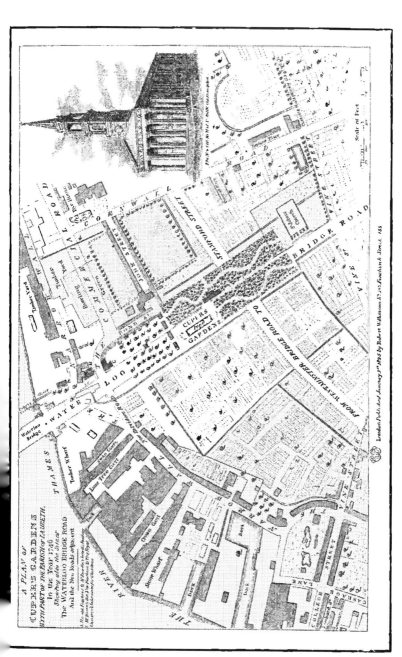

PLAN OF CUPER'S GARDENS.

1814 part of the ground was required for making the south approach to Waterloo Bridge. The " fireworks " building and the rest of Messrs. Beaufoys' works were then taken down and the Waterloo Road, sixty feet in width, was cut through the three acres, thus passing through the centre of Cuper's Gardens which had extended up to the site of the present St. John's Church (built in 1823) opposite Waterloo Station.

The Royal Infirmary for Children and Women erected in 1823 on the eastern side of the Waterloo Road stands on (or rather *over*) the centre of the site of the gardens. The Feathers was used during the building of the bridge for the pay-table of the labourers, and when it was taken down (about 1818 ?) its site was occupied by a timber-yard, close to the eastern side of the first land-arch of the Waterloo Bridge.

The public-house now called the Feathers, standing near the Bridge and rising two stories above the level of the Waterloo Road was built by the proprietor of the old Feathers in 1818.

[Wilkinson's *Londina Illustrata*, vol. ii. "Cuper's Gardens," Public Gardens Coll. in Guildhall Library, London (newspaper cuttings, &c.) ; Charles Howard's *Historical Anecdotes of the Howard Family* (1769), 98, ff. ; Pennant's *Account of London*, 3rd ed. 1793, 32–34 ; *Musical Times*, February 1894, 84, ff. ; Hone's *Every Day Book*, i. 603 ; E. Hatton's *New View of London*, 1708, ii. 785 ; Lysons's *Environs*, 1792, i. 319, 320 ; Walford, vi. 388, 389 ; *The Observator*, March 10, 1702–3 ; newspaper cuttings, W. Coll.]

VIEWS.

1. View of the Savoy, Somerset House, and the water entrance to Cuper's Gardens, engraved by W. M. Fellows, 1808, in J. T. Smith's *Antiquities of Westminster*, from a painting (done in 1770, according to Crace, *Cat.* 188, No. 219) by Samuel Scott.

2. Woodcuts in Walford, vi. 391, showing entrance to the gardens (the back entrance) and the "orchestra" during the de-

molition of the buildings ; cp. *ib.* 390. Walford also mentions, *ib.* p. 388, a view showing the grove, statues, and alcoves, of the gardens.

3. Water-colour drawings of Beaufoys' and Cuper's in 1798 and in 1809 (Crace, *Cat.* 648, Nos. 49, 50).

4. Wilkinson, *Lond. Illust.* (1825), vol. ii. gives three views, Pl. 155, view of the Great Room as occupied for Beaufoys' manufactory, with a plan of the gardens ; Pl. 156, another similar view ; Pl. 157, view of the old Feathers Tavern.

Close by Cuper's Stairs (where the visitors to
Cuper's Gardens landed) and opposite Somerset House,
there was generally moored during the summer months
a sort of castellated house-boat, notorious as The Folly.[1]

It consisted of a strong barge on which was a deck
platform, surrounded by a balustrade, and contained a
saloon provided with large windows and divided into
boxes and compartments. At each of the four angles
of the deck was a turret, giving the whole something of
the appearance of a floating castle.

This " whimsical piece of architecture " (as Thomas
Brown calls it) [2] was in existence soon after the Restoration, and in 1668 was visited by Pepys.[3] It was intended, says Brown, " as a musical summer-house for
the entertainment of quality where they might meet and
ogle one another . . . but the ladies of the town finding it as convenient a rendezvous for their purpose . . .
dash'd the female quality out of countenance and made
them seek a more retired conveniency " for their " amorous intrigues." Queen Mary (II.) once paid it a

[1] The Folly was occasionally moored off the Bank side (Wheatley, *London Past and Present*, " The Folly ").

[2] *Amusements Serious and Comical*, part ii. " The Thames."

[3] Pepys (*Diary*, 13 April, 1668) jots down in his daily expenditure
a shilling spent " in the Folly." From the circumstance that he
makes no special comment on the place it may perhaps be inferred
that he was already acquainted with it from previous visits.

visit, and the proprietor endeavoured to re-christen
it The Royal Diversion. It continued, however, to
be popularly known as The Folly, and already in 1700
had ceased to have any quality to boast of, at least
among its female frequenters.

Thomas Brown describes a visit that he made about
1700. Rowing up to the side in a boat he found himself scrutinised by a crowd of women both young and
old, and (as he puts it) " of all sorts and sizes." Some
of these ladies were dancing and tripping airily about

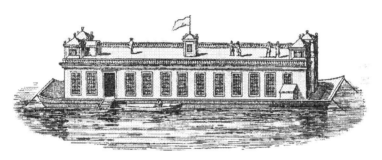

"THE FOLLY," BEFORE *circ.* 1720.

the deck, and some tattling to their beaux ; but many
of the company, including certain long-sworded bullies,
were crowded into the boxes in the saloon where they
sat, smoking, and drinking burnt brandy. " In short,
it was such a confused scene of folly, madness and
debauchery" that Thomas Brown, by no means a
squeamish person, stepped again into his boat " without
drinking."

The Folly in its later days was occasionally visited
by people who at least worked honestly for their
living, and the draper's apprentice, when his shop was
shut, would row up with his sweetheart for an evening's
amusement at this curious haunt.[1]

[1] Tom D'Urfey, *A Touch of the Times*, 1719.

The Folly was in existence till 1720, and perhaps for more than thirty years later, but the character of its frequenters, and the gambling that took place at what was known as its Golden Gaming Table, at last led to its suppression as a public resort.   It was suffered to fall into such decay that its material was burnt for fire-wood.

Near that part of the river where the Folly was usually moored the famous Chinese junk was anchored about 1848, and visited by thousands of sight-seers.[1]

[Thomas Brown's *Amusements Serious and Comical*, Part ii. "The Thames"; Wheatley's *London Past and Present*, "Folly"; E. Hatton's *New View of London*, 1708, ii. 785 ; Wilkinson's *Londina*, vol. i. No. 88 ; also vol. ii. "Cuper's Gardens"; Walford, iii. 290 ; Larwood and Hotten, *History of Signboards*, 509 ; manuscript notes, &c. in "Public Gardens" collection in Guildhall Library, London.]

VIEWS.

1. A view of Whitehall from the water, showing the Folly Musick House on the Thames. Engraved in Wilkinson's *Londina Illustrata*, vol. i. No. 88, from a drawing taken about the time of James II. "in the possession of Thomas Griffiths, Esq."

2. The Southern Front of Somerset House with its extensive Gardens, &c., showing the Folly. A drawing by L. Knyff, about 1720, engraved by Sawyer Junior, and published (1808) in J. T. Smith's sixty additional plates to his *Antiquities of Westminster*. This is copied, with a short account of the Folly, in E. W. Brayley's *Londiniana* (1829), vol. iii. 130, 300. It is substantially the same as the view on a larger scale engraved by Kip in Strype's *Stow*, 1720, ii. bk. 4, p. 105. Cp. also an engraving (W. Coll.) "Somerset House, La Maison de Somerset." L. Knyff del. I. Kip sc. undated, before 1720 ?

---

[1] Walford, iii. 290, 291.

BELVEDERE HOUSE AND GARDENS, LAMBETH

BELVEDERE HOUSE and Gardens were near Cuper's Gardens,[1] but a little higher up the river (south side). They were opposite York Buildings in the Strand, and extended from the present Belvedere Road (then called Narrow Wall) to the water's edge. Some modern writers speak of the gardens as a place of public entertainment in the reign of Queen Anne, but there seems no evidence of this, and in 1719 or 1720 the premises were in the possession of a Mr. English (or England), who at that time sold them to the Theobald family. In 1757, Belvedere House was the private residence of Mr. James Theobald.

In the early part of 1781, "the house called Belvedere" was taken by one Charles Bascom, who opened it as an inn, with the added attractions of "pleasant gardens and variety of fish-ponds." He professed in his advertisements, to accommodate his guests with choice wines and with eating of every kind in season, after the best manner, especially with "the choicest river-fish which they may have the delight to see taken."

[1] Walford's statement (*Old and New London*, vi. 388) that they adjoined Cuper's Gardens is not quite accurate. Four strips of land belonging to four different proprietors are marked in the map in Strype's *Stow* (1720) as lying between the Belvedere Gardens and Cuper's Gardens.

The gardens could not have been open later than 1785, for in that year part of the ground was turned into the Belvedere (timber) Wharf, and part was occupied by the machinery of the Lambeth water-works.

[Advertisement in *The Freethinker* for April 28, 1781, quoted in Wilkinson's *Londina*, vol. ii. "Cuper's Gardens," *notes*, and in Nichols's *Lambeth*, Nichols's *Bibl. Top. Brit.* ii. Appendix, 158 ; map in Strype's *Stow* (1720), vol. ii. book 6, p. 83, Appendix ; Manning and Bray, *Surrey*, iii. 467 ; Brayley and Mantell, *Surrey*, iii. 393 ; Howard's *Historical Anecdotes of some of the Howard Family*, 106 ; Wheatley's *London P. and P.* s.v. "Belvedere Road."]

RESTORATION SPRING GARDENS, ST. GEORGE'S FIELDS

THE Restoration Tavern was in existence in the early part of the reign of Charles II.[1] In 1714 there was a new cockpit in its grounds and a great match of cock fighting was announced to take place there ; "two guineas a battle, and twenty guineas the odd battle" all the week, beginning at four o'clock. The races and popular sports then frequent in St. George's Fields probably brought additional custom to the house.

In the gardens of the tavern was a purging spring which was advertised[2] in 1733 as already well-known for the cure of all cancerous and scorbutic humours. About the same year a second spring was discovered, a chalybeate "of the nature of Piermont Water but superior." The water was obtainable every day at the gardens,[3] and was declared to "far exceed" the water at the neighbouring Dog and Duck. Dr. Rendle says that it must have been the mere soakage of a swamp,

---

[1] The proprietor, William Hagley, issued a halfpenny token "at ye Restoration in St. George's Feilds." Boyne's *Trade Tokens of the Seventeenth Century*, ed. Williamson, p. 1036, No. 357.

[2] Advertisement in the *Country Journal or the Craftsman*, 31 March, 1733, where the celebrated "Purging Spring" and the Chalybeate Spring "lately discovered" are mentioned, "at Mr. Lewis's, commonly called the Restauration Gardens in St. George's Fields."

[3] The water was also to be obtained at a corkcutter's under Exeter Change in the Strand.

but whatever may have been the virtues of the spring it was probably before long eclipsed by its rival at the Dog and Duck, though the Restoration was in existence in 1755 and perhaps for some years later.

In 1771 the garden, or at any rate about an acre of it, was taken by William Curtis,[1] the author of *Flora Londinensis*, who formed a Botanical Garden there which was afterwards open to subscribers until 1789, when the botanist removed to another garden in the more salubrious air of Brompton.

Restoration Garden is marked in the map in Stow's *Survey*, 1755, as abutting on the western side of Angel Street (a continuation of the Broad Wall), southern end. In a map of the Surrey side of the Thames showing the proposed roads from Blackfriars Bridge (circ. 1768) the ground is marked as " Public House Gardens " and " Gardens." The Half-way House from the Borough to Westminster Bridge is marked immediately south of the gardens ; and still further south is the Westminster Bridge Road, the end east of the Asylum. St. Saviour's Union, Marlborough Street (near the New Cut), is now near the site.

[Rendle and Norman, *Inns of Old Southwark* (1888), pp. 367, 368 ; and see Notes.]

---

[1] Loudon's *Arboretum et frut. Brit.* vol. i. p. 75. Nichols, *Parish of Lambeth*, p. 84, says " about the year 1777."

THE FLORA TEA GARDENS (OR MOUNT GARDENS), WESTMINSTER BRIDGE ROAD

THE Flora Tea Gardens (or Mount Gardens), were on the right hand side of the Westminster Bridge Road going towards the Obelisk, and opposite the Temple of Flora. They were in existence about 1796-7. The gardens were well kept and contained "genteel paintings." They were open on weekdays and on Sundays till about 11 p.m., and the admission was sixpence.

Among the frequenters were democratic shopmen, who might be heard railing against King and Church, and a good many ladies respectable and the reverse. The "Sunday Rambler" (1796-7) describes the company as very orderly, but at some time before 1800 the place was suppressed on account of dissolute persons frequenting it.

Some small cottages were then built in the middle of the garden, which retained a rural appearance till shortly before 1827, when several rows of houses, "Mount Gardens," were erected on the site.

[The Flora Tea Gardens described in *A Modern Sabbath* (1797), chap. viii., are evidently identical with the Mount Gardens mentioned by Allen (*Lambeth*, 335), though he does not mention their alternative name (cp. Walford, vi. 389). Allen (*loc. cit.*) is the authority for the suppression of the gardens.]

THE TEMPLE OF FLORA

THE Temple of Flora stood hard by the Temple of Apollo, in the middle of Mount Row on the lefthand side of Westminster Bridge Road, going towards the Obelisk, and was separated by Oakley Street from the Apollo Gardens (Temple of Apollo). Concerts were given every evening in the season, and the place is described as "beautifully fitted up with alcoves and exotics."

In the hot house was "an elegant statue of Pomona," a transparency of Flora, and at the lower end of the garden, a natural cascade and fountain. "The entrance and the gardens," were advertised in July 1789 as being formed by the proprietor into an exact imitation of the admired Temple of Flora, which he had constructed at the Grand Gala at Ranelagh.

Some special entertainments were given in June and July in honour of the King's recovery, and the Grand Temple of Flora, an "elegant and ingenious imitation of Nature in her floral attire," was then illuminated with nearly a thousand variegated lamps amid wreaths of flowers twining round pillars "made in imitation of Sienna marble." Fireworks and waterworks were also displayed; a large star of lamps was suspended above the cascade, and (in the absence of nightingales) "a variety of singing birds" were imitated. The admission for these special entertainments was one shilling, and the gardens were illuminated from eight till the closing time at eleven. Light refreshments were served consisting of orgeat, lemonade, "confectionary," straw-berries and cream.

There is evidence [1] that in the first few years of its existence (1788–1791) the place was visited by some people of good position, but it afterwards became the haunt of dissolute characters and of young apprentices.[2] The author of *A Modern Sabbath* describes (*circ.* 1796) the boxes in the gardens as " neatly painted" like most of the company who were to be seen there about ten in the evening. The admission appears to have been now reduced to sixpence.

In 1796 the proprietor, a man named Grist, was indicted for keeping the place as a disorderly house, and was ordered (May 30) to be confined for six months in the King's Bench Prison,[3] and in all probability the Temple of Flora was then finally closed.

Mme. Lamotte, the heroine of the famous Diamond Necklace affair, ended her strange career (23 August, 1791) in her house near the Temple of Flora, a place of amusement that, it is likely enough, she frequented.[4]

[*A Modern Sabbath* (1797), chap. viii.; *Public Advertiser*, 2 July, 1789 (fêtes of June and July); Brayley and Mantell, *Surrey*, iii. 399; Allen's *Lambeth*, 321.]

---

[1] *Notes and Queries*, 7th series, xi. p. 87 (communication from Lieut.-Col. Capel Coape).

[2] This appears from the evidence brought forward in the prosecution of Grist; see *The Whitehall Evening Post* for May 7 to May 10, 1796 (referring to May 7).

[3] Newspapers cited by E. M. Borrajo in *Notes and Queries*, 7th ser. xi. 138.

[4] " The English translator of Lamotte's *Life* says she fell from the leads of her house, nigh the Temple of Flora, endeavouring to escape seizure for debt, and was taken up so much hurt that she died in consequence. Another report runs that she was flung out of window. . . . Where the Temple of Flora was, or is, one knows not " (Carlyle, *Diamond Necklace*, note near end). The Temple of Flora alluded to was certainly in London, and there can be no reasonable doubt that the popular resort now described is the place in question.

APOLLO GARDENS (OR TEMPLE OF APOLLO)

THESE gardens were on the left hand side of the Westminster Bridge Road going from Westminster to the Obelisk, and were situated nearly where the engineering factory of Messrs. Maudslay, Sons and Field now stands and opposite the present Christ Church Congregational Chapel.[1]

Walter Claggett, the proprietor (at one time a lessee of the Pantheon [2] in Oxford Street) opened the place in October 1788 with an entertainment given in the concert room, which is described as a fine building with "a kind of orrery in the dome, displaying a pallid moon between two brilliant transparencies." In this building was an orchestra containing a fine-toned organ, and in the opening concert, given before nearly one thousand three hundred people, a band of about seventy instrumental and vocal performers took part, the organist being Jonathan Battishill.

Previous to the opening for the season in April 1790, the gardens were much altered and a room was arranged for large dinner parties. In the gardens were a number of "elegant pavilions or alcoves" ornamented with the adventures of Don Quixote and other paintings.

---

[1] At the period when the gardens were open "The Asylum" (*i.e.* Female Orphan Asylum) stood where Christ Church now stands.

[2] Cp. Wilkinson, *Londina Illust.* vol. ii. "Pantheon Theatre."

In 1792 (May-July) there was music every evening and fantoccini were exhibited. In this year the concerts took place in a covered promenade described as the Grand Apollonian Promenade. Mr. Flack, junior, was the leader of the band ; Mr. Costelow the organist, and the vocalists were Mr. Binley, Miss Wingfield, Mrs. Leaver, and Mrs. Iliff, the last-named one of the Vauxhall singers in 1787. New overtures, &c., "composed by Messrs. Haydn and Pleyel since their arrival in this Kingdom" were advertised for performance.

The season began in April or May, and the visitor on entering at five o'clock or later, paid a shilling or sixpence (1792) receiving in exchange a metal check entitling him to refreshments. No charge was made for the concert. At about nine o'clock many persons who had "come on" from other public places visited the Apollo for hot suppers, and the gardens and promenade were illuminated, sometimes with two thousand lamps. The proprietor prided himself on "the superior excellence of the Music and Wines." He boasted, moreover, of the patronage of the nobility and gentry, and vaunted the "chastity and dignity" of the place, though it was probably owing to the presence of some of these late arriving visitors that the Apollo Gardens speedily acquired an unenviable reputation.

In 1792 the place was known to be a resort of cheats and pickpockets. We hear of one Elizabeth Smith, a smartly dressed young woman, about eighteen, being charged in 1792 at the Guildhall with "trepanning a Miss Ridley," a beautiful girl ten years of age, whom she had taken with her to the Apollo and the Dog and Duck, and left crying on Blackfriars Bridge, after stealing her fine sash.

The Apollo was suppressed by the magistrates, probably about 1793.[1] The proprietor himself became

[1] Allen (*History of Lambeth*, 319) states that the Apollo Gardens were suppressed about 1791, but this is certainly erroneous, as

bankrupt; the orchestra was removed to Sydney
Gardens, Bath;[1] and the Temple of Apollo fell into a
ruinous state and its site was eventually built upon.

[A collection of newspaper cuttings relating to London, &c.
(section, Apollo Gardens) in Guildhall Library, London (*Catal.* ii.
546); "Public Gardens" collection (newspaper cuttings, &c.) in
Guildhall Library (*Catal.* ii. 761); Brayley and Mantell, *Surrey*,
iii. 399; Allen's *Lambeth*, 319; Walford, vi. 343, 389; *A Modern
Sabbath*, chap. viii.]

VIEWS.

There appear to be no extant views. The site may be ascer-
tained from Horwood's *Plan*, 1799; and from Willis's *Plan*, 1808.
In the Crace Coll. (*Cat.* p. 122, No. 69) are "Two drawn plans
of a plot of land called the Apollo Gardens, lying next the
Westminster Bridge Road to the Obelisk," by T. Chawner.

the gardens were frequently advertised in 1792. Kearsley's
Strangers' Guide to London (1793?) mentions the place as "the
resort of company in the evenings," and says that music was occasionally performed there. The Temple of Apollo was described
about 1796–7 in *A Modern Sabbath* as already becoming ruinous,
and it is there stated that Claggett, the proprietor, had become
bankrupt. A newspaper paragraph of December 1796 refers to a
field opposite the Asylum, close by "the ditch that encircles that
place of late infamous resort, the Apollo Gardens."

[1] This was probably the orchestra that seems to have stood in
the centre of the gardens and not that in the concert room.

DOG AND DUCK, ST. GEORGE'S FIELDS
(St. George's Spa)

THE Dog and Duck was in existence as a small inn as early as 1642.[1] In its vicinity were three or four ponds in which, no doubt, the brutal sport of hunting ducks with spaniels was at one time practised,[2] and near the place were mineral springs whose properties were known as early as 1695, though the water does not appear to have been advertised for sale till about 1731,[3] when the Dog and Duck had taken to itself the imposing sub-title of St. George's Spaw. At this time the water was sold at the pump for fourpence a gallon, and was stated to be recommended by eminent physicians for gout, stone, king's evil, sore eyes, and inveterate cancers. A dozen bottles could be had at the Spa (*circ.* 1733–1736) for a shilling.

From about 1754 till 1770 the water was in considerable repute, and new buildings appear to have been

[1] Cp. a token of 1651 ("At the Dogg and Ducke in Southwarke," type, Spaniel with Duck in mouth) in Boyne's *Trade Tokens*, ed. Williamson, p. 1022, there assigned to The Dog and Duck in Deadman's Place, Southwark, by Mr. Philip Norman, who, however, suggests the possibility of its belonging to the Dog and Duck in St. George's Fields. A specimen is in the British Museum.

[2] The ponds are marked in Rocque's Map, *circ.* 1745. The duck-hunting probably took place at an early period, not later than *circ.* 1750.

[3] Newspaper cutting of 1731 (W. Coll.) : see also *The Country Journal or the Craftsman* for 12 Aug. 1732 ; also 26 Aug. 1732.

erected for the accommodation of visitors.   There was a long room for breakfasting (1754), a bowling-green, and a swimming-bath (1769) two hundred feet long and nearly one hundred feet broad.   Tea and coffee were to be had in the afternoon.   At this period people of good position seem to have frequented the Spa or to have sent for the water.   We find Miss Talbot writing about the place to Mrs. Carter, and Dr. Johnson suggested the use of the water to Mrs. Thrale.[1]

The proprietors issued (1760) to subscribers an admission ticket handsomely struck in silver with a portrait of Lazare Rivière, the famous Professor of Medicine, on its obverse.[2]

The *St. James's Chronicle* ranked the water with that of Tunbridge, Cheltenham, and Buxton.

Physicians of repute described its curative properties, and affirmed it to be excellent for cutaneous afflictions and for cancer which it would certainly arrest, even if it did not cure.   This water, which was advertised as an aperient (Epsom Salts being also kept on the premises), came at a much later date—1856—under the observation of Dr. Rendle, the historian, and, as it happened, the Officer of Health in that year for the Parish of St. George's, Southwark.   Rendle procured an analysis of water from the superficial well, formerly the spring, on the site of the old Dog and Duck and was forced to

---

[1] Johnson to Mrs. Thrale, 10 July, 1771, Letter viii. in Johnson's *Works* (ed. Murphy), xii. 338.

[2] A specimen in British Museum (from Miss Banks's Coll.). Silver, size 1·25 inch ; *Obverse: Lazarius Riverius.—Non omnibus dormio.—Miseris succurrere disco.*   Bearded head of Rivière, to left ; beneath head, the number " 18 " incised. *Reverse: The original Spaw in St. George's Fields so memorable in the Plague,* 1665.—*For the proprieters* (sic) *T. Townshend Alchymist to his Majesty,* 1760. Another specimen described in C. A. Rudolph's *Numismata* (relating to medical men), 1862, p. 45, has the words " Robert Baker, Esq., Twickenham," evidently the subscriber's name, engraved on the edge.

describe it as "a decidedly unsafe water" containing impurities, eighty grains per gallon, chiefly alkaline chlorides, sulphates and nitrates, gypsum and carbonate of lime, with a little phosphoric acid.

But we return to the year 1770, about which time the Dog and Duck took a new lease of life. A temporary circus established in St. George's Fields by Sampson, of The Three Hats, Islington, was the cause of much additional custom being brought to the tavern, and Mrs. Hedger who kept the house was obliged to send for her son who was then a youth in a stable-yard at Epsom. Young Hedger soon saw the possibilities of the place. He gradually improved the premises and in a few years was making a large income from the tavern and its tea-garden, which was much frequented, especially on Sundays.[1] The garden was well laid out and contained "a pretty piece of water" doubtless one of the old ducking ponds, and at one time a band played in the garden for the delectation of the weekday visitors. At night, the long room was brilliantly lighted for the company who assembled to dance, drink, and listen to the strains of the organ. Under Hedger, however, the character of the company went from bad to worse. The "rowdy" delights of the Dog and Duck are indicated, though probably with an exaggerated coarseness, in Garrick's Prologue to "The Maid of the Oaks" acted at Drury Lane in 1775 :—

> St. George's Fields, with taste and fashion struck,
> Display Arcadia at the Dog and Duck,
> And Drury misses here in tawdry pride,
> Are there "Pastoras" by the fountain side ;
> To frowsy bowers they reel through midnight damps,
> With Fauns half drunk, and Dryads breaking lamps.[2]

---

[1] The water continued to be advertised in newspapers of 1771–1779. Hedger afterwards put in his nephew Milis (or Miles) to conduct the house which is said to have yielded Hedger £1,000 a year, but evidently himself remained the moving spirit.

[2] On the "Maid of the Oaks," see Baker's *Biog. Dram.*

T

In about ten years the Dog and Duck had become a place of assignation and the haunt of " the riff-raff and scum of the town." One of its frequenters, Charlotte Shaftoe, is said to have betrayed seven of her intimates to the gallows. At last, on September 11, 1787, the Surrey magistrates refused to renew the license. Hedger, like the Music Hall managers of our own time, was not easily beaten. He appealed to the City of London, and two City justices claiming to act as justices in Southwark, renewed the license seven days after its refusal by the County magistrates. The legality of the civic jurisdiction in Surrey was tried in 1792 before Lord Kenyon and other judges, who decided against it. The license of the Dog and Duck was then made conditional on its being entirely closed on Sundays.[1]

In 1795 the bath and the bowling-green were advertised as attractions and the water might be drunk on the usual terms of threepence each person. About 1796 the place was again open on Sundays, but the license was lost. This difficulty the proprietor surmounted by engaging a Freeman of the Vintners Company, who required no license, to draw the wine that was sold on the premises. The " Sunday Rambler " who visited the place (*circ.* 1796) one evening about ten o'clock found a dubious company assembled. He recognised a bankrupt banker and his mistress; a notorious lady named Nan Sheldon; and another lady attired in extreme fashion and known as " Tippy Molly," though once she had been a modest Mary Johnson. De Castro (*Memoirs*), with a certain touch of pathos, describes the votaries of the Dog and Duck in its later days as "the children of poverty, irregu-

---

[1] The Dog and Duck may have been more respectably conducted for a time. On 28 May, 1792, a charity dinner of the Parish of St. Thomas, Southwark, was held there (engraved invitation ticket in W. Coll.).

"LABOUR IN VAIN" (ST. GEORGE'S SPA IN BACKGROUND, 1782.

larity and distress." [1]   It would, indeed, be easy to moralise on the circumstance that the place was soon to become the inheritance of the blind and the lunatic. In or before 1799 the Dog and Duck was suppressed, and the premises, after having been used as a public soup-kitchen, became in that year the establishment of the School for the Indigent Blind, an institution which remained there till 1811.

Meanwhile, the enterprising Hedger, had made a good use of his profits by renting (from about the year 1789) a large tract of land in St. George's Fields at low rates from the managers of the Bridge House Estate.   The fine for building was £500, but Hedger immediately paid this penalty, and while sub-letting a portion of the ground, ran up on the rest a number of wretched houses which hardly stood the term of his twenty-one years' lease.   From this source he is said to have derived £7,000 a year.   He died in the early part of the present century,[2] having obtained the title of The King of the Fields, and the reputation of a " worthy private character."   He left his riches to his eldest son, whom the people called the Squire.

The Dog and Duck was pulled down in 1811 for the building of the present Bethlehem Hospital, the first stone of which was laid on 18 April, 1812.   The old stone sign of the tavern, dated 1716, and representing a spaniel holding a duck in its mouth, and the Arms of the Bridge House Estate, was built into the brick garden-wall of the Hospital where it may still be seen close to the actual site of the once notorious Dog and Duck.

[1] The Dog and Duck and the Apollo Gardens were for a time within the Rules of the King's Bench Debtors' Prison (De Castro's *Memoirs*, pp. 126, 134).

[2] In De Castro's *Memoirs* (1824) it is stated that he died "about two years ago," which indicates the year 1822, or possibly the year 1810 (for part of the *Memoirs* were apparently written *circ.* 1812) as the date of his death.   He was certainly alive, however, during part of the year 1810.

[Trusler's *London Adviser* (1786), pp. 124, 164 ; Fores's *New Guide* (1789), preface, p. vi ; Allen's *London*, iv. 470, 482, 485 ; *A Modern Sabbath*, 1797, chap. viii. ; Wheatley's *London P. and P.* s.v. "St. George's Fields" and "Dog and Duck" ; Humphreys's *Memoirs of De Castro* (1824), 126, ff. ; Manning and Bray, *Surrey*, iii. 468, 554, 632, 701 ; Allen's *Lambeth*, p. 7, 347 ; *Gent. Mag.* 1813, pt. 2, 556 ; Rendle and Norman, *Inns of Old Southwark*, p. 368, ff. ; Walford, vi. 343, 344, 350-352, 364 ; Larwood and Hotten, *Signboards*, 196, 197 ; *Notes and Queries*, 1st ser. iv. 37 ; newspaper cuttings in W. Coll.]

VIEWS.

1. The old Dog and Duck Tavern, copied from an old drawing 1646, water-colour drawing by T. H. Shepherd, Crace, *Cat.* p. 646. No. 27.

2. The Dog and Duck in 1772. A print published 1772. Crace, *Cat.* p. 646, No. 28.

3. Woodcut of exterior, 1780, in Chambers's *Book of Days*, ii. 74.

4. "Labour in Vain, or Fatty in Distress" (St. George's Spa in the background), print published by C. Bowles, 1782, Crace, *Cat.* p. 647, No. 35, and W. Coll.

5. Engraving of the exterior, 1788 (W. Coll.).

6. Interior of the Assembly Room. A stipple engraving, 1789, reproduced in Rendle and Norman, *Inns of Old Southwark*, 373.

7. Sign of Dog and Duck, engraved in Walford, vi. 344 ; cp. Crace, *Cat.* p. 646, No. 32, and Rendle and Norman, *Inns of Old Southwark*, p. 369.

THE BLACK PRINCE, NEWINGTON
BUTTS

THE Black Prince at Newington Butts possessed,
about 1788, a pleasant garden frequented for trap-ball

THE BLACK PRINCE, NEWINGTON BUTTS, 1788.

playing.   There is a view (W. Coll.) of the tavern and
garden printed for C. Bowles, 22 Sept., 1788.

In the last century Lambeth Marsh and the fields in the neighbourhood were a favourite resort of Londoners for running-matches and outdoor sports, and the Lambeth Wells offered the special attractions of music and mineral water-drinking. The Wells (opened to the public before 1697) were situated in Three Coney Walk, now called Lambeth Walk, and consisted of two springs, distinguished as the Nearer and Farther Well. The water was sent out to St. Thomas's Hospital and elsewhere at a penny a quart, and the poor had it free.

The usual charge for admission for drinking the waters was threepence, including the music, which, about 1700, began at seven in the morning, and was continued on three days of the week till sunset, and on other days till two. The season began in the spring, usually on Easter Monday.

Attached to the Wells was a Great Room, in which concerts and dancing took place. During the season of 1697 there was a "consort" every Wednesday of " vocal and instrumental musick, consisting of about thirty instruments and voices, after the manner of the musick-meeting in York Buildings, the price only excepted," each person to pay for coming in but one shilling. These concerts began originally at 2.30 p.m., but afterwards at six, when no person was admitted in a mask.

About 1700 these shilling concerts seem to have been discontinued, but the Wells remained in some repute till about 1736, when they found a rival in the spring of the Dog and Duck, and the attendance fell off.

In 1740 the owner was named Keefe. About 1750, under his successor Ireland, a musical society under the direction of Sterling Goodwin, organist of St. Saviour's, Southwark, gave a monthly concert there. At the same period Erasmus King, once coachman to Dr. Desaguliers, read lectures there and exhibited experiments in natural philosophy (admission sixpence). There were gala dancing-days in 1747, and in 1752 (June 27), when a " penny wedding in the Scotch manner was celebrated for the benefit of a young couple."

At a later date (after 1755 ?[1]) the place was condemned as a nuisance, and the magistrates refused the dancing licence. The Great Room was then used for Methodist services, and the music-gallery for the pulpit, but the preacher (we are told) being disturbed greatly in his enthusiastic harangues was obliged to quit, and the premises were afterwards built on, or devoted to various purposes, with the exception of the dwelling-house, which (before 1786) was turned into a tavern, under the sign of the Fountain. The present Fountain public-house, erected on the site of the older Fountain in 1829, is No. 105 Lambeth Walk, nearly opposite Old Paradise Street (formerly Paradise Row). The Wells themselves, though long closed, were still in existence in 1829, but a house was subsequently built over them.

Brayley and Mantell (*Surrey*, iii. 400) writing about 1841, say that part of the grounds continued " long within memory " to be used as a tea-garden.

[Nichols's *Parish of Lambeth* (1786), p. 65, ff. ; *Gent. Mag.* 1813, pt. 2, p. 556 ; Manning and Bray, *Surrey*, iii. 468 ; Brayley and Mantell, *Surrey*, iii. 399, ff. ; Allen's *Lambeth*, p. 346, ff. ; Walford, vi. 389].

_____

[1] Lambeth Wells are marked in the map of 1755 in Stow's *Survey*.

MARBLE HALL was situated on the Thames, at the spot afterwards occupied by the southern abutment of Vauxhall Bridge. Part of the road to the bridge now occupies the site.

Joseph Crosier, the proprietor in 1740, "enlarged, beautified and illuminated" the gardens,[1] and built a Long Room facing the river, which was opened in May 1740, and used for dancing during the spring and summer.

From *circ.* 1752–1756 the proprietor was Naphthali Hart,[2] teacher of music and dancing, who held assemblies at Marble Hall in the season, devoting his energies in the winter to Hart's Academy, Essex House, Essex Street, Strand, where (as his advertisements state) "grown gentlemen are taught to dance a minuet and country dances in the modern taste, and in a short time." "Likewise gentlemen are taught to play on any instrument, the use of the small Sword and Spedroon." "At the same place is taught musick, fencing, French, Italian, Spanish, Portuguese, High German, Low Dutch, Navigation, or any other part of the Mathematicks." "A sprightly youth is wanted as an apprentice."

[1] They were of smaller extent than the Cumberland Gardens, their river-side neighbour situated a little further south.

[2] One account calls him Nathan Hart.

In the spring of 1756 Marble Hall was opened as a coffee house and tavern, but little appears to be known of it after this date, though it was in existence till about August 1813, when the abutment of Vauxhall Bridge on the Surrey side was begun.

[Advertisements in " Public Gardens " collection in Guildhall Library, London ; Manning and Bray, *Surrey*, iii. 484, and map, p. 526 ; Allen's *Lambeth*, 368 ; Walford, vi. 339.]

THE CUMBERLAND TEA-GARDENS AND TAVERN, VAUXHALL

(ORIGINALLY SMITH'S TEA-GARDENS)

THESE small gardens, about one acre and a half in extent, were pleasantly situated on the south bank of the Thames, immediately to the south of Vauxhall Bridge (built 1811–1816). Under the name of Smith's Tea-Gardens they were probably in existence some years previous to 1779. "A Fête Champêtre, or Grand Rural Masked Ball," with illuminations in the garden and the rooms, was advertised to take place on 22 May, 1779, at 10 P.M., the subscription tickets being one guinea.

About May 1784 the gardens were taken by Luke Reilly, landlord of the Freemasons' Tavern in Great Queen Street, who changed the name to the Cumberland (or Royal Cumberland) Gardens.[1] At this time they were open in the afternoon and evening, and visitors to Vauxhall Gardens sometimes had refreshments there in the arbours and tea-room while waiting for Vauxhall to open ; or adjourned thither for supper when tired of the larger garden.

In August 1796 a silver cup given by the proprietor was competed for on the river by sailing boats. In

[1] "Riley's Gardens, Vauxhall," mentioned in Trusler's *London Adviser*, 1786, are doubtless identical with Reilly's Cumberland Gardens.

1797 a ten years' lease of the gardens and tavern was advertised to be sold for £1,000.

From 1800 to 1825 the gardens were much frequented by dwellers in the south of London. Between three and four o'clock in the morning of May 25, 1825, the tavern was discovered to be on fire. The engines of Vauxhall Gardens and of the various Insurance Offices came on the scene, but the fire raged for more than an

WATERSIDE ENTRANCE TO CUMBERLAND GARDENS.

hour, and the tavern and the ball-room adjoining were completely destroyed and the plantation and garden greatly injured. In October of the same year the property on the premises was sold by the lessors under an execution and at that time the gardens were, it would seem, finally closed.[1]

[1] In the *Picture of London* for 1829 the Cumberland Gardens are named in the list of places of London amusement, but it is probable that this entry has been inadvertently copied from a previous edition (1823) of the work. Cp. Allen, *Lambeth* (1827), p. 379.

The South Lambeth Water Works occupied the site
for many years and the Phœnix Works of the South
Metropolitan Gas Company are now on the spot.[1]

[Newspaper cuttings in W. Coll. ; Walford, vi. 389, 449 ; Timbs,
Curiosities of London (1868), p. 18, and *Club Life*, ii. 261 ; *Picture
of London*, 1802, 1823 and 1829 ; the *Courier* for 25 and 26 May,
1825 ; Allen, *Lambeth*, p. 379.]

VIEWS.

"Cumberland Gardens, &c." A view by moonlight of the
waterside entrance to the gardens. Undated (*circ.* 1800 ?). W.
Coll.

The gardens are well marked in Horwood's *Plan*, D. 1799.

---

[1] Timbs (*Curiosities of London*, 1868, p. 18) says that Price's
Candle Manufactory occupied the site, but in the Post Office
Directory map of 1858 the "Phœnix Gas Works" are marked
immediately south of Vauxhall Bridge and the Candle Works still
further south, *i.e.*, beyond the Vauxhall Creek which formed the
southern boundary of the gardens.

VAUXHALL GARDENS

§ 1. 1661–1728

THESE, the most famous of all the London pleasure gardens, were known in their earliest days as the New Spring Garden at Vauxhall, and continued till late in the eighteenth century to be advertised as Spring Gardens.[1]

The Spring Garden was opened to the public shortly after the Restoration, probably in 1661.[2] It was a

---

[1] In the advertisements the name Vauxhall Gardens first appears in 1786, but many years before that date the place was often popularly known as Vauxhall Gardens.

[2] The place was at first generally called The New Spring Garden. Cunningham (*Handbook of London*, s.v. "Vauxhall Gardens") and other modern writers suppose that it was called *New* to distinguish it from the old Spring Garden at Charing Cross, and this view seems to receive some countenance from a passage in Evelyn's *Fumifugium*, 1661, quoted by Cunningham. It must be borne in mind, however, that there existed at Vauxhall shortly after the Restoration, *two* Spring Gardens which seem to have been distinguished as the Old and New. This appears very distinctly from the following passage in Pepys, under date 29 May, 1662 :— "Thence home and with my wife and the two maids and the boy took the boat, and to Fox-hall, where I had not been a great while. To the Old Spring Garden, and there walked long, and the wenches gathered pinks. Here we staid, and seeing that we could not have anything to eate but very dear, and with long stay, we went forth again without any notice taken of us, and so we might have done if we had had anything. Thence to the new one, where I never was before, which much exceeds the other ; and

prettily contrived plantation, laid out with walks and arbours : the nightingale sang in the trees ; wild roses could be gathered in the hedges, and cherries in the orchard. The Rotunda, the Orchestra, and the Triumphal Arches, distinctive features of the later Vauxhall, were then non-existent, and the proprietor's house from which refreshments were supplied was probably the only building that broke the charm of its rural isolation. It was a pleasant place to walk in, and the visitor might spend what he pleased, for nothing was charged for admission. It soon became one of the favourite haunts of Pepys, who first visited it on 29 May 1662. On hot summer days, he would take water to Foxhall with Deb and Mercer and his wife, to stroll in the garden alleys, and eat a lobster or a syllabub. On one day in May (29, 1666) he found two handsome ladies calling on Mrs. Pepys. He was burdened with Admiralty business—" but, Lord ! to see how my nature could not refrain from the temptation, but I must invite them to go to Foxhall, to Spring Gardens."

In a few years the Spring Garden became well known.

here we also walked, and the boy crept through the hedge and gathered abundance of roses, and after a long walk, passed out of doors as we did in the other place."

Somewhat earlier (2 July, 1661), Evelyn in his *Diary* has the entry " I went to see the New Spring Garden at Lambeth, a pretty contrived plantation." This probably, if not quite certainly (for compare the mention in Evelyn's *Fumifugium* noticed above), refers to Vauxhall Gardens. Monconys, the French traveller (1663), briefly describes " Les Jardins du Printemps " at Lambeth, but it can hardly be made out whether he is alluding to the garden called by Pepys the Old Spring Garden at Vauxhall or to the New Spring Garden, *i.e.*, Vauxhall Gardens (cp. Tanswell's *Lambeth*, p. 181). The supposed site of the Old Spring Garden at Vauxhall (or Lambeth) is indicated in a map in Manning and Bray's *Surrey*, iii. p. 526 (cp. Walford, vi. 340). The statement of Aubrey and Sir John Hawkins, usually accepted by modern writers, that Sir Samuel Morland occupied in 1675 a house on the site of Vauxhall Gardens, is evidently erroneous (cp. *Vauxhall Papers*, No. 4, p. 28).

Fine people came thither to divert themselves and the citizen also spent his holiday there, " pulling off cherries [says Pepys] and God knows what." The song of the birds was charming, but from about 1667 more sophisticated harmony was furnished by a harp, some fiddles, and a Jew's trump. About this time the rude behaviour of the gallants of the town began to be noted at the Spring Garden. Gentlemen like "young Newport" and Harry Killigrew, "a rogue newly come back out of France, but still in disgrace at our Court," would thrust themselves into the supper-arbours and almost seize on the ladies, " perhaps civil ladies," as Pepys conjectures. "Their mad talk [he adds] did make my heart ake," though he himself, at a later time, was found at the gardens eating and drinking with Mrs. Knipp, " it being darkish."

During the last thirty years of the seventeenth century, the Spring Garden, if less perturbed by the Killigrews and Newports, was not a little notorious as a rendezvous for fashionable gallantry and intrigue. " 'Tis infallibly some intrigue that brings them to Spring Garden " says Lady Fancyful in ' The Provoked Wife' (1697), and Tom Brown (*Amusements*, 1700, p. 54) declares that in the close walks of the gardens " both sexes meet, and mutually serve one another as guides to lose their way, and the windings and turnings in the little Wildernesses are so intricate, that the most experienced mothers have often lost themselves in looking for their daughters." It is not hard to picture Mrs. Frail " with a man alone " at Spring Garden ; Hippolita eating a cheese-cake or a syllabub " with cousin," and the gallant of Sedley's ' Bellamira' (1687) passing off on Thisbe the fine compliments that he had already tried on " the flame-coloured Petticoat in New Spring Garden."

On the evening of 17 May, 1711, Swift (it is interesting to note) visited the gardens with Lady Kerry

and Miss Pratt, " to hear the nightingales."[1]   The visit
of Addison's Sir Roger in the spring of 1712 is classical.[2]
" We were now arrived at Spring Garden, which is
exquisitely pleasant at this time of year.   When I
considered the fragrancy of the walks and bowers, with
the choirs of birds that sung upon the trees, and the
loose tribe of people that walked under their shades, I
could not but look upon the place as a kind of
Mahometan Paradise."   You must understand, says the
Knight, there is nothing in the world that pleases a
man in love so much as your nightingale.   " He here
fetched a deep sigh, and was falling into a fit of musing,
when a mask, who came behind him, gave him a gentle
tap upon the shoulder, and asked him if he would
drink a bottle of mead with her."   The old Knight
bid the baggage begone, and retired with his friend
for a glass of Burton and a slice of hung beef.   He
told the waiter to carry the remainder to the one-legged
waterman who had rowed him to Foxhall, and, as he
left the garden animadverted upon the morals of the
place in his famous utterance on the paucity of nightingales.

In 1726 the Spring Garden is singled out as one of
the London sights,[3] but it would seem that it had
fallen into disrepute, and that fresh attractions and a
management less lax were now demanded.[4]

---

[1] *Swift to Stella*, 17 May, 1711.
[2] *The Spectator*, 20 May, 1712, No. 383.   As notices of the
Spring Garden are rare at this period, the following advertisement
may be worth quoting :—"Lost in Fox Hall, Spring Garden, on
the 29th past a little Spaniel Dog, Liver Coloured and white
long Ears, a Peak down his Forehead, a small Spot on each knee"
(*The Postman*, May 3-6, 1712).   The pleasant walks of the Spring
Garden are referred to in 1714 in Thoresby's *Diary*, ii. 215.
[3] *A New Guide to London* (1726).   Guildhall Library, London.
[4] Lockman in his *Sketch of the Spring Gardens* (1753 ?) praises
Jonathan Tyers for having reformed the morals of the Spring
Garden when he became proprietor in 1728.

§ 2.   1732–1767.

In 1728 Mr. Jonathan Tyers, the true founder of Vauxhall Gardens, obtained from Elizabeth Masters a lease of the Spring Gardens for thirty years at an annual rent of £250, and by subsequent purchases (in 1752 and 1758) became the actual owner of the estate. He greatly altered and improved the gardens, and on Wednesday 7 June 1732 opened Vauxhall with a Ridotto al fresco.   The visitors came between nine and eleven in the evening, most of them wearing dominoes and lawyers' gowns, and the company did not separate till three or four the next morning.   The later Vauxhall numbered its visitors by thousands, but at this fête only about four hundred people were present, and the guard of a hundred soldiers stationed in the gardens, with bayonets fixed, was an unnecessary precaution. Good order prevailed, though a tipsy waiter put on a masquerading dress, and a pick-pocket stole fifty guineas from a visitor, "but the rogue was taken in the fact."   A guinea ticket gave admission to this entertainment, which was repeated several times during the summer.

From about 1737 the Spring Gardens began to present certain features that long remained characteristic. The admission at the gate was one shilling, the regular charge till 1792, and silver tickets were issued admitting two persons for the season, which began in April or May.[1]

---

[1] Several of the Vauxhall season tickets were designed for Tyers by Hogarth.   They are engraved in Nichols's *Lambeth*, pl. xv. p. 100, and in Wilkinson's *Londina Illustrata*.   A good though not complete collection of Vauxhall tickets is in the British Museum, including the series of silver tickets brought together by Mr. Edward Hawkins.   Tyers presented Hogarth as a return for his services with a gold ticket, inscribed *in perpetuam beneficii memoriam*, which was a free pass to the gardens for ever.   Mrs. Hogarth had it after her husband's death, and in 1856 it was in the possession

An orchestra containing an organ was erected in the garden, and the concert about this time lasted from five or six till nine. About 1758 this orchestra was replaced by a more elaborate 'Gothic' structure " painted white and bloom colour " and having a dome surmounted by a plume of feathers. The concert was at first instrumental, but in 1745 Tyers added vocal music, and engaged Mrs. Arne, the elder Reinhold, and the famous tenor, Thomas Lowe, who remained the principal singer at Vauxhall till about 1763.

On the opening day of the season of 1737 " there was (we read) a prodigious deal of good company present," and by the end of the season Pinchbeck was advertising his New Vauxhall Fan with a view of the walks, the orchestra, the grand pavilion, and the organ.

VAUXHALL TICKET BY HOGARTH (AMPHION ON DOLPHIN).

The proprietor was fortunate in the patronage of Frederick Prince of Wales, who had attended the opening Ridotto and often visited Vauxhall till his death in 1751.[1] On 6 July, 1737, for instance, His Royal Highness with several ladies of distinction and noblemen of his household came from Kew by water to the Gardens, with music attending. The Prince walked in the Grove, commanded several airs and retired after supping in the Great Room.

Of fashionable patronage Vauxhall had, indeed, no

of Mr. F. Gye who bought it for £20 (cp. Nightingale in *The Numismatic Chronicle*, vol. xviii (1856), p. 97). In 1737 the season tickets admitting two persons cost one guinea ; in 1742 they were twenty-five shillings ; in 1748, two guineas.

[1] In honour of Frederick, Tyers constructed the "Prince's Pavilion " at the western end of the Gardens facing the orchestra.

lack till a very late period of its existence ; but the place was never exclusive or select, and at no other London resort could the humours of every class of the community be watched with greater interest or amusement. "Even Bishops (we are assured) have been seen in this Recess without injuring their Character." To us, some of its entertainments seem insipid and the manners and morals of its frequenters occasionally questionable, but the charm of the place for our forefathers must have been real, or Vauxhall would hardly have found a place in our literature and social history. The old accounts speak of Spring Gardens not only with naïve astonishment, but with positive affection. "The whole place" (to borrow the remark, and the spelling, of a last century writer) "is a realisation of Elizium." One of the paintings in the gardens represented "Two Mahometans gazing in wonder at the beauties of the place." Farmer Colin, after his week's trip in town (1741) returned to his wife full of the wonderful Spring Gardens :—

> Oh, Mary ! soft in feature,
>   I've been at dear Vauxhall ;
> No paradise is sweeter,
>   Not that they Eden call.
>
> Methought, when first I entered,
>   Such splendours round me shone,
> Into a world I ventured,
>   Where rose another sun :
>
> While music, never cloying,
>   As skylarks sweet, I hear :
> The sounds I'm still enjoying,
>   They'll always soothe my ear.

The account of *England's Gazetteer* or 1751 is naturally more prosaic, but takes the exalted tone that characterises the old descriptions of the gardens : —" This (Fox-hall) is the place where are those

called Spring Gardens, laid out in so grand a taste
that they are frequented in the three summer months
by most of the nobility and gentry then in and near
London ; and are often honoured with some of the
royal family, who are here entertained, with the sweet
song of numbers of nightingales, in concert with the
best band of musick in England. Here are fine pavilions,
shady groves, and most delightful walks, illuminated
by above one thousand lamps, so disposed that they all
take fire together, almost as quick as lightning, and
dart such a sudden blaze as is perfectly surprising.
Here are among others, two curious statues of Apollo
the god, and Mr. Handel the master of musick ; and
in the centre of the area, where the walks terminate, is
erected the temple for the musicians, which is encompassed all round with handsome seats, decorated with
pleasant paintings, on subjects most happily adapted
to the season, place and company."

The usual approach to the gardens until about 1750,
when it became possible to go by coach, was by water.
At Westminster and Whitehall Stairs barges and boats
were always in waiting during the evening. Sir John,
from Fenchurch Street, with his lady and large family,
came on board attended by a footman bearing provisions
for the voyage. The girls chatter about the last city-
ball, and Miss Kitty, by her mamma's command, sings
the new song her master has taught her. Presently,
" my lady grows sick " and has recourse to the citron
wine and the drops. At the Temple Stairs a number
of young fellows, Templars and others, hurry into the
boats, and Mr. William, the prentice, takes the water
with Miss Suckey, his master's daughter. The deep-
ness of their design is an inexhaustible fount of merriment, for *she* is supposed to be gone next door to drink
tea, and *he* to meet an uncle coming from the country.[1]

[1] This description is adapted from the *Scots Magazine* for
July 1739.

More refined would be the party of Mr. Horatio Walpole, in a barge, " with a boat of French horns attending," or (at a later date) of Miss Lydia Melford, who describes how "at nine o'clock in a charming moonlight evening we embarked at Ranelagh for Vauxhall, in a wherry so light and slender that we looked like so many fairies sailing in a nutshell." The pleasure of the voyage was marred by the scene on landing, for, although the worthy beadles of the gardens were present at the waterside to preserve order, there

was at all periods on landing at Vauxhall Stairs " a terrible confusion of wherries," " a crowd of people bawling, and swearing, and quarrelling," and a parcel of ugly fellows running out into the water to pull you violently ashore. But you paid your shilling at the gate, or showed your silver ticket, and then passed down a dark passage into the full blaze of the gardens, lit with their thousand lamps.[1] This was the great moment, as every Vauxhall visitor from first to

VAUXHALL TICKET BY HOGARTH ("SUMMER").

last, has testified. An impressionable young lady[2] found herself dazzled and confounded by the variety of the scene :—" Image to yourself. . . . a spacious garden, part laid out in delightful walks, bounded with high hedges and trees, and paved with gravel ; part exhibiting a wonderful assemblage of the most picturesque and striking objects, pavilions, lodges, groves, grottos, lawns, temples, and cascades ; porticos, colonnades, and

[1] The lamps about the middle of the eighteenth century were about 1,000–1,500 in number ; they afterwards greatly exceeded this total.
[2] Smollett's *Humphry Clinker*.

rotundas ; adorned with pillars, statues, and paintings ; the whole illuminated with an infinite number of lamps, disposed in different figures of suns, stars and constellations ; the place crowded with the gayest company, ranging through those blissful shades, or supping in different lodges on cold collations, enlivened with mirth, freedom and good humour, and animated by an excellent band of music." Among the vocal performers you might perhaps have the happiness to hear the celebrated Mrs. ——— whose voice was so loud and shrill that it would make your head ache " through excess of pleasure."

Goldsmith's Chinese Philosopher [1]—for foreigners always visited Vauxhall and even imitated it in Paris and at the Hague—received a similar impression on entering the gardens with Mr. Tibbs, the second-rate beau, and the pawnbroker's widow. " The lights everywhere glimmering through the scarcely moving trees ; the fullbodied concert bursting on the stillness of the night ; the natural concert of the birds in the more retired part of the grove vying with that which was formed by art ; the company gaily dressed, looking satisfaction, and the tables spread with various delicacies."

For an hour or two the promenade and the concert were sufficiently amusing, and the crowd gathered before the orchestra, when Lowe or Miss Stevenson came forward with a new song. Music is the food of love, and the Vauxhall songs were (as Mr. Dobson has remarked) " abjectly sentimental." Incidents like the following described by an amorous advertiser in the *London Chronicle* for 5 August, 1758, must have been not uncommon at the gardens :—" A young lady who was at Vauxhall on Thursday night last in company with two gentlemen, could not but observe a young gentleman in blue and a gold laced hat, who being near her by the orchestra during the performance, especially

---

[1] Goldsmith's *Citizen of the World*, Letter lxxi.

the last song, gazed upon her with the utmost attention. He earnestly hopes (if unmarried) she will favour him with a line directed to A. D. at the bar of the Temple Exchange Coffee-house, Temple Bar, to inform him whether fortune, family and character may not entitle him upon a further knowledge, to hope an interest in her heart."

At nine o'clock a bell rang, and the company hurried to the north side of the gardens to get a view of the Cascade.   A curtain being drawn aside disclosed a land-scape scene illuminated by concealed lights.   In the foreground was a miller's house and a waterfall.   " The exact appearance of water " was seen flowing down a declivity and turning the wheel of a mill : the water rose up in foam at the bottom, and then glided away. This simple exhibition was a favourite at Vauxhall, though it lasted but a few minutes and was spoken of contemptuously in *The Connoisseur* and other journals as the " tin cascade." [1]

The concert was then resumed, and some hungry citizens and their families had already taken their seats in the supper boxes. During supper the citizen [2] expressed his wonder at the number of the lamps, and said that it must cost a great deal of money every night to light them all.   The eldest Miss declared that for her part she liked the dark walk best of all because it was *solentary*. Little Miss thought the last song pretty, and said she would buy it if she could but remember the tune : and the old lady observed that there was a great deal of good company indeed, but the gentlemen were so rude that they perfectly put her out of countenance by staring at her through their spy-glasses.   The more fashionable visitors arrived later and had their supper after the concert, often hiring a little band of French

---

[1] The cascade was varied in the course of years.   In 1783 the background was a mountain view with palm trees.

[2] *The Connoisseur*, 15 May, 1755.

CONNOISSEUR

THE CITIZEN AT VAUXHALL, 1755.

horns to play to them.   An interesting supper-party
might have been seen at the gardens on a June night in
1750, Horace Walpole, Lady Caroline Petersham and
" the little Ashe, or the Pollard Ashe as they call her."
In the front of their box—one of the best boxes, of
course, near the orchestra and in full view of the company—sat Lady Caroline " with the vizor of her hat
erect, and looking gloriously jolly and handsome."
" She had fetched (says Walpole) my brother Orford
from the next box, where he was enjoying himself with
his *petite partie*, to help us to mince chickens.   We
minced seven chickens into a china dish, which Lady
Caroline stewed over a lamp, with three pats of butter
and a flagon of water, stirring and rattling and laughing,
and we every minute expecting the dish to fly about
our ears.   She had brought Betty, the fruit girl, with
hampers of strawberries and cherries from Rogers's, and
made her wait upon us, and then made her sup by
us at a little table. . . . In short the whole air of our
party was sufficient, as you will easily imagine, to take
up the whole attention of the Gardens ; so much so,
that from eleven o'clock till half an hour after one we
had the whole concourse round our booth ; at last, they
came into the little gardens of each booth on the side
of ours, till Harry Vane took up a bumper and drank
their healths, and was proceeding to treat them with
still greater freedoms.   It was three o'clock before we
got home " (Walpole to Montague, 23 June, 1750).

At this point it seems appropriate to furnish some
details of the Vauxhall commissariat, and we cannot do
better than transcribe an actual Bill of Provisions sold
in the gardens about the year 1762.[1]

	s.	d.
Burgundy, a bottle	6	0
Champagne	8	0
Frontiniac	6	0

---

[1] From *A description of Vauxhall Gardens*, London, S. Hooper, 1762.

	s.	d.
Claret	5	0
Old hock, with or without sugar .	5	0
Two pound of ice		6
Rhenish and sugar	2	6
Mountain . . .	2	6
Red port . .	2	0
Sherry	2	0
Cyder	1	0
Table beer, a quart mug . . .		4
A chicken	2	6
A dish of ham . . .	1	0
A dish of beef	1	0
Salad		6
A cruet of oil . .		4
Orange or lemon . .		3
Sugar for a bottle		6
Ditto for a pint . . .		3
A slice of bread . .		1
Ditto of butter .		2
Ditto of cheese . . .		2
A tart	1	0
A custard . . .		4
A cheese cake . .		4
A heart cake		2
A Shrewsbury cake .		2
A quart of Arrack . .	8	0

When Tyers leased the gardens in 1728 there was in the dwelling-house a "Ham Room," so that this famous Vauxhall viand must have been already in request. The thinness of the slices was proverbial. A journal of 1762, for instance, complains that you could read the newspaper through a slice of Tyers's ham or beef. A certain carver, hardly perhaps mythical, readily obtained employment from the proprietor when he promised to cut a ham so thin that the slices would cover the whole garden like a carpet of red and white.

The chickens were of diminutive size. Mr. Rose, the old citizen in *The Connoisseur* (15 May, 1755), found them no bigger than a sparrow and exclaimed at every mouthful: "There goes twopence—

there goes threepence—there goes a groat . . . . why it would not have cost me above fourpence halfpenny to have spent my evening at Sot's Hole."

Chicken, ham and beef remained the staple of Vauxhall fare, but from about 1822 onwards the chicken cost four shillings instead of the half-crown, at which the old citizen had grumbled. Ham remained steady at one shilling a plate, and was cut no thicker. Thackeray speaks of " the twinkling boxes in which the happy feasters made believe to eat slices of almost invisible ham."

In 1774 the same liquors were in demand, at the same prices as in 1762. In 1822 the claret sold was half a guinea a bottle and Frontiniac had risen from six shillings to ten shillings and sixpence a bottle. By this time, arrack—the famous rack punch that Jos. Sedley drank so freely—had risen from eight to twelve shillings a quart. In 1859 it was ten shillings a bowl, and rum and whisky, and of course, Guinness and Bass had taken their places in the bill. About 1802 Vauxhall Nectar was a common summer beverage. It was " a mixture of rum and syrup with an addition of benzoic acid or flowers of benjamin " and was taken with water.

Having thus given a general sketch of the company and amusements at Vauxhall, we must say something of the gardens themselves and of the character of the musical entertainments.

The gardens [1] occupied about twelve acres and were laid out in gravel walks flanked by a number of fine trees. On passing through the principal entrance, that connected with the manager's house [2] at the western end

[1] Further details as to the form of the Gardens may be seen in the guides of Lockman and "Hooper." Mr. Austin Dobson (*Eighteenth Century Vignettes*, 1st series) gives the best modern account of the Vauxhall geography.

[2] From about 1827 the entrance chiefly used by the public was the "coach-entrance " at the corner of Kennington Lane.

of the gardens, the visitor beheld the Grand (or Great) Walk, planted on each side with elms and extending about nine hundred feet, the whole length of the garden, to the eastern boundary fence, beyond which could be seen pleasant meadows with the hay-makers at their task. At the eastern end of this walk there was a gilded statue of Aurora, afterwards (before 1762) replaced by a Grand Gothic Obelisk bearing the inscription *Spectator fastidiosus sibi molestus*. This latter erection would hardly have borne inspection by daylight, for, like much of the ' architecture ' of Vauxhall, it consisted merely of a number of boards covered with painted canvas.

Parallel to the Grand Walk was the South Walk with its three triumphal arches through which could be seen a painting of the ruins of Palmyra.

A third avenue, the Grand Cross Walk, also containing a painted representation of ruins, passed through the garden from side to side, intersecting the Grand Walk at right angles. This cross walk was terminated on the right by the Lovers' (or Druid's) Walk, and to the left were the Wildernesses and the Rural Downs.

The lofty trees of the Lovers' Walk formed a verdant canopy in which the nightingales of Spring Gardens, the blackbirds, and the thrushes were wont to build. This was the principal of the Dark Walks so often mentioned in the annals of Vauxhall. In 1759 complaints were made of the loose characters who frequented these walks, and in 1763 Tyers was compelled to rail them off. When Vauxhall opened for the season in 1764 some young fellows, about fifty in number, tore up the railings in order to lay the walks open.

The Rural Downs, at least in the earlier days of Vauxhall, were covered with turf and interspersed with firs, cypresses and cedars. On one of the little emi-

nences was a leaden statue of Milton [1] seated, listening
to music, and at night-time the great Bard was illuminated by lamps.   Here were also the Musical Bushes
where a subterraneous band used to play fairy music
till about the middle of the eighteenth century when
this romantic entertainment ceased, "the natural damp of
the earth being found prejudicial to the instruments."

The Wildernesses were formed by lofty trees and were
(about 1753) the verdant abode of various "feathered
minstrels, who in the most delightful season of the
year ravish the ears of the company with their harmony."

The orchestra, open in the front, stood, facing the
west, in the centre of what was called The Grove, a
quadrangle of about five acres formed by the Grand,
Cross, and South Walks and by the remaining side of
the garden.

On each side of this quadrangle were the supper-
boxes and pavilions, placed in long rows or arranged in
a semicircular sweep.   These were decorated, about
1742, with paintings chiefly by Francis Hayman.
Hogarth allowed his "Four Times of the Day" to be
copied by Hayman for the boxes, and is said to have
given Tyers the idea of brightening Vauxhall with
paintings.   It is doubtful if any of the pictures in the
boxes can be traced directly to his hand, though an
undoubted Hogarth, "Henry VIII. and Anne Boleyn"
was presented by the artist to Tyers and hung in the
Rotunda.   The pictures in the boxes chiefly represented
scenes in popular comedies and a number of common
sports and pastimes such as the play of seesaw, the play
of cricket, the humorous diversion of sliding on the ice,
leap-frog, and the country dance round the maypole.

---

[1] This has been attributed to Roubillac, but Mr. Dobson thinks
that it was probably by Henry Cheere who made such leaden
statues for gardens.   The statue was cleared in 1779 of the bushes
that had grown round it, and it was still in the gardens in 1817.

Some of the larger boxes, denominated temples and pavilions, were more elaborately designed and decorated. Such were the Temple of Comus (in the semi-circle of boxes on the left of the garden) and the Turkish Tent behind the orchestra.

Roubillac's celebrated marble statue of Handel, as Orpheus, stood in various positions in the gardens (sometimes under cover) from 1738 to 1818.[1]

The principal structure was the Rotunda, entered through a colonnade to the left of the Grand Walk. It was a circular building, seventy feet in diameter, elegantly fitted up and containing an orchestra in which the band performed on wet evenings. When first opened it was known as the New Music Room or the Great Room, and in early days was nicknamed the Umbrella from the shape of the roof. With the Rotunda was connected a long room, known as the Saloon, or the Picture Room. This projected into the gardens, parallel to the Grove.

Under Tyers's management the concert began at five or six and lasted till nine or ten. It consisted of sixteen pieces, songs alternating with sonatas and concertos. An overture on the organ, always formed part of the entertainment. Not much is known of the instrumental music, for the Vauxhall advertisements, until late in the eighteenth century, never gave the details of the programme. Arne, and Dr. John Worgan, (the Vauxhall organist) were the composers during this period. Valentine Snow, serjeant-trumpeter to the king, was a favourite about 1745, and Burney remarks that "his silver sounds in the open air, by having room to expand, never arrived at the ears of the audience in a manner too powerful or piercing."

The songs consisted chiefly of sentimental ballads,

---

[1] In 1818 it was removed to the house of Dr. Jonathan Tyers Barrett in Duke Street, Westminster; it was described lately (1894) as being in the possession of Mr. Alfred Littleton.

and of a few more sprightly ditties, such as Miss
Stevenson's song " You tell me I'm handsome " :—

> All this has been told me by twenty before,
> But he that would win me must flatter me more.

The verse is highly conventional, but sometimes shows
a glimmering of poetic form that raises it somewhat
above the level of our own drawing-room ballads.
The average Vauxhall song seems to our ears sufficiently thin and trivial, but on the lips of Lowe or Mrs.
Weichsell, may easily have been successful. Of the
popularity of the songs at the time, there can be no
question. The magazines, especially *The London
Magazine*, regularly published the words, and often
the music, of " A new song sung at Vauxhall," and
the contemporary collections of Vauxhall songs, such
as *The Warbler* published at a shilling in 1756, were
numerous.

In the period 1745-1767, when the singers were few
in number, the chief male vocalist was Thomas Lowe,
who possessed an inexhaustible répertoire of Delias and
Strephons which he sang with great applause from
1745 till about 1763, when he entered on the management of the Marylebone Gardens.[1] Mrs. Arne sang
for a few years from 1745, and Miss Stevenson frequently *circ.* 1748-1758. Miss Isabella Burchell,
better known as the Mrs. Vincent of Marylebone
Gardens, sang at Vauxhall from 1751 to 1760. She
was originally a milk-girl employed on Tyers's estate
in Surrey, and it was through his instrumentality that
she obtained instruction in music.

In 1764, the chief singers were Vernon and Miss
Brent, who belong rather to our next period. Miss
Wright's " Thro' the wood, laddie," was popular in
1765.

Jonathan Tyers died on 1 July, 1767. He had

---

[1] On Lowe, see *supra*, p. 50, p. 101 f., and p. 243

amassed a large fortune and owned the estate of Denbies at Dorking, where he laid out a curious garden containing a hermitage, called the Temple of Death, and a gloomy valley of the Shadow of Death. In spite of these lugubrious surroundings this " Master-builder of Delight" retained his love for Vauxhall till the last, and shortly before his death had himself carried into the Grove to take a parting look at the Spring Gardens.

He was succeeded at Vauxhall by his two sons, Thomas and Jonathan. ' Tom ' Tyers, as he was called by Dr. Johnson, with whom he was a favourite, had been bred to the law, but he was too eccentric and vivacious to confine himself to practice. " He, therefore (says Boswell), ran about the world with a pleasant carelessness," amusing everybody by his desultory talk and abundance of anecdote. He furnished many songs for the gardens, but in 1785, sold his interest to his brother Jonathan's family. Jonathan was manager of Vauxhall from 1785 till his death in 1792.

§ 3. 1768-1790.

During this period the character of the entertainments of Vauxhall and the arrangement of the gardens themselves, underwent no very material changes,[1] and people of all ranks frequented the place as of old. The singers, however, were more numerous, and there seems to have been a general tendency to stay late. In 1783, the concert began at eight and ended at eleven, and a London guide-book of 1786,[2] states that the company at that time seldom left the garden till two in the morning, if the weather was fine.

From about 1772-1778, a good deal of rowdyism appears to have disturbed the harmony of Vauxhall,

[1] As to the introduction of the covered walk see *infra*, § 4.
[2] Trusler's *London Adviser*, p. 163.

though it must be said that the company under old
Tyers had not always been distinguished for urbanity.
The rude treatment to which Fielding's Amelia was
subjected at the gardens (*circ.* 1752), can hardly have
been an isolated occurrence, and in the summer of 1748
a party of ladies, apparently of good position, used to
crow like cocks when visiting Vauxhall, while their
friends of the male sex responded with an ass's bray.
One Mrs. Woolaston, attained special proficiency in
her imitations.[1]

At this time (1772-1778), it was the custom to
violently emphasize the importance of the *last night* of
the season. Young Branghton, in *Evelina* (*circ.* 1778),
declares that the last night at Vauxhall is the best of
any ; " there's always a riot—and there the folks   ʌ
about—and then there's such squealing and squalling !
and there all the lamps are broke, and the women run
skimper scamper."[2]

From the newspapers we learn that on the 4th of
September, 1774, " upwards of fifteen foolish Bucks
who had amused themselves by breaking the lamps at
Vauxhall, were put into the cage there by the proprietors, to answer for the damage done.   They broke
almost every lamp about the orchestra, and pulled the
door leading up to it off the hinges."

The Dark Walk and Long Alleys were also not
without their terrors.   Evelina, who had unwittingly
strayed thither, was surrounded by a circle of impudent
young men, and the Branghton girls were also detained,
though they had gone more with their eyes open.
" Lord, Polly," says the eldest, " suppose we were to
take a turn in the Dark Walks ? "   " Ay, do," an-

[1] *Notes and Queries*, 6th ser. ix. (1884), p. 208.
[2] *Evelina*, Letter xlvi. Cp. *The Macaroni and Theatrical Magazine*
for September 1773, p. 529, which gives a plate showing "the
Macaroney Beaus and Bells in an Uproar, or the last Evening at
Vauxhall Gardens " (W. Coll.).

swered she, " and then we'll hide ourselves, and then
Mr. Brown will think we are lost." A quarrel in
public between two angry gentlemen was also a not
uncommon incident, and the affair sometimes assumed
the heroic proportions of a Vauxhall "Affray." For
example, one day in June 1772 two gentlemen, Captain Allen and Mr. Kelly, created a scene. The words
" scoundrel " and " rascal " were heard, and Allen who
had a sword would have overpowered Kelly who had
only his cane, if the bystanders had not interposed.[1]
But the Vauxhall Affray *par excellence*, was the affair
of Bate, " the fighting parson," and Mr. Fitzgerald.[2]
The Rev. Sir Henry Bate Dudley, Bart. (as he afterwards was) was at Vauxhall on the evening of 23 July,
1773, in company with Mrs. Hartley and some friends.
A party of gentlemen sat down near them, and made a
deliberate attempt to stare the beautiful actress out of
countenance. Captain Crofts and Mr. George Robert
Fitzgerald were among the offenders, or at any rate
took their part. Bate expostulated loudly with Crofts,
and a crowd gathered round. The next day Bate and
Crofts met at the Turk's Head Coffee House in the
Strand, where matters were being peaceably adjusted,
when Fitzgerald appeared on the scene insisting on
satisfaction for his friend Captain Miles, who wanted
to box the parson. Bate declared that he had offered
no insult to Miles, but ultimately the party adjourned
to the front dining-room of the Spread Eagle Tavern
close by, and there in fifteen minutes Bate had completely beaten Miles. A few days afterwards Bate
discovered that the supposed Captain Miles was Fitzgerald's footman, esteemed an expert bruiser. Bate

---

[1] *The Gazeteer and New Daily Advertiser*, 29 June, 1772.
[2] *The Vauxhall Affray, or the Macaronies defeated*, London, 1773 ;
Westminster Magazine for September 1773, p. 558 ; *The Macaroni
and Theatrical Magazine* for August 1773, where there is a copper-
plate showing the parson fighting the footman (W. Coll.).

published an account of the affair in the papers, and
Fitzgerald's conduct was generally condemned, though
he tried to make out that the footman had only pre-
tended to be beaten.   A further quarrel arising out of
this incident led to a meeting between Fitzgerald and
a Captain Scawen in Flanders.   As a finishing touch
to our picture of the Vauxhall manners of the period,
we must recall an evening in August 1782, when the
Prince of Wales and a party of gay friends visited the
gardens.   When the music was over the Prince was
recognised by the company, and being surrounded,
crushed, and pursued, had to beat a hasty retreat.   The
ladies followed the Prince, the gentlemen pursued the
ladies ; the curious and the mischievous increased
the tumult, and in a few minutes the boxes were
deserted, the lame overthrown, and the well-dressed
demolished.[1]

On May 10, 1769, a Ridotto al fresco was given at
which not less than ten thousand people are said to
have been present.   The Rotunda was lit with nearly
five thousand glass lamps, and a platform under an
awning was laid down in the gardens for dancing.   The
fancy dresses were not numerous, and Walpole, who
was there with his friend Conway, only walked twice
round, and was glad to get out of the mob and go
home.   Some years later, on 29 May, 1786, there was
another Ridotto to celebrate (approximately) the
Jubilee of Vauxhall Gardens.   Fourteen thousand additional lamps were displayed, and most of the company appeared in dominoes, as at the original Ridotto
of 1732.

During this period (1768–1790) the principal tenor
was Vernon, who had taken Lowe's place in 1764.   His
répertoire appears to have been somewhat less conventional than that of his predecessor, and his gay and

---

[1] *British Magazine*, 6 August, 1782.

A Collection,

of Favorite

SONGS

Sung by

Mr Dignum. Mr Denman. Mr Franklin.

The Two Miss Howells, & Mrs Mountain.

AT

VAUXHALL GARDENS,

Composed by

Mr Hook.

Entered at Stationers Hall. ——— Book 1st 1798 . ——— Prix 3.

London, Printed & Sold at A Bland & Weller's Music Warehouse, No 23 Oxford Street.

energetic manner rendered him popular in such songs as
the " English Padlock," the " Crying and Laughing "
Song, and " Cupid's recruiting Sergeant."   He was a
constant singer at Vauxhall till the end of the season
of 1781.   In 1783 Arrowsmith, a young tenor, pupil
of Michael Arne, aspired with some success to take
Vernon's place.   He sang till 1785, but in the summer
of next year (1786) a more celebrated tenor, Charles
Incledon, then only twenty-two, made his appearance,
and sang till 1790.

The principal female singers were Mrs. Baddeley
(about 1768); Mrs. Weichsell (1769–1784); Miss
Jameson (1770–1774); Miss Wewitzer (*circ.* 1773);
Mrs. Hudson (1773–1776); Mrs. Wrighten (1773–
1786); Mrs. Kennedy (1782–1785); Miss Leary
(1786–1789); Mrs. Martyr, the actress (1786–1789).
Of these vocalists, Mrs. Baddeley and Mrs. Kennedy
were the well-known actresses.   The latter possessed a
powerful voice, and often assumed male parts at Covent
Garden.   Mrs. Wrighten had a vivacious manner and
a bewitching smile, and her " Hunting Song" was
popular.   Mrs. Weichsell, the mother of Mrs.
Billington the actress, was an especial favourite at
the gardens.   A magazine poet of 1775 [1] celebrates
her among the best Vauxhall singers .—

> Sweet Weichsell who warbles her wood-note so wild,
> That the birds are all hushed as they sit on each spray,
> And the trees nod applause as she chaunts the sweet lay.

In 1774 James Hook was appointed organist and
composer, and remained at Vauxhall Gardens till 1820,
exerting his facile, if not very distinguished powers, as
a music-writer.   In 1775 Catches and Glees were for
the first time introduced into the concert.   On an evening of July of this year Lord Sandwich and a party of

---

[1] *Westminster Magazine*, May 1775.

friends amused themselves by starting some Catches and Glees of their own, which they sang from their box near the orchestra. General Haile, who sat in the next box, then requested a young lady who was with him to sing a song, which the band obligingly accompanied, to the great delight of the audience.[1] A favourite catch, "They say there is an echo here," was performed in 1780, by two sets of singers and musicians, the stanzas of the principal band being answered by an invisible band of voices and wind instruments stationed over the Prince's box at the bottom of the garden.

In 1783 Barthelemon led the orchestra, and a band of drums and fifes, horns and clarionets, was introduced to perambulate the gardens after the regular concert. These supplementary bands generally formed part of the later Vauxhall entertainments.

§ 4. 1791–1821.

In 1792 the ordinary admission was raised from one shilling to two shillings, and Grand Galas and Masquerades became features of Vauxhall.[2] On 31 May, 1792, there was a successful masked ball, and the gardens were a blaze of light. Amid a crowd of Haymakers, Punches, Chimney Sweeps, and Sailors, Munden, the actor, attracted attention in the character of a deaf old man.

People of all classes took part in these masqueradings. Deputy Gubbins went as a very fat Apollo, and his spouse, a portly matron, as Diana with a huge quiver. Master Gubbins was Cupid. But these characters were misunderstood by the newspaper-reporter, who described

---

[1] *Middlesex Journal*, July 23–25, 1775.
[2] On the gala nights the charge was three shillings.

the Deputy as the Fat Knight, accompanied by his lady as Mother Quickly, and by the hope of all the Gubbinses as an awkward Toxophilite.[1]

The "Dashalls" and "Tallyhos" sometimes caused trouble, and a newspaper of 1812, describes how at a ball of this year, a crowd of masks followed "Mr. Cockadoodle Coates" with crowing and exclamations of "Romeo, Romeo, wherefore art thou, Romeo."

An imposing festival took place on 20 June, 1813, to celebrate the Battle of Vittoria and Wellington's victories. The Prince of Wales, and all the Royal Dukes were present at the banquet.

During this period (1791–1821) some capable vocalists made their appearance at Vauxhall ; Darley (who had already sung at the gardens in 1789) ; Mrs. Franklin (who had previously appeared as Miss Leary) ; Mrs. Mountain,[2] the actress (1793) ; the well-known Charles Dignum (1794) and Mrs. Bland[3] the popular ballad-singer (1802). Dignum and Mrs. Bland remained Vauxhall favourites for some years.[4]

Fireworks, which had long before been usual at Cuper's Gardens, Marylebone Gardens, and Ranelagh, were not introduced at Vauxhall till 1798. From about 1813, they became a permanent institution. In 1816, Mme. Saqui of Paris appeared at Vauxhall, and was the principal attraction for several seasons. A mast about sixty feet high was erected on the firework platform at the eastern end of the gardens, and from its top depended an inclined rope 350 feet long. At twelve o'clock a lady of muscular and masculine appearance,

---

[1] A burlesque account in the *Bon Ton Magazine*, June 1791, with plate (W. Coll.).

[2] Her husband, Mr. Mountain, was leader at Vauxhall from 1792.

[3] On Mrs. Bland, see *supra*, p. 137 (White Conduit House).

[4] Miss Tunstall, another singer, was in repute at the gardens about 1820.

Engraved by W.Ridley, from an Original Picture in the Possession of Mrs.Martyr.

M^{RS} MARTYR.

Printed for J.Parsons 21.Paternoster Row.Jan.t 1794.

bedecked with spangles and waving plumes, might be
seen ascending this rope to the platform, amid a glare

Painted by Aug't Earle.   Engraved by Fairland.

CHARLES DIGNUM.

of blue flame.　Her　appearance　was almost　super-
natural :—

> Amid the blaze of meteors seen on high,
> Etherial Saqui seems to tread the sky ;[1]

---

[1] *Sketches from St. George's Fields* (1821), 2nd ser. p. 216.

Having now reached the highest point, she made her descent in a shower of Chinese Fire, and "in the face of a tempest of fireworks." This exciting performance became a necessity at Vauxhall, and Saqui's feats were afterwards reproduced by Longuemare and Blackmore.

At this period (*circ.* 1817) the newspapers describe the orchestra as a " pagoda of lustre," and the covered walks as arches of fire. The songs, and the music, and the fireworks were the attractions till about one o'clock, when the ordinary visitors withdrew. But the noisy and the dissipated sometimes kept up the fun with reels and waltzes till nearly four in the morning.[1]

We have now wandered far from the old Spring Garden of Jonathan Tyers and the later history of Vauxhall must, in the present volume, be very briefly summarised.

In the gardens themselves, some important changes had already been effected. In 1786, a Supper Room had been added to the left of the Rotunda, and in 1810-11 many of the trees in the Grove were cut down, and part of the Grand Walk and two sides of the Grove were covered in by a vaulted colonnade supported by cast-iron pillars. This colonnade was brilliantly lit with lamps, and was convenient in the wet weather that was proverbial at Vauxhall, but it greatly tended to destroy what Walpole calls, "the gardenhood " of the place.[2] The last of the old trees of Tyers's period is said to have survived till 1805.

In 1821 Vauxhall Gardens passed out of the possession of the Tyers family. After the death of

---

[1] In 1806 the opening of the gardens on Saturdays was discontinued on account of the disorderly persons staying on late into Sunday morning. From about this time the gardens were for a long period usually open on three days of the week only.

[2] Already in 1769 an awning or other covering was placed over one of the walks, and "covered walks " are afterwards alluded to. The permanent colonnade was not erected till 1810.

Madame Saqui

The celebrated Performer on the Rope, at Vauxhall.

Engraved by Alais, from an Original Painting by Hutchisson of Bath.

Published for La Belle Assemblee N.º 132. Feb.y 1.st 1820.

by J. Bell, & Sold at N.º la Brydges S.t Covent Garden.

Jonathan Tyers the younger in 1792, his place was taken as proprietor and manager by his son-in-law Bryan Barrett, who died in 1809. Barrett's son, George Rogers Barrett then acted as manager of the gardens for many years. In 1821, the property was purchased from the Barrett family for £30,000 [1] by T. Bish (the lottery-office keeper), F. Gye, and R. Hughes.

§ 5. 1822-1859.

The gardens opened [2] for the season of 1822 on June 3rd, and for the first time received the appellation of The Royal Gardens, Vauxhall. This change in the name was made with the approval of George IV. who as Prince of Wales had been a regular frequenter of the gardens and had received from a grateful management public recognition of his patronage. In 1791, a gallery had been constructed in the gardens and named after him.[3] This was the shrine of an allegorical transparency portraying him leaning against a horse held by Britannia. Minerva bore his helmet; Providence fixed his spurs, and Fame blew a trumpet and crowned him with laurel. The good-natured Darley came to the front of the orchestra (August 1792) and sang in his best manner, " The Prince of the People " :—

> Endow'd with each virtue, the dignified Youth,
> Ere Reason enlighten'd his mind,
> Burst forth on the world in example and truth,
> The boast and delight of Mankind.

The gardens had now (1822) completely assumed their nineteenth-century aspect and Vauxhall, lit with " 20,000 additional lamps," began to supply a constant succession of variety entertainments.

---

[1] Some accounts say £28,000.
[2] Admission, three shillings and sixpence.
[3] This Prince's Gallery was burnt down in 1800.

DARLEY IN THE ORCHESTRA AT VAUXHALL.

The Rotunda was decorated as an Indian Garden Room, and at a later date was fitted up with seats and boxes and used for the equestrian performances. In the Saloon (or Picture Room) adjoining, where historical pictures by Hayman were still hanging, was an exhibition called by the erudite managers Heptaplasiesoptron. On plates of glass ingeniously distributed manifold reflections were produced of revolving pillars, palm-trees, twining serpents, coloured lamps and a fountain.

The old Cascade had been abolished about 1816, and a stage for rope-dancing occupied its site (1822). A Submarine Cavern and a new exhibition of Waterworks appear to have covered the Rural Downs.

At the eastern end of the garden was a building of wood and canvas representing a Hermit's Cottage, wherein might be seen—all in transparency—the Hermit himself pursuing his studies by the aid of a lamp, a blazing fire and a brightly-shining moon. At this end of the gardens was the Firework Tower, where the fireworkers Hengler, Mortram and Southby were now (1822) at work, preparing for the ascent of Longuemare, which was to take place at twelve o'clock à la Saqui.

The South Walk (so much of it at least as remained uncovered) was now known as the Firework Walk, and the three Triumphal Arches had disappeared.

The Dark Walk of Vauxhall now began at the Submarine Cavern, passed along the left hand and eastern boundaries of the garden and terminated at the right hand end of the Grand Cross Walk, the last branch of it being thus identical with the Lovers' Walk of old days. The Cross Walk was now usually denominated the Chinese Walk from its being lit with Chinese lanterns. Four cosmoramas had taken the place of its Ruins.

The boxes and pavilions containing Hayman's paint-

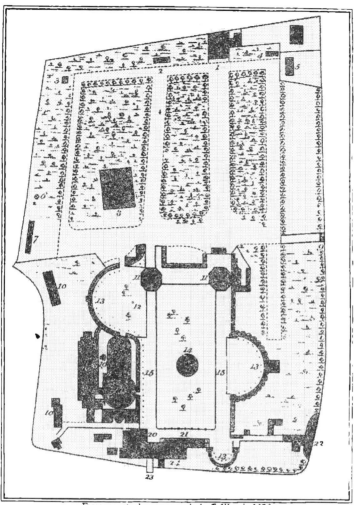

From an actual survey made by T. Allen, in 1826.

VAUXHALL GARDENS.

1 Fire work Tower	13 Circles of Boxes
2 Evening Star	14 Orchestra
3 Hermitage	15 Collonade
4 Smugglers Cave	16 Rotunda
5 House in which Mr Barrett died	17 Picture Room
6 Statue of Milton	18 Supper Room
7 Transparency	19 Ice House
8 Theatre	20 Bar
9 Chinese entrance	21 Princes Pavillion
10 Artificers work shops	22 Entrance
11 Octagon temples	23 Water Gate
12 Fountain	24 House

ings remained much as of old.   Among other note-
worthy features of the later Vauxhall was the gilded
cockle-shell sounding-board over the orchestra (from
1824) ; a new avenue called the Italian Walk (from
about 1836), and the Neptune Fountain.

In 1822 Ramo Samee, the Indian juggler and sword-
swallower, made his appearance, and next year a Shadow
Pantomime and Grey's Fantoccini were introduced.
From this period, Vauxhall was enlivened or vulgarised
by the performance of comic songs.   Mallinson (*circ.*
1823), W. H. Williams (from 1824), and J. W. Sharp
(from 1846) being some of the best-known singers.

In 1826 the admission was raised to four shillings, on
account of the engagement of Braham and Miss Stephens
and of Mme. Vestris, whose "Cherry Ripe" was popular.
In 1827 the space in front of the firework tower was
cleared of shrubs, and a representation of the Battle of
Waterloo took place there.   Cooke's stud and a thousand
horse and foot soldiers engaged in this action.   The
" Waterloo " ground afterwards (1834) became the
Polar Regions, and subsequently the space was covered
by other scenic displays, including (1847) a view of
Venice with "imitation water."

In 1828 Ducrow's stud was engaged, and in the next
year ballets became a feature.

In 1830–1832 the musical director was Sir Henry
Bishop, who composed operettas for the gardens, such
as " The Sedan Chair," " The Bottle of Champagne,"
and the " Magic Fan."   In the last-named Mrs. Way-
lett and Paul Bedford took part.   George Robinson, the
alto, made Bishop's " My Pretty Jane " popular.   On
August 2, 1833, when a one shilling night was tried,
upwards of 27,000 people paid for admission.

The 19th of August, 1833, is notable in the Vauxhall
annals as the benefit night of old Simpson, for more
than thirty-six years Master of the Ceremonies at the
gardens, and himself one of the sights and institutions.

He was a man of short stature and his plain face was
pitted with the smallpox, but his manner and dress
made ample amends.   He wore a shirt with an
enormous frill, a coat of antique cut, and black silk
knee-breeches and hose.   In his uplifted left hand he
carried his tasselled and silver-headed cane, and with
his right raised his hat to every one he met, as a welcome to the Royal Property.   His habitual attitude has
been immortalised by Cruikshank and he was exhibited
(from 1833) in the gardens in coloured lamps—an
immense effigy, forty-five feet high.   Simpson's Vauxhall Addresses and his letters to newspaper editors were
masterpieces of florid humility.   To the editor of *The
Times* he wrote to say that he had given directions that
the illustrious editor's " much-beloved family " were to
be admitted " to any number " at the Vauxhall Juvenile
Fêtes—a communication which amused Thomas Barnes
who had no children.   Simpson died, almost in office,
on 25 December, 1835, after expressing a wish that the
managers of the Royal Gardens would dispose as they
deemed fit of his " humble body."   Thackeray calls
him " the gentle Simpson, that kind, smiling idiot." [1]

In 1836 the gardens were open in the daytime, but
Vauxhall by daylight, as " Boz " observed, is " a porter-
pot without porter ; the House of Commons without
the Speaker ; a gas-lamp without gas."   Ballooning

[1] Among the curious characters of Vauxhall Gardens must be
noticed a youth named Joseph Leeming, who called himself " the
Aeriel " and " the Paragon of Perfection," and offered himself for inspection to artists and surgeons as a model of bodily perfection.   On
2 July, 1825, and on subsequent occasions he mingled with the
other visitors at Vauxhall and created excitement by his extraordinary Spanish costume and by distributing three or four hundred
" Challenges " to the people in front of the orchestra.   One of
these curious challenges is in my collection.   It is a small card
printed with the words " The Aeriel (*sic*) challenges the whole
world to find a man that can in any way compete with him as
such.   No. —." (cp. Hone's *Every Day Book*, i. p. 1456, ff.).

was the chief feature of these afternoon fêtes.[1] On
7 November, 1836, Charles Green, accompanied by

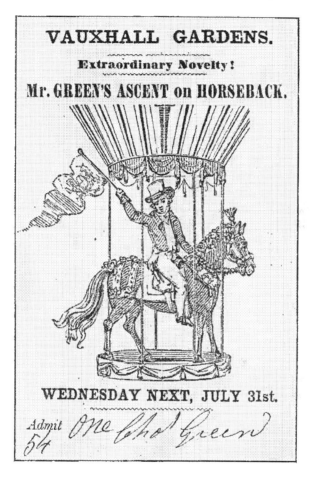

ADMISSION TICKET FOR GREEN'S BALLOON ASCENT, 31 JULY, 1850.

Monck Mason and Robert Hollond, M.P., ascended
from the gardens at 1.30 P.M. in the balloon, after-

[1] An earlier balloon ascent from Vauxhall Gardens by Garnerin
in 1802 may be noted.

wards named " the Nassau," and descended next morning near Weilburg in the Duchy of Nassau after a voyage occupying eighteen hours.[1]   On 24 July, 1837, Green, Edward Spencer, and Robert Cocking ascended in a balloon with a parachute attached, and Cocking in descending in the parachute was killed.

In 1839 the proprietorship of Gye and Hughes came to an end, and Vauxhall was closed in 1840. The gardens were again open in July 1841 with Alfred Bunn as stage-manager.   During this season Bunn and " Alfred Crowquill " published at the gardens their amusing series of *Vauxhall Papers*, " a daily journal published nightly, every other evening, three times a week." [2]   The Ravel Family and Ducrow's horsemanship were among the attractions of this season, which came to an end on 8 September, when the announcement was made that Vauxhall would " positively close its doors for ever."

On 9 September (1841) the gardens were offered for sale by auction, but were bought in at 20,000 pounds. The furniture and fittings were, however, disposed of at this time, notably, twenty-four of the paintings by Hayman, which realised sums from £1 10s. to £9 15s. Four busts of the celebrated Simpson were sold for half-a-crown apiece.

From 1842 till the final closing of the gardens, galas, masquerades, and a great variety of entertainments were advertised in bold letters of many colours, but Vauxhall was now rapidly declining.   In 1845, Musard conducted Promenade Concerts, and in that year and

[1] A detailed account of the voyage is given in Monck Mason's *Aeronautica*, London, 1838.

[2] The publication came to an end on 23 August, 1841.   It consisted of sixteen parts, sixpence each.   A set of these is in my collection.   Mr. H. A. Rogers, of Stroud Green, has recently undertaken an interesting facsimile reprint of this scarce little journal.

during most of the years following, Mr. Robert Wardell
was the lessee. In 1846, gas lamps took the place of
the oil lamps, and about this time the musicians in the
orchestra ceased to wear the cocked hats that had long
been their characteristic head-dress. In 1849, there was

Manners and Customs of y᷒ Englyshe (New Series) No. 9.

VAVXHALL.

VAUXHALL IN 1850, DOYLE'S VIEW FROM *Punch*.

a Grand Venetian Carnival, and 60,000 lamps were
advertised.

In October 1853, when the annual license for the
Royal Gardens was applied for, great complaints were
made of the nuisance caused by the bals masqués which
lasted from 11 P.M. till 5 or 6 A.M., and were frequented
by many disreputable characters. The license was renewed on the somewhat easy conditions that the fireworks should not be let off after eleven, and that the

gardens should close at three in the morning. In 1858, Mr. R. Duffell was the director. Monster galas were announced, and the gardens were opened on Sundays for a promenade.

Monday, 25 July, 1859, witnessed the last entertainment at Vauxhall Gardens. One of the vocalists at the concert then given was Mr. Russell Grover, who died lately, in April 1896. After the concert and the equestrian performances in the Rotunda, dancing was continued till past midnight : the fireworks displayed the device *Farewell for Ever*, and Vauxhall was closed.

On 22 August following, the auctioneer ascended his rostrum in the gardens at noon and announced that the site had been let for building, and that all the property on the premises must be sold. Three "deal painted tables with turned legs," made for the gardens in 1754, went for nine shillings each. The dancing platform realised fifty guineas, the ballet theatre seventeen guineas, and the orchestra ninety-nine pounds. The pictures that still remained in the supper boxes were purchased by Edward Tyrrell Smith, who placed them in the Banqueting Hall at Cremorne. The whole sale realised about £800.

The builders soon went to work upon the twelve acres of Vauxhall Gardens, and in 1864 the church of St. Peter, Vauxhall, erected on part of the site, was consecrated. Numerous streets of small houses have for many years completely obliterated all traces of the gardens, the boundaries of which, it is, however, interesting to trace. The western boundary is marked by the present Goding Street, and the eastern by St. Oswald's Place. Leopold Street and a small portion of Vauxhall Walk define their northern limit, and Upper Kennington Lane marks their southern extent. The space within these boundaries is occupied by Gye Street, Italian Walk, Burnett Street, Auckland Street,

The Farewel to VAUX HALL.

the Words by Mr Sam Dedwyn   the Music by Mr Lampe

Farewel dear Scenes of gay Delight, adieu ye ever pleasing Shades, since now no more my

ravish'd Sight Surveys y lovely tuneful Glades: Sweet Philomel no more, complains, nor chants her

soft love labour'd Song nor round y Muse's warbling Fanes attend y in-raptur'd listning Throng.

(2)

No more y fragrant Zephyrs spread,
Their Sweets along th'illumin'd Groves,
Nor Cynthia glimmers thro' y Shade,
That witness'd to a thousand Loves.
No longer each Sweet thrilling Sound,
Lulls the forsaken Lover's Care,
Nor Airs melodious help to wound,
The Bosoms of the lovely Fair.

(3)

But Oh! thou beauteous Source of Day,
Quickly thy Winter's Journey run,
With hast restore the blooming May,
And thy own Choir once more attaine
Then seen as Vesper gilds the West,
Let me with Dear Corinna move,
Along y Thames fair dimply Breast,
To Scenes of Harmony and Love.

Glynn Street, and part of Tyers Street,[1] and also by St.
Peter's Church and the Lambeth District School of
Art.

As late as 1869 "the Supper Colonnade of Vauxhall " was advertised to be sold cheap,[2] and with this
prosaic detail of our own time, we must perforce take
leave of the pleasure gardens of a past century.

AUTHORITIES AND VIEWS.

The literary and pictorial matter available for a history of
Vauxhall Gardens is almost inexhaustible and, except in a mono-
graph, it would be impossible to set forth a detailed list of authorities and views. The present sketch is primarily based on the
materials furnished by an extensive collection in the writer's
possession, consisting of views, portraits, songs, bills, and cuttings
from newspapers and magazines, and covering the period 1732–
1859. Among many other authorities that have been consulted,
the following may be mentioned :—Pepys's *Diary : A Sketch of the
Spring Garden, Vauxhall* (by John Lockman, 1753 ?) ; *A Description
of Vauxhall Gardens*, London, S. Hooper, 1762 (Guildhall Library,
London) ; Kearsley's *Stranger's Guide* (1793 ?) ; *Sale Catalogues of
Vauxhall Gardens*, 1818 (Brit. Mus.) and 1841 (W. Coll.) ; *A Brief
Historical and Descriptive Account of the Royal Gardens, Vauxhall*,
1822 ; *The Vauxhall Papers*, 1841 ; the histories of Lambeth and
Surrey ; W. H. Husk in Grove's *Dict. of Music*, art. "Vauxhall
Gardens" ; Austin Dobson's *Eighteenth Century Vignettes*, 1st ser.
p. 230, ff. ; Cunningham's *Handbook of London ;* Wheatley's *London
Past and Present ;* Walford, vi. 447, ff. ; Blanchard in *Era Almanack*
for 1870, p. 9, ff.

---

[1] This part of Tyers Street was formerly called Brunel Street.
[2] *Punch* for 21 August, 1869, " The Lament of the Colonnade."

INDEX

THE END

Printed in Great Britain
by Amazon